# The praier and complaynte of the ploweman vnto Christe

Sixteenth-century English Protestant reformers were hard-pressed to establish a historical pedigree that would provide their ideas with weight and legitimacy. Many of those reformers turned back to early fifteenth-century Lollard texts, recycling and reprinting them to serve the needs, both political and spiritual, of the burgeoning English Protestant reform movement. The anti-clerical and reformist Lollard text *The praier and complaynte of the ploweman vnto Christe* was one of the works used by sixteenth century English Protestants in their struggle for religious reform.

This is an old-spelling, critical edition of the version of *The praier and complaynte of the ploweman vnto Christe* that resurfaced in the 1530s. Demonstrating the continuity of ideas between the Lollards and the Reformists, Douglas Parker situates *The praier and complaynte* firmly in the tradition of English Reformist borrowing of texts, and argues for William Tyndale as editor of the sixteenth-century version of *The praier and complaynte.* Parker examines the two extant copies of the manuscript, and comments on the work's structure and reformist content. He presents full historical, literary, and biographical information in his introduction, and a full line-by-line commentary on the text.

This careful, meticulous work is a revealing look at the ideology of Protestant religious struggles in England from the fourteenth to the sixteenth century.

DOUGLAS H. PARKER is a professor of English at Laurentian University. He is also the editor of *A proper dyaloge betwene a Gentillman and an Husbandman* (UTP 1996).

# The praier and complaynte of the ploweman vnto Christe

*Edited by Douglas H. Parker*

UNIVERSITY OF TORONTO PRESS
Toronto Buffalo London

Reprinted in paperback 2014

ISBN 978-0-8020-4268-2 (cloth)
ISBN 978-1-4426-5500-3 (paper)

Printed on acid-free paper

---

**Canadian Cataloguing in Publication Data**

Main entry under title:

The praier and complaynte of the ploweman vnto Christe

Includes bibliographical references and index.

ISBN 978-0-8020-4268-2 (bound) ISBN 978-1-4426-5500-3 (pbk.)

1. Reformation – Sources. I. Parker, Douglas H. (Douglas Harold), date

BR303.P73 1997 270.6 C97-931530-1

---

University of Toronto Press acknowledges the financial assistance to its publishing program of the Canada Council for the Arts and the Ontario Arts Council.

This book has been published with the help of a grant from the Humanities and Social Sciences Federation of Canada, using funds provided by the Social Sciences and Humanities Research Council of Canada.

For Hilary, again

With hym ther was a Plowman, was his brother,
That hadde ylad of dong ful many a fother.
A trewe swynkere and a good was he,
Lyvynge in pees and parfit charitee.
God loved he best with al his hoole herte
At alle tymes, thogh him gamed or smerte,
And thanne his neighebore right as hymselve.
He wolde thresshe, and therto dyke and delve,
For Cristes sake, for every poure wight,
Withouten hire, if it lay in his myght.

Geoffrey Chaucer, 'General Prologue,' *The Canterbury Tales*

# Contents

# Acknowledgments

I am indebted to the generosity and kindness of the administrators and librarians of the following institutions: The British Library, London; The Bodleian Library, Oxford; the Huntington Library, San Marino, California; The Pierpont Morgan Library, New York City; Osterreicheische Nationalbibliothek, Vienna, Austria; University of Ottawa, Ottawa, Ontario; Carleton University, Ottawa, Ontario; and Laurentian University, Sudbury, Ontario. I also am indebted to the estate of the Duke of Bath, Longleat, Warminster, Wiltshire, for permission to use items from his library, and to his librarian, Dr Kate Harris. Dr Geoffrey Tesson, Vice-President, Academic, Laurentian University, generously supported this project as did the Laurentian University Research Fund. Suzanne Rancourt and Barbara Porter, University of Toronto Press, have been helpful, efficient, and encouraging. Joan Bulger, copyeditor, has been remarkably astute in her careful reading of a difficult manuscript. And finally, special thanks to Matt and Diane Bray for their hospitality, companionship, and innumerable kindnesses.

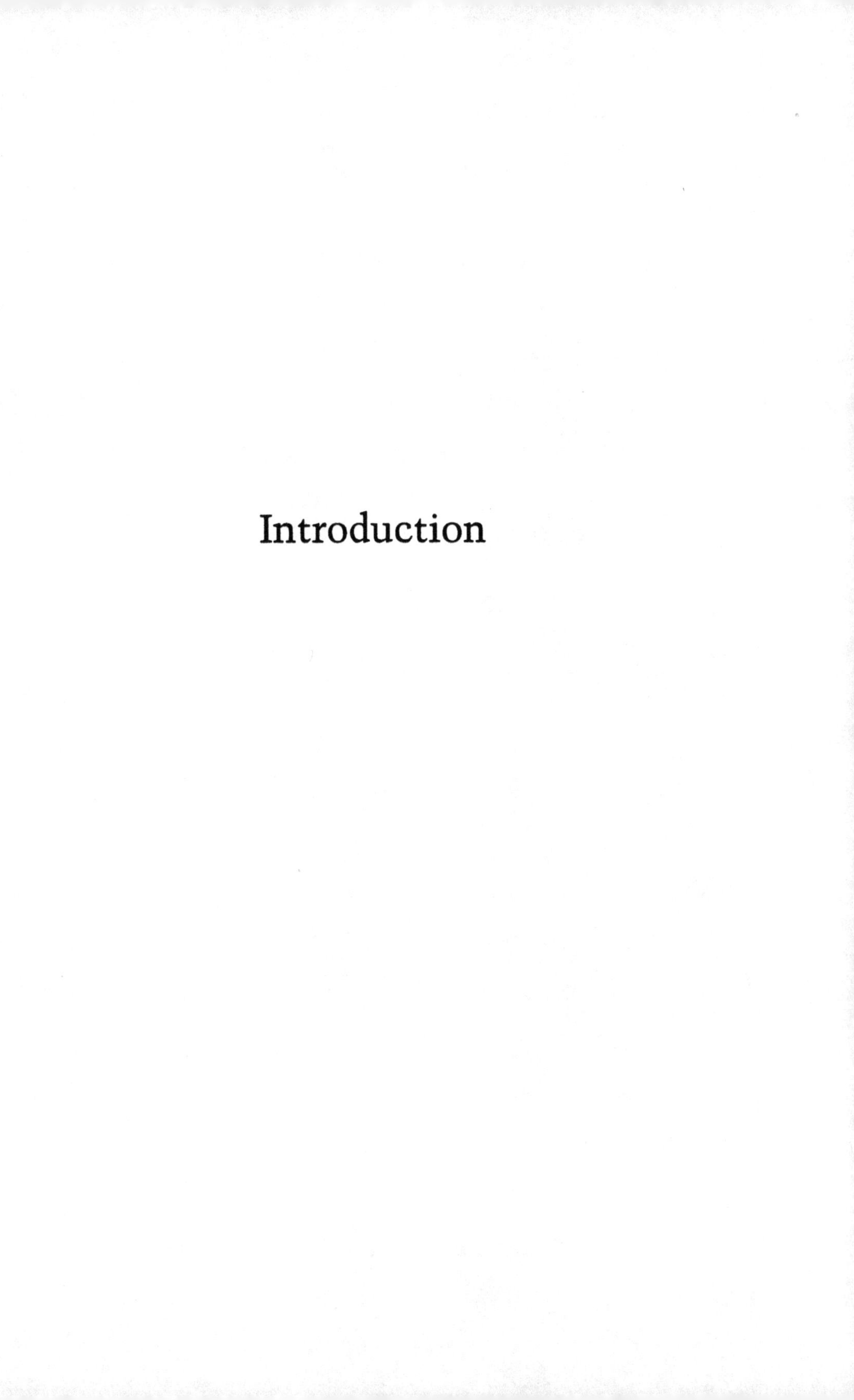

# Introduction

# Contents and Structure

*The praier and complaynte of the ploweman vnto Christe* is an interesting and significant Protestant reformist tract probably written in Lollard times well before it first appeared in print in 1531 from the press of Martinus de Keyser of Antwerp. This anonymous work must have been seen as important for the reformist cause in England since it was published again in 1532, this time in England itself by the mainstream printer Thomas Godfray, although Godfray's name appears nowhere in the second edition. The first printer of the work, de Keyser of Antwerp, was one of several printers, including Peter Quentell of Cologne, Peter Schoeffer of Worms, Johann Schott of Strassburg, and Johannes Hoochstraten, Johannes Grapheus, and Govaert van der Hagen all of Antwerp, who published English Protestant books on the continent between 1525 and 1535. According to Anthea Hume in 'English Protestant Books Printed Abroad,' de Keyser seems to have flourished as a printer between 1530 and 1535, and may have been responsible for printing as many as fourteen of the forty-one Protestant tracts that appeared in 1525–35.[1]

*The praier and complaynte of the ploweman* is divided into two main parts, a four-page anonymous preface entitled 'To the reader,' and the much longer 'praier and complaynte' itself, some ninety pages in length.[2] The title page and preface of both the first and second editions mention that the prayer was written 'not longe after the yere of our Lorde A thousande and thre hundred' (3–6), a date that is impossibly early. Probably it was actually written by a Lollard sympathizer, possibly in the third-quarter of the fourteenth century or, more likely, in the early years of the fifteenth when Wycliffite and

Lollard tracts flourished.[3] Certainly the presence of a ploughman as prominent speaker in the tract suggests that it was written after William Langland's *The Vision of William Concerning Piers the Plowman*, and was probably meant to capitalize on the popularity of Langland's poem, as were so many other Lollard or Protestant tracts dating from the later fourteenth century through the mid-sixteenth (see The Ploughman Tradition of Complaint, below). The early but wrong date of 'A thousande and thre hundred' was probably deliberately used to suggest that the sixteenth-century Protestant complaints against the church and the persecution of those views stretched well back into history, a point that the author of the preface is at pains to make.[4]

There is some conflicting speculation as to who may have written the anonymous sixteenth-century preface to the complaint. Two names are often connected with it: John Bale and John Foxe attribute the preface and the editorship of the tract to William Tyndale;[5] the initials 'W.T.' do appear at the head of the preface itself in the second edition, although this is by no means proof that Tyndale was actually responsible for it. Hume thinks that the work more properly belongs to George Joye, basing her claim on two pieces of possible evidence: Joye often wrote anonymously, and Martinus de Keyser printed Joye's work in the same type face that was used in *A praier and complaynte*. As Hume acknowledges, however, de Keyser also printed some of Tyndale's tracts in the same bastard type face (Hume 'English Protestant Books Printed Abroad' 1078–9).[6]

The preface is an informative document despite its brevity. With the exception of the final paragraph, the entire preface is an extended analogy which works to establish a connection between the iniquitous persecution that Christ and his apostles endured at the hands of their enemies and the present misfortunes inflicted by a corrupt church on those who hold reformist views. Even though Christ and his apostles 'taught no thinge which was not taught in the law and the prophetes more than a thousande yeres before' (17–18), they were accused of promulgating 'new lerninge' (23) and persecuted by 'the Phareses/ the Byschops/ the prestes/ the lawyers/ and the elders of the people' (21–2). The author is guilty of deliberate historical distortion and anachronism in his use of the word 'Byschops' – and perhaps even the word 'prestes' – in the list of those who spoke against

Christ in his own time.[7] He includes it, nevertheless, one feels, to force the first part of the analogy into line with the second, where 'holy byschops' (44–5) are seen as one category of enemy to the truth propounded by the reformers, who themselves are analogous to Christ and his apostles. In short, just as Christ and his apostles were condemned by those whose interests were threatened by the truth, so are present-day followers of Christ attacked by contemporary Pharisees, namely 'fryers,' 'monkes,' 'holy byschops,' 'vertuous prestes,' 'aunciente doctors' (67–8), and the like. In addition, the true descendants of Christ – Lollards and other early English reformers – are, like Christ himself, condemned for spreading 'newe lerninge' and misleading the people.[8]

The author of the tract spins out the analogy: Christ's crucifixion and death, instigated by his ideological enemies and abetted by an easily misled crowd, find their sixteenth-century counterpart in the persecution of noteworthy contemporary reformers. 'Thomas hitton' (84–5) of 'maydeston in kente' (86–7) is mentioned as an example of a present-day martyr who died for his beliefs at the hands of William Warham, Archbishop of Canterbury, and John Fisher, Bishop of Rochester.[9] The author of the preface is willing to ask God to forgive those benighted souls who were foolish enough to participate in Christ's condemnation, but, interestingly, he is unwilling to supplicate for contemporary 'malicious tyrauntes that persecute against their awne conscience' (90–1). These, including Warham and Fisher, must be left 'to the iudgemente of god as manyfest synners against the holy goost' (91–2).

Another important element in the analogy, especially significant for the emphasis it places on the socio-economic ranking of ideological adversaries, occurs when the author points out that Christ's enemies undermined his teaching by assuming that 'laye men /ydiotes fyschers /carpenters and other of the rascall sorte' (42–3), as they chose to call them, could not possibly have anything of significance or merit to say to anyone. For the author of *A praier and complaynte*, dealing with contemporary persecution, this is an important point, since the church in its present corrupt state writes off those who protest against abuse and excess by suggesting that their humble socio-economic status disqualifies them from access to the truth. Since, as Dickens has made clear, Lollardy flourished among the lower orders, and residual Lollard thought in the sixteenth-century also appealed to those of less than splendid means,[10] it seems clear that the author is here attempting to establish a direct line of descent from Christ to Lollards and others of a reformist bent. Such a privileging of the lower classes serves as an appropriate introduction to a protesting tract narrated by a humble Ploweman who himself does much to validate his own socio-economic group.[11]

In summary, Christ's teachings, dismissed scornfully as new learning by his enemies, were not new but based in part on 'the law and the prophetes more than a thousande yeres before' (17–18). Present-day reformist views spurned as new learning are even less entitled to that pejorative title than Christ's, since present-day learning is based on Christ's message, itself old and hallowed even in Christ's own time. Further, the wisdom that Christ and his apostles attempted to teach was largely ignored by those who assumed that intelligence was intimately tied to wealth and social status. The contemporary church makes the same mistake by dismissing the wisdom of poor folk because of their modest socio-economic condition, failing to recognize that they are part of a tradition of spiritual enlightenment stretching back to Christ's time and honoured by Christ himself.

The preface closes by employing a rhetorical technique not dissimilar to ones found in other reformist tracts of the sixteenth century. In order to solidify his argument that contemporary reformist colleagues are not 'a secte new fangled,'[12] the author points to the antiquity of the work which follows to prove that such complaints have a noble ancestry. A similar technique of bringing an old work to the service of a new – or rather revived – cause can be found, for example, in Jerome Barlowe and William Roye's *A proper dyaloge betweene a Gentillman and an husbandman*. In that work two disaffected speakers – a gentleman and a farmer – call upon and cite an old Lollard tract to justify their complaints about the pernicious practice of clerical impropriation; later in the work another old prose tract, probably written in the last quarter of the fourteenth century and arguing for the Bible in the vernacular, is appended to the contemporary document to demonstrate that the call for a vernacular Bible is not a recent invention of upstart reformers.

In the final sentence of the preface to *The praier and com-*

*playnte,* which places the old tract that follows within a contemporary reformist context, the Protestant author assures the reader that, if any 'more soch holy reliques' (115) come into his hands, he will do his best to see that they are published. In signing off in this manner the author is, I feel certain, echoing a sentiment found in another important and well-known reformist tract, *Rede Me and Be Nott Wrothe,* which appeared in 1528, and which was also published anonymously on the continent. Near the conclusion of the prefatory letter in *Rede Me and Be Nott Wrothe* the letter writer encourages his correspondent to send him other tracts similar to the one that follows so that he can work to ensure that they get into print 'yf in englonde they maye not be publisshed' (150). It seems unlikely that the author of the preface to *A praier and complaynte* would not have known about Barlowe and Roye's controversial work, and he probably borrowed this idea to demonstrate the close connection between reformers of like stripe.

The Ploweman's prayer itself is less prayer *and* complaint, as the title suggests, and more prayer or complaint, as the running titles state, because, as the tract unfolds, it becomes clear that one term is synonymous with the other. Throughout the work the Ploweman addresses himself to God: his prayer is a complaint in which corrupt manifestations within the church are explained to God as if God himself were ignorant of them. God is a silent listener, as is the reading audience to whom this monologue is actually addressed. The fact that the Ploweman seems to be speaking to God in prayer is a skilful rhetorical device: we the readers hear an uninterrupted exposé of church iniquities – the real point of the tract; at the same time, we are assured of the Ploweman's honesty and integrity and know the state of his soul because the complaint is in the form of a prayer.

The opening of the work appears to be little more than a display of the Ploweman's impressive knowledge of Old Testament texts. However, this string of biblical verses anticipates other lists in the work; in this work the list is a major technique employed to enhance unity among occasionally wayward materials. The Ploweman begins by calling on 'Iesu Christ' (152) whom he claims was never needed more than he is at this present time to help 'thy pore servantes ... in her gret nede to fight agens synne/ and agens the deule' (152–4). It is not uncommon in religious complaint literature to see the present state of affairs as in dire need of assistance, and in beginning his tract in this manner the Ploweman is working within a well-established tradition. Then immediately follow a number of references from 'Isaye' to make clear how Old Testament persecutions of God's people find their present-day counterpart in the as yet unspecified iniquities carried out against those on whose behalf the Ploweman prays to God. At this early stage Isaiah is evidently the prophet whom the Ploweman feels best anticipates contemporary injustices; he cites him at length four times in the space of two pages. Then follows a not altogether relevant summary of Old Testament narratives beginning with a brief reference to the Adam and Eve story (217ff), mention of the flood (229ff), Abraham's injunction from God to slay Isaac (233ff), the descendants of Isaac (241ff), and the captivity of the chosen people in Egypt (245ff). The Ploweman, who, up to this point, has yet to establish a clear thesis for his complaint and seems simply to be floundering among Old Testament narratives, then claims that the Old Testament 'was but a schadewe and a fygure of a newe testamente' (300–1). A citation from Paul and a brief comment on Christ's birth, death, and resurrection (318ff) follow to prove this point. In some unspecified way these biblical stories are meant to serve as 'the bred of spirituall lyfe' (336–7) for all Christian men, a metaphor that allows the Ploweman to use figurative language in his tract so that it might escape closer rational or logical analysis. In addition to this 'bred' God has also provided us with 'a draught of water of lyfe to drinke' (340–1). This water turns out to be the seven commandments, which the Ploweman proceeds to list – his second list in nine pages.

The relevance of this opening section of the Ploweman's *complaynte* becomes clear only after one has read the tract through to the end. What the Ploweman wants to show by focusing on the Old and New Testaments and the commandments is that these are the only elements to which one need subscribe in order to lead a true and fulfilling Christian life. As he attempts to show from here on, anything beyond the Scriptures and the commandments is not only unnecessary but actually harmful to the simple Christian's quest for salvation.

The Ploweman now begins to sharpen his focus and, as a result, the tract becomes increasingly more interesting and meaningful.

After having regaled God with a summary of Old Testament texts, the history of the chosen people, the essential message of the New Testament, and the commandments – all of which God logically should know already – the Ploweman slowly turns his attention to the true enemies of Christianity. He begins by mentioning in general terms those who have claimed that they themselves were Christ and, as a result, 'haue begyled thus thy puple' (387). No sooner has he started to warm to the attack than he is tempted again to create a list and does so by briefly mentioning what three things 'The heringe of god stondeth in' (398). Those who trust in God can be certain that he will forgive their sins, 'For his mercy ys endeles' (422). This mention of the forgiveness of sins leads the Ploweman finally to turn his attention to the first of the church's abuses, auricular confession, a practice universally attacked by those with strong reformist tendencies from Wycliffe's day down to the sixteenth century and beyond (see Commentary, below). The Ploweman makes clear that well before the church appropriated to itself the power to forgive sins and impose penances, Christ had already forgiven Peter and Mary Magdalene without the church's help or approbation. Since no one has greater power than Christ, those who presume to forgive sins are putting themselves 'above God' (435). As a true Lollard, entirely devoted to the notion of 'sola scriptura,' the Ploweman rarely tires of quoting scripture. He rejects the claim of the priests that Christ validated the sacerdotal forgiveness of sins when he exhorted lepers to show themselves to priests,[13] arguing that 'the old lawe [does not] betokeneth synne in this new lawe' (442), and that 'This nys nothinge to the purpos of schriuinge' (457). The true distinction is between leprosy of the body, which priests are charged to deal with, and 'the lepre of the soule' (459), which only Christ can heal.

Not only do priests have no right to forgive sin, but also they have no power to impose penances. Those who place their faith in fraudulent sacerdotal powers rather than in God's legitimate power to forgive sin tend to sin more frequently because they know that forgiveness is as close as the next confessional box (463–72).

Then follows another list of three abuses associated with auricular confession. Because of confession, some people believe that certain priests have greater power to forgive sin than others (473–5), that certain priests can forgive both sin and the temporal punishment attached thereto (476–9), and that many priests feather their own nests by selling 'forgeuenes of mennes synnes and absolucions for money' (481ff), a 'heresye' (482) that the Ploweman calls 'symonye' (482), a somewhat broad definition of the term which is usually associated with the selling of ecclesiastical preferments, especially benefices.

The abuse of penance by priests leads the Ploweman to consider the appropriation of God's power by the church in general and the pope in particular, the major subject of attack in the work and one which weaves its way in and out of subsequent discussions of other topics of moment. The pope, here and elsewhere, is referred to as Christ's 'viker in erth' (528) and is accused of undoing Christ's 'law of mercy/ and of loue' (513). He is vilified as a formidable curser and blasphemer of those who offend him. Assuming the title of 'fadur of fadurs' (531), he behaves in a most unfatherly way; moreover, through his active support of other disreputable clergy he creates many more uncaring fathers devoid of love not only for those whom they are supposed to tend but also, ironically, for those of other spiritual orders whom they see as rivals.[14]

This attack on the clergy – friars in particular, one feels – is directed against those who forsake the poor, whom they are supposed to aid, in order to ingratiate themselves with the rich through lengthy and ostentatious prayer for 'both quycke and deed' (565–6). Such public display of prayer is analogous to the practice of the Pharisees who worshipped God 'with her lippes. and her herte ys fer frome the' (578–9). In behaving in this manner these hypocritical religious figures follow not the commandments but 'mennes tradicions' (579–80), an expression with a biblical source that one also finds in Tyndale, in Barlowe and Roye's *Rede Me and Be Nott Wrothe*, and in *A proper dyaloge betwene a Gentillman and an Husbandman.*

The Ploweman turns to an analysis of true prayer, pointing out that it is a private affair in which no currency need change hands. Once again the pope is attacked, this time for encouraging fraudulent and profitable prayer and for formalizing it in such contexts as 'matens evensonge and masse' (616–17). The mention of the mass leads the Ploweman to attack the always controversial doctrine of transubstantiation. For him the mass has no sacrifical value, and the body and blood of Christ, it would appear, have merely symbolic significance (see Commentary). The Ploweman pauses for one brief paragraph in his list of complaints against the church to explain how the church inverts the truth of God's word so that everything about Christianity 'ys turned vpso doune' (678), an important expression used twice more in this tract.

The list begins again as the Ploweman attacks unmarried clergy – a perennial source of complaint and salty humour in many sixteenth-century satiric and reformist tracts (see Commentary). He then devotes considerable space to exposing another abuse, associated with pilgrimages, shrines, and churches. The Ploweman, like many of his Lollard contemporaries and reformist descendants, abominates the invocation of saints and regards the worship of images as a money-making scheme devised by a greedy church. The Ploweman's two contemptuous references to 'mawmetys of stockes and of stones' (727–8, 739) echo similar attitudes and expressions found in the Lollard tract *The Plowman's Tale* and the sixteenth-century dialogue *Rede Me and Be Nott Wrothe* (see Commentary).

Hard upon this section of the complaint follows a list of six illustrations all introduced by the same phrase, or a slight variant of it – 'A lorde what dome ys it' (863ff) – to show how Christ's law 'ys turned vpso downe' (862), the second time this phrase is used in the tract. The Ploweman argues that, although cattle thieves are slain, a priestly 'spousebreker' (864) and 'a lechour' (865) flourish. Horse thieves are slain too, but those members of the church hierarchy who 'robbeth thy pore puple of here lyfelode' (870) are not punished. Those who break laws established by a corrupt church are condemned as heretics, but those who ignore Christ's commandments are praised as good men. Unlearned men who insult priests are cursed, but priests who abuse the unlearned escape punishment. Simple people are cursed if they dabble in tithing, but tithing is legal for priests, as are idolatrous paintings 'of stonen walles' (881) and 'songes of laten that the puple knowen not' (881–2). Poor men are punished for their sins, but the rich are allowed to continue in theirs if they pay the clergy a sufficient amount.

A large portion of this tract, indeed almost half the work, is devoted to an exposé of corruption within the papacy, and the Ploweman seems to be unable to shake himself free from his preoccupations with the pope. Consequently he is not embarrassed by redundancy even when it threatens to undermine the structural integrity of the piece as a whole. The last part of this tract is considerably less integrated than the first. Once one manages to get beyond the Ploweman's tentative start, where numerous scriptural citations replace a firm and clear thesis, the work picks up momentum as it begins to detail and highlight various manifestations of corruption in the church through a confident linear progression from one point to the next. In the latter part of the work, however, the discussion at times loses direction, as the focus on the pope's enormities turns back on itself too often. The pope is responsible for encouraging the martyrdom of those who disagree with his doctrines (922ff). Rather than taking up swords against a common enemy, the church hierarchy, encouraged by the 'vyker,' slays honest and simple Christians. This 'vyker,' supposedly Peter's successor, behaves in a manner quite unlike Peter, who was himself once upbraided by Christ for raising his sword in anger. Steadfast in his refusal to show patience and kindness to those he has been chosen to lead, he 'fedeth thy puple/ with cursinge and with smytinge' (1041–2). In addition to the pope's cruelty, the Ploweman focuses once again on his greed and the fact that he 'hath ybroke the commaundement of charite' (1064–5) by insisting that all those who accept the faith give their goods and chattels to him when he already has more than he needs or is entitled to. The Ploweman reminds us that King Saul had his kingdom taken away from him (1094ff) and asks God to do the same thing to the pope. The pope is the new 'Nabugodnosor' (1105) who has made 'hymself a false god on erthe' (1104); he is 'Nabugodnosor' on two later occasions, and in one of these his kingdom is compared to Babylon. Relentlessly the Ploweman keeps up his attack, showing his revulsion with the papacy. The pope is the source of all that is inimical to true Christian belief. As the tract draws to a close the frequent ironic references to the pope as 'vyker' give way to the term 'byschop of Rome,'[15] which in turn gives way to that ubiquitous term of opprobrium for the pope, 'Antechrist' (1563; see Commentary).

Not until about five pages from the end of the work is new material briefly introduced. Perhaps feeling pressured to complete a work which has already gone beyond the length a succinct presentation of facts would call for, the Ploweman attacks the doctrine of purgatory and criticizes simony, 'the sellinge of byschoprychеs and personages' (1610–11). The tract comes to an end with an extended commentary on clerical celibacy, something mentioned much earlier in the work, and offers some tangential comments on the nature of marriage itself.

# The Persona of the Ploweman

One of the devices that helps to hold this sometimes wayward and repetitive tract together is the figure of the Ploweman himself and especially the frequent manifestations of his social class within the work. In general terms the most pervasive dichotomy that the narrator establishes in *The praier and complaynte*, and the one on which he focuses, is the contrast between an uncaring, wealthy, and self-serving church on the one hand, and the poor, humble, simple Christian in need of spiritual sustenance on the other. The Ploweman situates himself in this latter category and sees the former as ruled over by the pope, the uncaring father, variously called Christ's vicar, the bishop of Rome, and Antichrist. In a very real sense this works pits Ploweman against pope, one social class against another. Since the Ploweman is the narrator of this work, in the guise of a humble suppliant before God he can control and direct the reader's responses and as a result gain victory – albeit a literary one – over the apparently insuperable pope himself.

Despite insisting on the need of simple Christians for spiritual guidance from caring shepherds, the Ploweman himself, although ostensibly aligned with the poor and the humble, proves to be significantly more independent, perceptive, and intellectually acute than those with whom he associates and about whom he shows so much care. Even though his situation in life is modest, he is, nevertheless, a keen observer of church abuses and not deceived by fraudulent manifestations of sanctity on the church's part. This Ploweman-narrator is clearly a student of the Bible and can quote and paraphrase from it with ease and frequency. Moreover, he is also able to judge the relative merits of the Old Testament and the New and is adept enough at exegesis to see the typological significance of the Old Testament, which he regards as 'but a schadewe and a fygure of a newe testamente' (300–1). He is also aware of perceived abuses in the church against which articulate Lollards and Protestants regularly fulminated: he attacks auricular confession, the mass, the doctrine of transubstantiation, the practice of tithing, the invocation of saints, pilgrimages, immoral clergy who are bound by non-scriptural laws of celibacy, and uncharitable behaviour in general found throughout the entire spiritual hierarchy from priest, to monk, to friar, to the pope himself. Thus, although this narrator is a ploughman, he is not just any ordinary ploughman, nor does he conform to our prejudices concerning the intellectual powers of humble tillers of the soil. Speaking on behalf of the social class from which he comes, he is an articulate, informed, and critical observer of the human spiritual scene at the beginning of the fifteenth century. His criticisms of the church in his own day well served the needs of like-minded reformers a century later. He knows that the Roman Catholic Church is what is wrong with the world, and like several of his literary-ploughman colleagues, he is prepared to expose that church to the general view in order to reveal its iniquities. The literary ploughman, here as elsewhere, represents a manifestation of the Lollard priesthood of the laity, a notion clearly at odds with the elitist church's appropriation of truth to itself and to a coterie of those belonging to the spiritual hierarchy.

Throughout the tract the Ploweman shows enormous concern, support, and respect for fellow members of his socio-economic class. The work begins with the Ploweman sympathizing with Christ's 'pore servantes' (153) who are in need of help and spiritual guidance in these troubled times. Here 'poor' is nicely ambiguous, one feels, referring not only to those who have been downtrodden, abused, and marginalized by the church, but also to those (invariably the same people) of an inferior social station who feel the full effects of a wealthy, uncaring church. In the tract the Ploweman refers regularly to 'lewed men'[16] – the expression takes on the prominence of a mantra – and compares their humble condition to those who focus their attention on self-aggrandizement and wealth. He also often uses the word 'lewd' ironically to show that the unlearned are nevertheless intelligent enough to see how the church violates the word of God as found in the Scriptures. For instance, in discussing auricular confession, the Ploweman makes clear that 'we lewed men' know that those who claim to be able to forgive sin are placing themselves above God (433ff). Unlike the selfish church, 'lewed men that ben laborers' (547–8) do not work solely for their own self-interest. 'Lewd men' know that ostentatious praying is of no value, and that the Lord's goodness is endless to those who keep his commandments. The Ploweman argues that 'a lewed man maye serue God as well as a man of religion' (591). In addition, 'good husbande men that well gouern her housholdes' (669–70) are not unlike worthy priests; through their caring attitude towards those for whom they are responsible 'they lyvedeyn as trew Christen men every daye they eten Christes body and dronken hys blode to the sustenance of lyvynge of here soules' (673–5). The Ploweman addresses God and hopes that he will not neglect a 'pore mannes soule' (722) simply because he works with his hands 'for hys lyuelode' (722). 'Lewed men' are unjustly treated by the clergy and are thrown in prison for preaching God's word. God's efficacious word, found in the scriptures, is hidden 'by quaynte gloses from thy lewed puple' (1184). Those who do preach, however, do so in the presence of the rich rather than 'before pore men' (1221–2). Despite their lack of formal training, 'lewed men' do not acknowledge the pope and only recognize one God. Christ himself, the Ploweman states – and the preface reiterates – appeared on earth as a poor man. The Ploweman reminds Christ of his words in the sermon on the mount where he honoured the poor by promising them the kingdom of heaven (1262–3). The New Testament is eloquent on the virtues of poverty; nevertheless, in this world, under the aegis of the pope, 'pore men and porenesse ben yhated/ and rych men ben yloued and honoured' (1274–6). Poor men are deemed to be without 'grace' (1277) and those who seek out poverty are regarded as fools. In these times, when 'the worlde ys turned vpsedowne' (1341), everyone studies how to be rich and all men are ashamed to be seen as poor.

Finally, as if speaking for himself, and with a view to justifying this very tract, the narrator-Ploweman implores God to receive his prayer even though it is uttered by a poor man who is neither committed to the religious life nor in any position to pay for spiritual favours. The Ploweman is never more moving and at the same time more bitingly ironic in this tract than in this personal appeal to be heard: 'And so Lorde oure hope ys/ that thou wilt as sone yhere a plowmans prayer/ and he kepe thyne hestes/as thou wilt do a mans of religion: though that the plowman ne maye nat haue so much syluer for his preyer as men of religion. For they kunnen not so wel preysen her preyers as these other chapmen: But Lorde oure hope ys/ that oure preyer be neuer the worse though it be not so well sold as other mens preyers' (592–8).

Of all of the works written within the ploughman tradition of complaint none pays more manifest and overt tribute to the working classes than *The praier and complaynte of the ploweman.* Despite its structural flaws and sometimes maddening repetitions, occasioned in large part by the author's uncontrollable hatred of the papacy, it is an eloquently subversive tract, pitting the repressed common man imbued with the simple truths of the Bible and a knowledge of the commandments against the mighty monolithic and conservative church.[17] *The praier and complaynte* is a strong statement of Lollard belief obviously well suited to the needs of the early-sixteenth-century English reformers who would have seen their battle against a powerful church as similar to and perhaps derived from those earlier struggles that the Lollards waged against the various manifestations of Antichrist.[18]

With a view to sustaining and enhancing the emphasis in the tract on the inherent nobility of poverty, simplicity, and labour and the compatibility of these qualities with the Christian message, the author makes skilful use of a metaphor designed to appeal to those to whom the tract is in fact addressed.[19] Time and again, he invokes and alludes to the metaphor of the shepherd who tends his sheep. The choice is a brilliant one: for one thing the metaphor has biblical authority, a *sine qua non* for Lollard reformers and their sixteenth-century descendants; for another, it serves to capture the attention of those who make their living by ploughing, working the land, and tending their crops and livestock. In addition, both ploughman and shepherd endure the rigours of economic injustice and poverty. For the ploughman this fact is everywhere apparent in this tract; for the shepherd it is evident in a work such as the Wakefield *Second Shepherd's Play.* Always aware of the members of his audience and their socio-economic category, the author of *The Praier and complaynte* never forgets his persona as Plowеman: by employing the metaphor of good and bad shepherds he dramatically increases the appeal of this work for those to whom it is really addressed.

# Analogues and Sources

By the time *The praier and complaynte of the ploweman* made its first appearance in print in 1531, a number of early English Protestant books published on the continent and dealing with reformist subjects similar to those found in *The praier* had seen the light of day. The fact that many of these works expressed views identical to those found in *The praier*, a work first written during Lollard times, indicates that not only Lutheran but specifically Lollard views were well known among early Protestants, and *The praier* would have found a congenial home among these other tracts.[20] Discounting biblical works and their prefaces published during this period, such as Tyndale's New Testament (*STC* 2823, 2824), his preface to Paul's Epistle to the Romans (*STC* 24438), the psalter of David (*STC* 2370), and Tyndale's Genesis (*STC* 2350), there were eleven non-biblical but polemical works published on the continent prior to the appearance of *The praier*. Of these, five were altogether original: Tyndale's three great works, *The Parable of the Wicked Mammon* (*STC* 24454; *Doctrinal Treaties* 29–126), *The Obedience of a Christian Man* (*STC* 24446; *Doctrinal Treatises* 127–344), and *The Practice of Prelates* (*STC* 24465; *Expositions and Notes* 249–344); Jerome Barlowe and William Roye's *Rede Me and Be Nott Wrothe* (*STC* 21427); and Simon Fish's *A Supplicacyon for the Beggers* (*STC* 10883; More vii). Six, however, were, like *The praier and complaynte*, borrowed in whole or in part and appropriated by English Protestants either to meet the needs of their reformist constituents or to proselytize. Four of these six were works originally written by continental reformers: William Roye's *A Lytle treatous or dialoge very necessary for all christen men to learne and to knowe* (*STC* 24223.3) is a modified translation of a dialogue by Wolfgang Capito that appeared first in Latin in August 1527 under the title 'De Pueris Instituendis Ecclesiae Argentinensis Isagoge' and immediately after in German as 'Kinder bericht vnd fragstuck von gemeynen puncten Christlichs glaubens' (Hume 'William Roye's "Brefe Dialoge"' 308); *The summe of the holye scripture* (*STC* 3036), a translation of Henricus Bomelius's *Summa der Godliker Scrifturen*, sometimes attributed to Simon Fish; William Roye's translation of Erasmus's *Paraclesis*, which Roye entitled *An exhortation to the diligent studye of scripture*, to which is added Roye's translation of Luther's seventh chapter of the first Epistle to the Corinthians (*STC* 10493); and finally John Frith's English translation of Luther's *The Revelation of Antichrist* (*STC* 11394).

Although these four translations of continental Protestant works leave no doubt that German reformist thought in its various manifestations left its mark on early English Protestant thought – a view which has never been questioned – the presence of other works with clear Lollard roots indicates that Wycliffite ideas were prevalent in English reformist minds as well, and coexisted with continental views, some of which were identical with them. Excluding *The praier and complaynte of the ploweman*, two other Lollard tracts, both published in 1530, appear among the borrowed works published on the continent for English Protestants. The first is *A proper dyaloge betwene a Gentillman and an Husbandman* (*STC* 1462.3; 3021; 1462.5),[21] a work made up of a discussion between a reformist gentleman and his interlocutor, an equally reformist farmer, on the unfortunate economic and social effects of clerical impropriation. Added to this altogether original tract, written, I believe, by Jerome Barlowe and William Roye, is what the husbandman calls 'an olde treatyse made aboute the tyme of kinge Rycharde the seconde.' This prose treatise, clearly a Lollard document, also argues against clerical impropriation by invoking biblical and historical precedents for its illegality and immorality. Barlowe and Roye add the Lollard tract to their own dialogue to support their claim that impropriations are wrong and to give historical authority to their position.

The second of the two Lollard documents is made up of two fifteenth-century tracts: *The examinacion of Master William*

*Thorpe* ... and *The examinacion of the honorable knight syr Ihonn Oldcastell Lorde Cobham* (*STC* 24045), perhaps edited by William Tyndale, although Hume believes it to be the work of George Constantine ('English Protestant Books' 1077–8).[22]

Although his identity cannot be finally determined, the editor of *The praier and complaynte of the ploweman* was clearly a part of the group of English reformist writers publishing their work from the relative safety of the continent, and would have been aware of all these original and borrowed contributions to the English reformist cause generated by like-minded colleagues; in addition, he probably would not have hesitated to introduce to his countrymen a Lollard document since two of them had been published in Antwerp, as his would be, only one year earlier.

Although Foxe reprints *The examinacion of Master Thorpe* (III 250–85), which was probably first written in 1407, he does not reproduce the 1530 preface composed by a contemporary reformist editor. The preface is important for the two links it creates with *The praier and complaynte*, both of which suggest that the editor of the latter might have borrowed some of the Thorpe material. In the preface to *The praier and complaynte* the editor mentions the martyrdom of 'Thomas hitton whom willyam werham/ byschop of Canturbury and Iohn fyscher byschop of Rochestur morthered at maydeston in kente the last yere' (84–7). In the introduction to Thorpe's examination, the editor, writing in 1530, the very year of Hitton's death according to the editor of *The praier*,[23] puzzles over the reason for Hitton's martyrdom and states: 'Who can tell wherfore that good preaste and holy martyr Syr Thomas hitton was brente/ now thys yere at maydstone yn Kent' (A2r). The editor of *The praier and complaynte* justifies introducing this Lollard tract to sixteenth-century readers by arguing that it both demonstrates the antiquity of the church's abuses against the true doctrine of Christ and also shows how the church, in Lollard times and earlier, as now, stigmatized the teachings of Christ and his disciples with the dismissive terms 'new lerninge' and 'new masters.' He states: 'Now good reader/ that thou maist se playnly that it ys no new thinge/ but an olde practyse of oure prelates lerned of their fathers the byschops/ phareses and prestes of the olde law/ to defame the doctrine of Christe with the name of new lerninge and the teachers thereof with the name of new masters' (99–104). Similarly in Thorpe's examination the editor makes clear how the tract will serve not only to expose the antiquity of the church's pernicious abuses but also to emphasize, through its focus on Thorpe's examination, the deceit and secrecy involved in contemporary sixteenth-century abuses. History proves that the church's methods have not changed; it also proves that now, as earlier, people continue to suffer unjustly for their beliefs:

> Wherfore I exhorte the good brother/ who soeuer thou be that redest thys treatyse/ marke hit well and consyder it seryouslye/ and there thou shalt fynde not onelye what the chyrche ys/ theyre doctryne the Sacramente/the worshyppynge off ymages/ pylgremage/ confessyon/ swerynge and payinge of tythes. But also thou mayst se what stronge and and substancyall argumentes off scripture and doctoures/ and what clerkely reasons/ my lorde/ that hadde and prymate of the holye chyrche in England (as he wilbe taken) bryngeth agenst this pore/ folysh/ symple/ and madde losell/ knave/ and heretike as he calleth hym. And also the verye cause wherfore all their examynacions are made in darkenes. And the lorde of all lyght shall lighten the with the candle of his grace/ for to se the trewth. (A2r–A2v)

Finally, it is possible that there is direct indebtedness between Thorpe's examination and *The praier and complaynte*. Both editors are aware of linguistic differences between the period in which the works were first written and the era in which they are, as it were, reborn. Both hasten to add that, although they have altered the English, they have not changed the content, a claim that all reborn works of this era could not honestly make.[24] The editor of Thorpe states:

> This I haue corrected and put forth in the english that now is vsed in Englande/ for ower sothern man/ nothynge ther to addynge nor yet mynysshyng. And I entende hereafter with the helpe of God to put it forthe in his owne olde english/ which shal well serue/ I doute not/ bothe for the northern men and the faythfull brothern of scotlande. (A2v)

And in *The praier and complaynte* the editor states:

> I haue put forth here in printe this prayer and complaynte of the plowman which was written not longe after the yere of our Lorde a thousande and thre hundred/ in his awne olde english/ chaingynge there in nothinge as ferforth as I coulde obserue it other the english or ortographie/ addinge also ther to a table of soch olde wordes as be now antiquate and worne out of knoulege by processe of tyme. (104–10)

If the sixteenth-century editor of *The praier and complaynte* knew Thorpe's examination, as seems likely, he would have found in it considerable encouragement for the publication of his own tract only one year later since both works are written solidly within the Lollard tradition and share a common ideology. In his examination before his accusers, the chief of whom is Archbishop Arundel, Thorpe openly praises John Wycliffe's learning and the effects of his teaching on 'so many men and women' (Foxe III 257–8). Later in the tract one of the other bishops acting with Arundel encourages Thorpe to renounce 'Lollard opinions' (279) by pointing out how one 'Nicoll Herford' has profited since abandoning such pernicious views.

The charges brought against Thorpe clearly reflect his Lollard bias. The certification against him reads as follows: 'The thirde Sundaie after Easter, A.D. 1407., William Thorpe came vnto the towne of Shrewesburie, and through leaue granted vnto him to preach, he saide openlie, in S. Chads church in his sermon, that the sacrament of the aultar, after the consecration was natural bread. And that images should in no wise be worshipped; and that men should not goe on pilgrimages; and that priests haue no title to tithes; and that it is not lawfull to sweare in any wise' (258). Thorpe denies the charges as baldly stated as they are in 'this roll,' but in the course of his response to each individual accusation it is clear that, despite his qualifications and logic chopping, he is a firm adherent to Wycliffite views.[25] Furthermore, even though it is not one of the specific charges brought against him, it is also evident near the end of his examination that Thorpe is opposed to the church's position on the efficacy of auricular confession. In *The praier and complaynte* the Ploweman, like Thorpe, stands opposed to confession, transubstantiation, swearing, images in churches, and the associations these have with pilgrimages, and tithing. Both Thorpe's examination and *The praier and complaynte* are reborn Lollard tracts but one of the major differences between them is the way in which *The praier and complaynte* attacks the church hierarchy as such, and especially the pope. Thorpe avoids the subject, perhaps because of the very form and occasion of the treatise itself. In his examination Thorpe is defending himself against the charge of heresy in front of judges who are themselves members of the hierarchy that the Ploweman so vigorously attacks. To attack the pope and, by implication, the entire spiritual hierarchy of the church would have immediately destroyed what little credibility Thorpe has as the tract opens and proceeds. In short, such an attack would have made Thorpe appear mean-spirited and grossly intolerant in front of his judges, and would have left little room for them to give him the benefit of the doubt.[26] The Ploweman in *The praier and complaynte*, however, is speaking ostensibly to a silent and friendly listener, whom he addresses as a proreformist Lollard God.

*The examinacion of the honourable knight syr Ihonn Oldcastell Lorde Cobham*, printed along with Thorpe's examination and reprinted in Foxe (III 329–35), would have well served the editor of *The praier and complaynte* too since it is an even more strident denunciation of the church than Thorpe's examination. Less careful about offending his interlocutors and accusers, Cobham speaks out forthrightly against the four particular charges brought against him. His position on transubstantiation is closer to what would later be designated Lutheran rather than Zwinglian; he is opposed to auricular confession, denies the efficacy of pilgrimages, relics, and images of saints, and is most outspoken – unlike Thorpe in his examination – on the church hierarchy, which he describes in terms that would doubtless please the editor of *The praier and complaynte*. Mentioning Christ's meekness, mercy, and poverty – characteristics of Christ that *The praier and complaynte* articulates – Cobham states: 'And let all men consider well this, that Christ was meek and merciful; the pope is proud and a tyrant: Christ was poor and forgave; the pope is rich and a malicious manslayer, as his daily acts do prove him: Rome is the very nest of Antichrist; and out of that nest come all the disciples of him; of whom prelates, priests, and monks, are the body, these pilled friars are the tail behind' (333).

Another tract, published only one year before the first edition of *The praier and complaynte*, may also have encouraged the editor of the latter to bring his Lollard work to the public attention. Barlowe and Roye's *A proper dyaloge betwene a Gentillman and an Husbandman* is a hybrid work made up of a dialogue and two early prose tracts, the first of which is a Lollard piece devoted to pointing out the prevalence of clerical greed, especially as manifested in the impropriation of secular lands and the abuses attendant upon it. As in *The praier and complaynte*, one of the principals is a farmer or husbandman, a clear relative of the Lollard ploughman. It is the farmer who draws to the attention of the gentleman the Lollard tract that makes up a large portion of the work. Additionally, he uses the Lollard tract both to show that the complaint against impropriations is of considerable antiquity as well as to demonstrate, like the editor of *The praier and complaynte*, that the present complaints cannot be written off as the ravings of an upstart group of contemporary grumblers. Just as the editor of *The praier and complaynte* is at pains to show that the doctrine of Christ preached by present-day reformists is not 'newe lernynge,' but rather part of a well-established tradition stretching back to Christ and his apostles, so both the husbandman and the gentleman cite the Lollard tract to establish a clear sense of history and continuity between present and past reformist thought, a clear indication of the indebtedness of Lutheranism to Lollardy. The gentleman points out how the church tries to convince others of the 'newness' of contemporary complaints, thereby working to discredit them:

They resorte to lordes and great estates
With whom they are dayly checke mates
  Ye to saye the trouthe their soueraynes.
Where amonge other communicacion
They admonishe them with protestacion
  To beware of thes heretikes Lutheranes.
Whom they saye is a secte new fangled
With execrable heresyes entangled
  Sekinge the chirches perdicion.
Which oure fore fathers as wise as we
Were content with humble simplicite

To honour/ obeynge their tuycion.
Also none presumed till nowe a late
Against the clergye to beare any hate
Or grudged at their possession. (641–55)

The husbandman responds, providing an approximate date for the tract that follows, as does the editor in *The praier and complaynte:*

By seynt mary syr/ that is a starcke lye
I can shewe you a worcke by and by
Against that poynte makinge obiection.
Which of warantyse I dare be bolde
That it is aboue an hundred yere olde
As the englishe selfe dothe testifye
Wherin the auctour with argumentes
Speaketh against the lordshippes and rentes
Of the clergye possessed wrongfully. (656–65)

To which the gentleman adds the following in order to clinch the point that contemporary complaints cannot be dismissed as new and, therefore, of no value:

Is it so olde as thou doest here expresse
Reprouynge their pompous lordlynes
So is it than no new found heresy. (666–8)

Although Barlowe and Roye's mélange of dialogue and old prose tracts does not take on and expose as wide a spectrum of church corruption as *The praier and complaynte,* it does, nevertheless, overtly articulate the marriage between Lutheran and Lollard ideologies more than any other reformist work published between 1525 and 1531. Apart from reproducing a large chunk of an identifiable Lollard document, it also harks back to perceived church atrocities which have clear Lollard roots: as well as mentioning the difficulties King John had with the clergy over clerical temporalities, it also alludes to the troubled life of the Lollard Sir John Oldcastle and mentions the Lollard persecutions under Henry v.

Given the similarities in the topics discussed, range of reference, historical precedents, and sensitivity to linguistic differences between eras, it is likely that the editor of *The praier and complaynte* knew both Thorpe's examination and *A proper dyaloge* and saw his reborn Lollard tract as altogether consistent with the other two Lollard pieces transported into the sixteenth century to advance the cause of religious reform.

If the editor of *A praier and complaynte* was encouraged to publish his Lollard tract because of similar rebirths occurring only one year before the appearance of the first edition of his work, it is also possible that he saw within reformist – if not necessarily overtly Lollard – works published on the continent between 1527 and 1530 material that was consistent with the subjects of complaint in his tract. Several of these works are themselves openly derived from German sources. Three of them involve William Roye to some extent, and two of these three are translations. The first is *A Lytle treatous or dialoge very necessary for all christen men to learne and to knowe* (*STC* 24223.3), which appeared from the press of Johann Schott of Strassburg in 1527 (Hume 'English Protestant Books' 1069). This translation of Wolfgang Capito's dialogue between a father and his son contains radical reformist material appearing at a surprisingly early stage in the history of sixteenth-century English reformist thought. There is little in the tract to differentiate it from Lollard opinion except for the emphasis on the Lutheran doctrine of justification by faith. Like *The praier and complaynte, A Lytle treatous* attacks confession, pilgrimages, images, and the mass. In addition, the work is virulently anti-clerical, although Roye does not fix on the pope for special attack as *The praier and complaynte* does. The vexed issue of transubstantiation is given a decidedly Zwinglian emphasis in Roye's text. According to the author, Christ's corporal presence does not inhere in the bread and wine, a denial of both transubstantiation and the doctrine of the real presence, and a departure from the Lutheran view, the so-called consubstantiation position.[27]

Roye's other translation is his English rendering of Erasmus's *Paraclesis* and Luther's exposition of the seventh chapter of St Paul's first Epistle to the Corinthians (1529; *STC* 10493). These two pieces published together have less relevance for *The praier and complaynte*. The former deals with the importance of a vernacular Bible and the latter with justification by faith, both of which subjects have little apparent interest for the editor of *The praier and complaynte*, a work, as we have seen, that is largely devoted to attacking abuses within the church and the clerical hierarchy.

A work of the late 1520s that probably had some effect on the appearance of *The praier and complaynte of the ploweman* is Barlowe and Roye's dialogue and verse satire, *Rede Me and Be Nott Wrothe* (*STC* 21247), which first appeared in 1528. This work incensed English authorities, especially Cardinal Wolsey against whom it was directed primarily, but even the reformer Tyndale, with whom Roye had worked in some capacity on the New Testament, was disturbed by what he called its 'railing rhymes.'[28] Like *The praier and complaynte*, *Rede Me* is a strong indictment of clerical improprieties and an attack on traditional church practices. In it we hear the usual Lollard complaints: the pope is Antichrist; bishops, priests, monks, and friars are corrupt and greedy; auricular confession is fraudulent; pilgrimages and images are designed to separate the unsuspecting from their money; church impropriations are wrong; unmarried clergy take sexual advantage of the wives and daughters of others when they are not involved in gross indecencies among themselves; the mass is a device used to extort funds from the simple; transubstantiation is a fable. The fact that the work itself has a practical orientation and is made up of simple rhyme, combined with humour and song, suggests that it was designed to have a popular appeal. And since Lollardy itself was, according to Scattergood, 'almost exclusively a lower-class movement' (250), the clear implication is that the work drew its inspiration from Lollardy, and was meant to appeal, at least in part, to a Lollard audience. There is nothing in *Rede Me* that the editor of *The praier and complaynte* would find foreign to his own reborn tract and much in it that would support his ideological agenda. The main differences between the two works are in form and tone. *Rede Me* is a satirical dialogue, *The praier and complaynte* an impassioned prayer to God devoid of both humour and sustained satire. That the editor of *The praier* may have known Barlowe and Roye's work is suggested by the possible borrowing from it in the closing lines of the preface. Addressing the 'good reder,' he signs off by saying, 'And if here after there shall chaunce to come into my handes any more soch holy reliques perceauinge this to be accepted. I shall spare nother laboure nor cost to destribute it in as many partes as I haue done thys/ by the help of god' (114–17). Near the end of their prefatory letter, written ostensibly by someone on the continent to a reformist colleague in conservative England, Barlowe and Roye also express their commitment to extend the reformist agenda by publishing works which support it: 'Wherfore dere brother, yf eny mo soche smale stickes come vnto youre hondes, which ye shall iudge apt vnto the augmentacion of this fyre, sende them vnto me (yf in englonde they maye not be publisshed) and by goddes grace with all my power and possibilite, I shall so endever my sylfe to kyndle theym, that as many as are of the sede of abraham shall se their light, and therby gloryfy their father celestiall' (56).[29]

The 1529 tract *The summe of the holye scripture* (*STC* 3036), possibly Simon Fish's translation of Henricus Bomelius's *Summa der Godliker Scrifturen*, is largely a theoretical discussion of Luther's view on justification by faith. As such, one would not expect it to influence greatly the publication of *The praier and complaynte*, since Lollardy appeared to take little interest in the theory of justification by faith.[30] The first fifteen chapters of *The summe* are devoted to a discussion of the relationship between faith and good works and the central importance of the former in the scheme of salvation. However, chapters 16 to 21 turn to more practical concerns, concerns which would have attracted the interest of the editor of *The praier and complaynte*. The author of *The summe* opens chapter 16 by explaining the origins of monasticism and comparing its original purity with its present degradations. Chapter 17 ponders 'Whether the life of a monke be better then the life af [*sic*] a commen Cytezyn' and answers the question in the negative. Chapter 18 explains why monks 'go not forward in spirituall life/ but waxe often worsse.' And chapters 20 and 21 turn their attention to present-day 'Nonnes and Chanonesses' who prove to be no better than their male monastic counterparts.[31] If the editor of *The praier and complaynte* knew *The summe of the holye scripture*, chances are he would have been interested in the work's focus – narrow as it was – on clerical corruption as manifested in the lives of present-day monks and nuns.

More likely, however, the editor of *The praier and complaynte* would have been drawn to John Frith's *The Revelation of Antichrist*, a translation of Luther's work that Frith, under the pseudonym of Richard Brightwell, first published in 1529 (*STC* 11394). The very title of the work suggests that the focus of attack will be the pope, a subject that gets extensive critical treatment in *The praier*. However, Frith's translation discusses as well perceived abuses in the church on which *The praier* also feels compelled to comment. Pardons and purgatory come under fire (A8v, F6r), as do fasting (B1r, d5v), the mass (D5r–D5v), relics and pilgrimages (D6v), purgatory (F8v), miracles (G1r), auricular confession (K2v), and clerical celibacy (D6r–D6v). As in *The praier*, the papacy is attacked for its cruel persecution of those who profess true Christian beliefs (B1v–B2r) and the pope is called 'the vicare of god in the erth' and the 'vicare of Christ' (E6v), as he is in *The praier and complaynte*.

More significant, perhaps, from the point of view of analogues between the two works is the admiration for Christian poverty and simplicity and the use of the New Testament imagery of sheep and shpeherd. In what Frith entitles 'an Epitome' (L8r) appended to the end of *The Revelation*, he establishes an 'Antithesis' between Christ and the papacy, an antithesis which echoes many of the contrasting characteristics of Christ and the pope found in *The praier and complaynte*. In the first antithesis (L8v) he states: 'Christ was poore/ saienge. The foxes have holes/ and the birdes of the aier have nestes/ but the sonne of the man hath not where on to laye his hede. The Pope and his adherentes are rich.' One term of the second antithesis reads: 'Christ was meake and lowe,' while the other states by way of contrast, 'The Pope is full; hygh and proude' (L8v–M1r). Antitheses 3 and 4 pursue the contrast between wealth and pomp on the one hand and meekness and humility on the other. Antithesis 3 states, 'Christ full lowlye and meakly/ wasshed his disciples feate. The Pope saieth. The Emperours and kinges/ shall knele and kysse my feate' (M1r). And antithesis 4 adds, 'Christ cam not to be served but to serve ... The Pope will be served' (M1r).

A number of antitheses explore the sheep-shepherd metaphor. Two examples will suffice to indicate the nature and direction of the imagery. Antithesis 23 reads, 'Christ charged peter thryes/ to kepe well and noryssh his shepe. The pope chargeth moch more to kepe well his monye/ As for the shepe he shereth and punissheth with infinite exactions' (M4v). And antithesis 73 states: 'Christ sayth I am a good shepard. A good shepard geveth his lyffe for his shepe. The Pope and Bisshopes saye also that they are good shephardes/ how be it they pille and shere their shepe so nighe/ that they leve not one loke of wolle on theyr backes' (N4v).

Some mention must be made of another sixteenth-century reborn Lollard tract, *The Lanterne of Lyght* (*STC* 15225), whose date of publication, given as 1530 by Aston ('Lollardy and the Reformation'), makes it possible for it to have been a source of inspiration for the editor of *The praier*. Research more recent than Aston's, however, suggests that the date of publication of *The Lanterne* may have been 1535 (Hudson '"No Newe Thyng"'), and *The Short-Title Catalogue* would seem to agree with this later date, in which case the publication of *The praier* in England in 1532 may rather have served as the inspiration for the rebirth of *The Lanterne*.[32] In any case, the latter is an interesting Lollard tract which shares many of the same concerns as *The praier*. Indeed, Hudson states that in many ways it 'presents the fullest picture of Lollard beliefs' ('"No Newe Thyng"' 158). Throughout the Lollard author attacks the pope and the Roman Catholic Church as Antichrist. Criticism is directed against absolution, indulgences, pardons, and idolatry as manifested in pilgrimages and 'mawmetry' (B1v). The church is criticized for not letting the people read 'goddes lawe in theyr mother tonge' (B2v). Temporal lordships greedily sought by the clergy are attacked (G3r), as are churches and their unnecessary and costly ornaments (C7r), singing instead of preaching (D8v), simony (E2r), oaths (F6r), and the persecution of true believers (B2v). Fidelity in marriage, a subject which comes near the end of *The praier*, is also introduced near the end of *The Lanterne* (I2rff). The reference to the world being upside down, alluded to three times in *The praier*, is heard as well in *The Lanterne*, as is *The praier*'s reference to 'Sodom and Gomer' and the allusion to Naaman from 2 Kings 4 and its application to the contemporary simoniacal church.

The strong emphasis in all Lollard tracts on the importance of preaching and the persecution that often follows from it is evident as well in *The Lanterne*. Indeed, the tract associates unauthorized preaching with Lollardy as, for instance, in the following comment:

> For there ben many prechours but theyr ben fewe trewe prechours/ and yf any preche the trouthe/ the multytude shal agayne say him/ and thus men abyden styl in theyr gostly hungre for they wete neuer whom to folowe: theyr prechynge is

> so wonderful/ ioynynge in theyr curyous wordes the trouth to the falshede who that hauntyth to thys brede for to sleke hys hungre thoughe he were so holye as euer was saynt Iohn the baptyst he shulde not fayle to be sclaundrede for a cursed lollarde/ and pursued as an heretyke of these cruell enmyes. (G5v)

The author's attitude towards the church hierarchy is evident right the from beginning of the tract. Devoid of any subtlety when vilification of the church is the subject, he establishes a correspondence between the church hierarchy and the beast of Revelation: 'the courte of Rome/ is the heed of Antechryst/ and in archebysshoppes and bysshopes/ is the body of Antechrist/ but in these patched/ and clouted sectes as Monkes Chanons and Freers/ is the venemous tayle of Antechriste' (B1r).[33]

If the sixteenth-century editor of *The praier and complaynte* was not William Tyndale himself (see The Editor and Early English Editions, below), he probably would have received considerable inspiration from Tyndale to publish his Lollard work given the prevalence of Lollard and Wycliffite views in Tyndale's writings. Although there is no final or altogether decisive statement on the extent to which Tyndale may have been influenced by Lollard thought, it seems evident from Donald Dean Smeeton's study, *Lollard Themes in the Reformation Theology of William Tyndale*, that Tyndale either borrowed much from the native tradition or that there was much in his work that was remarkably similar to Wycliffite and Lollard views. The thesis of Smeeton's book is that 'Tyndale's theology can be understood more completely by looking at his English context, which included Lollard dissent, rather than only at contemporary continental events' (15). Smeeton's initial survey of critical opinion shows that some commentators are still convinced that Tyndale borrowed mainly from Luther and continental reformers. However, Smeeton's book is the most thoroughgoing study of possible Lollard influence on Tyndale, and it shows convincingly and with copious documentation the similarities of thought between Tyndale and Lollardy. Its one drawback, in my view, is that for the most part Smeeton is content to show similarities between Lollardy and Tyndale without regularly factoring Luther and continental reformers into the equation.[34] In other words, the reader would be better served by knowing whether a position shared by Tyndale and Lollardy might not also be similar to or identical with Lutheran or continental thought. This is especially true in those areas where one feels that all the reformers were in general agreement, for instance, on the subjects of clerical immorality and greed and the papacy.[35]

Nevertheless, despite this reservation, Smeeton makes a clear case for a relationship between Lollard and Tyndalian thought. He tells us that Tyndale referred to Wycliffe positively a half dozen times in his writings (75). Tyndale's plain style is similar to Wycliffe's (78). The audience for both Lollard literature and Tyndale's 'was not the titled or the trained but the tailor, the tinker, and the trader' (80). Both Lollardy and Tyndale recognized the inevitability and the value of persecution by the conservative enemy (84–6).

Smeeton points out that both Wycliffe and Tyndale recognized the importance of a vernacular Bible: Wycliffe was the inspiration for the one which has traditionally carried his name, and Tyndale produced his own version in 1526. Both regarded the Bible as the source of mediation between Christ and mankind (97), as a unified whole with no incompatibility or contradictions between the two Testaments (98ff), as a source of ultimate truth standing opposed to man's laws and inventions (99ff), and as a valuable tool when read in the literal sense (101), stripped of the pernicious glosses of scholastic theologians.

Smeeton claims that, although the doctrine of salvation 'does not occupy the dominant place in the Lollard literature that it does in Tyndale's, there are themes common to both sets of writings' (123–4). Tyndale and the Wycliffites both gave God 'the credit for the initiative in salvation' (124), and to that extent at least both subscribed to the notion of election. Both also saw the importance of a 'feeling faith' in Christian life, although it played a larger part in Tyndale's scheme than it did in Wycliffe's or the Lollards who followed him (127). On the vexed question of the relationship between works and faith Tyndale was less doctrinaire on justification than Luther and, like the Wycliffites, he saw a place for works within the scheme of salvation (136ff). On the law Smeeton sees a significant difference between Luther and Tyndale and aligns Tyndale's well-developed theory with its 'silhouette' in Lollard writings. In summarizing the Wycliffite and Lollard views on soteriology Smeeton states: 'For Tyndale and the Wycliffite tradition, love and works flowed from a right understanding of salvation; Luther, on the other hand, distanced faith and experience. Tyndale, however, went beyond the Lollards as well as Luther in elaborating the work of the Holy Spirit in the application of salvation and the manifestation of justification. Tyndale also re-emphasized the Lollard concern for obedience to law, and, in so doing, parted company from Luther's understanding of what became known as the law's "third" function. And finally, Tyndale expanded the idea of covenant tied to Christian baptism in a way which certainly would have made Luther uncomfortable, but which was not at variance with those views already expressed by English dissenters' (157).

Smeeton next turns to Lollard and Tyndalian attitudes towards the church. Both Tyndale and Wycliffe and his Lollard followers regarded the church as less a formal institution and more an informal collection of the whole body of the elect. Both placed supreme importance on preaching as opposed to ceremonies. The Lollard position on 'the priesthood of all believers' (168) was reflected in Tyndale's concern about the priestly function being held in the hands of a select and self-interested few. Attitudes towards church practices are similar in both Wycliffe and Tyndale. Both attacked the tyranny inherent in the notion of prelacy by which members of the various spiritual orders asserted mastery over the people rather than providing them with spiritual assistance (175–6). Nowhere was their criticism more intense than on the papacy which both saw as Antichrist (178ff). Both were also critical of the mendicant orders because of their laziness, sexual immorality, and competitive sectarianism (181ff). Clerical sins, especially those tied to greed and sex, were the objects of attack by both Wycliffe, his Lollard descendants, and Tyndale (186ff). Images, saints, costly church buildings, and pilgrimages were attacked by both Wycliffe and Tyndale alike (190ff). Both Lollardy and Tyndale were critical of the church doctrine of transubstantiation (206), although it would be stacking the cards in favour of this argument to suggest that there was unanimity on this issue, since individual Lollards held different views of the Eucharist. Both the Lollards and Tyndale were suspicious of auricular confession, and for the same reasons (213ff).

On the issues of politics and the philosophy of history Tyndale's views show 'striking similarities to Lollard thought' (221), particularly in the areas of kingship (222ff) and the uses of war (235). On their attitudes towards history – especially church history – both Wycliffe and Tyndale saw a falling off from the original purity of the church, although each chose different occasions to mark the onset of the period of degradation.

Smeeton's analysis of similarities between Wycliffe, Lollardy, and Tyndale and his attempt to show that 'Tyndale was [not] an uncritical conduit of Luther's thought in England' (250) may at times be overargued and insufficiently aware of the difficulty of separating strands of theology into native and continental camps, but Smeeton clearly shows that the views of Tyndale, England's most renowned Protestant reformer, would have served as adequate inspiration for the editor of *The praier and complaynte* to issue his Lollard text in 1531.[36]

Before turning to the prevalence of Lollard thought in *The praier and complaynte* and its links with other Wycliffite writings written probably around the same period or slightly before *The praier*, it is important at least to mention another source of inspiration for the editor of the work, over and above the literary ones I have detailed heretofore. Clearly, there would have been no market for this tract had there not been those interested in and receptive to Lollard views. Although Wycliffe was long dead when *The praier and complaynte* reappeared in the sixteenth century, there is much to suggest that his thought, or rather its latter-day manifestation in Lollardy, was still very much alive in England, not only in literary rebirths of earlier Lollard works, but also in the presence of Lollardy as a subversive force within the country. Smeeton mentions that Westerham in Kent 'was an area of strong Lollard influence' (71) in the early sixteenth century, as were the areas of Norwich and East Anglia (71). Thomson's record of prosecutions for major heresies also suggests considerable Lollard activity in the early sixteenth century. A count indicates that between 1499 and 1522 there were about 225 abjurations and 23 burnings in eleven English counties compared to 120 abjurations and 10 burnings (including 6 executions) from the end of the Oldcastle uprising in 1414 to 1496 (237–8).[37]

An examination of *The praier and complaynte* shows that it

reflects much of the thought, imagery, and diction of other Lollard works probably written around the same time. Without knowing the exact dates of composition and the identity of the authors of *The praier* and many of its Lollard relatives, it is impossible to speak of one or some as source or sources for others. However, what one can see from the following sampling is that Lollards and Lollard writings drew from a common pool of ideas and images which appear time and again in the literary, polemical, and theological tracts that have come down to us.

On the matter of auricular confession, for example, *The praier* argues that confessing one's prayers to a priest and being 'assoiled' (a word that is ubiquitous in Lollard writing) are not necessary to receive God's forgiveness. The author states: 'A Lorde thou forgaue some tyme Peter hys synnes and also Marye magdaleyne/ and other many synfull men withouten schryuinge to prestes/ and takynge penaunce of prestes for her synnes' (428–31). In the Lollard tract 'Of Confession' we read: 'Whenne crist forgaue marie magdeleyne hir synnes, he vsed not siche rownynge; and whenne he forgaue petir hise synnes, and poule his, and other men heren that he clensid, he vsed not sich rownyng in ere, ne siche asoylyng as prestis vsen nowe' (*The English Works of Wyclif* 328).

For those who argue that priests have received power from Christ to forgive sins by distorting the biblical texts on the cleansing of the lepers, *The praier* says:

> But hereto seyn prestes/ that when Christ made clene leprous men/ he bade hem goo and show hem to prestes. And therfore they seyn that it ys a commaundement of Christ/ that a man schuld shewen his synne to prestes. For as they seyn/ lepre in the old lawe betokeneth synne in this new lawe ... And as me thinketh the lawe of lepre/ ys nothinge to the purpos of schriuinge: for prestes in the old law hadden certein pointes and tokenes to know whether a man weer leprous or not and yif they were leprous/ they hadden power to putten hem awaie from other clene men. (438–53)

The Lollard tract 'On Confession' makes the same point using the same imagery:

> But yitt argueth antecrist that this sentence is heresie, for crist bad ten leprouse men go and shewe hem to the prestis; and bi this he taught opynly that it nedith to be shriuen at prestis ... crist bad ten leprouse men go and shewe hem to prestis, as it was boden in the olde lawe, but thise prestis in the oolde lawe assoileden not rownyngly, as we don nowe, but bi signes of goodis lawe thei sheweden wheche men weren leprouse, and which weren not leprouse, and to her iugement shuld stonde. (342–3)

On the relationship between absolution and simony *The praier* states: 'A nother myschefe ys/ that these prestes sellen ... absolucions for money/ and this ys an heresye accursed that ys ycleped symonye' (480–2). In a Lollard tract entitled 'Of Servants and Lords' the author states: 'In confessouris regneth moche gile for thei conforten and norischen grete men of this world in here synnys for to gete a benefice, worldly wynnynge ... and vnder colour of holynesse leden men to the gatis of helle and sellen soulis to sathanas' (*The English Works of Wyclif* 237).

In order to illustrate how the Bible speaks out against simony, the author of *The praier* warns simoniacal clergy to beware: 'for Helyse the prophet toke no money of Naaman when he was made clene of his lepre: But giesi his seruant and therfore the lepre of Naaman abode with hym and with his eyres ever more after' (485–88). In the Lollard tract 'The Clergy May Not Hold Property' we read: 'criste commendid and confermyd the dede of the blessid prophete helyse, that refusid the giftis proferid to hym of Naaman after the miracle and grace that god had done by hym to Naaman ... And oo grete cause whi helize wold not assent to Naaman to take eny giftis of hym in this case was for than helize had been a symonient, sith his man giezi, that ran aftir naaman and toke giftis of hym thorow occasion of that grace so minystred, was a symonyent, notwithstondynge that that grace was not geuen by hym in eny wise to Naaman, but that he toke tho giftis bi occasion of that grace' (*The English Works of Wyclif* 378).

On the subject of fraudulent religious events that occur within the confines of the church *The praier* states: 'A lorde he that clepeth hym selfe thy viker vpon erth hath yordayned an ordre of prestes to do thy seruyse in church to fore thy lewed puple in singinge matens evensonge and masse' (614–17). In 'Of Prelates' the author says: 'Also prelatis ben more bounden to this prechynge, for that is commaundement of crist bifore his deth and eke aftir, than to seie matynes, masse, euen song, or placebo, for that is mannus ordynaunce' (*The English Works of Wyclif* 57). And in 'The Order of Priesthood' we read in a similar vein: 'Also thei disceyuen the peple to holde forth here olde cursed lif and synne; for thei seyn that thei wolen preie for hem, and thei schullen ben excused to-fore gof for the almes that thei don in fyndynge hem to seie mass and matynes and euensong and placebo and dirige' (*The English Works of Wyclif* 177).

A regular complaint of the Lollards was clerical immorality and laziness. In *The praier* the author comments: 'And younge prestes and men of religion for defaute of wives maken many wymen horen ... And lorde me thinketh that these ben quaynte orders of religion and none of thy secte/ that wolen taken horen/ whilke god forfendes/ and forsaken wyues that god ne forfendeth not. And forsaken traueyle that god commaundes/ and gyuen her selfe to ydelenes that ys the moder of all noughtines' (707–16). In 'The Order of Priesthood' we hear essentially the same comment: 'Also many prestis vnwisly taken a vow of chastitie and defoulen wyues, widewis and maydens; For thei taken presthod for to lyuen esely and fare wel, and take no reward to here heighe hoot complexon, but norischen it in welfare of mete and drynk of the beste and riche clothis and softe beddis and traueilen not' (170).

As regards images, *The praier* states: 'But Lorde god/ men maketh now greet stonen houses full of glasene windowes/ and clepeth thylke thyne houses and chirches. And they sette in these houses mawmetys of stockes and of stones/ and to fore hem they knelen priuylich and apert/ and maken her preyers/ and al this they seyen ys thy worschup' (725–30). A few lines later we read: 'Lorde god what heryenge ys it/ to cloth mawmettes of stockes and of stones yn syluer and in golde and in other good coloures' (738–40). In the Lollard tract that Matthew entitles 'Of Poor Preaching Priests' we read: 'That the pore comons be not chargid with taxis, the while clerkis, and namely religiouse, han superfluyte of riches of gold and siluer and riche vesselis and othere iewelis ... That the wast tresour hanged on stockis and stones be wisly spendid in defence of the rewme, and releuynge of the pore comouns; that the peple of oure lond be not brought to maumetrie' (*The English Works of Wyclif* 279).

With a view to showing that clerical sin is greater than the sin of those who know no better the author of *The praier* states: 'Lorde the synne of the prest or of the clerke ys a gretter trespas then it ys of a lewed vnkunnynge man and gretter ensample of wickednesse to the comune puple' (888–91). We hear an echo of this sentiment in 'Of Servants and Lords': 'the synne of clerkis is more than the synne of othere lewid men, thanne lordis owen more to ponysche synne of clerkis thanne the synne of other men' (*The English Works of Wyclif* 241).

In discussing the iniquity and injustices of church courts *The praier* states: 'But lorde as thou saidest some tyme that it schulde ben lighter at domes daye to Tyro and to Sydon and Gomorra than to the cities where thou wrought wondres and miracles/ so I drede/ it shalben more lighte to Pilate in the dome then to our kynges and domes men that so demen withoute witnesse and prefe' (952–7). In 'Why Poor Priests Have No Benefice' we read: 'it is gret wonder that god suffrith so longe this synne vnponyschid opynly, namely of prelatis courtis that ben dennys of theues and larderis of helle ... this is a thousand fold more vengaunce than yif god distroie bodely bothe partis and alle here goodis and erthe ther-with as he dide bi sodom and gomor; for the lengere that thei lyuen thus in synne, the grettere peynes schullen thei haue in helle but yif thei amenden hem' (*The English Works of Wyclif* 251).

On the question of purgatory *The praier* has the following to say: 'And lorde me thinketh/ that yif there were a purgatorye/ and eny erthlyche man had power to delyueren synfull men from the peynes of purgatorye/ he schulde/ and he were in charite/ sauen everich man that were in waye of saluacion from thilke peynes/ syth they make hem gretter then any bodilych peynes of thys worlde' (1596–1601). On the same topic the Lollard author of 'Of Prelates' states: 'Also it semeth that the pope and his ben out of charite yif there dwelle ony soule in purgatorie, for he may with ful herte withouten ony other cost delyuere hem out of purgatorie and thei ben able to resceyue suche helpe sith thei ben in grace; than yif he delyuere hem not out of purgatorie him lackith charite' (82).

Finally, on three occasions in *The praier and complaynte* (678, 862, 1341) the author, deploring the regrettable influence of the traditional church on society, refers to the world as being upside down. The expression 'upside down' seems to be a common one in Lollard literature. In Matthew's edition of *The English Works of Wyclif* the expression occurs on four separate occasions, once in 'Of Prelates' (98), once in 'Of Clerks Possessioners' (119), once in 'Satan and His Children' (210), and finally in 'How Satan and His Priests' (268).

In would be exciting to think that the Lollard author of *The praier and complaynte* borrowed all the concepts mentioned above directly from Wycliffe. However, even though the text from which I have cited various Lollard works is entitled *The English Works of Wyclif*, its editor is quick to point out that many of the tracts that he prints may or may not be by Wycliffe. All we can say, and all that my comparison can show, is that *The praier and complaynte* is clearly in the Wycliffe-Lollard tradition, and that it seems likely, based on my brief comparative study, that a goodly number of ideas, images, and allusions were common property amongst the Lollard writers who expressed their views some time after Wycliffe provided the imaginative religious spark that initiated this religious tradition.

# The Editor and Early English Editions

Regrettably, based on the evidence – or rather the lack of it – we can come to no firm conclusions as to the identity of the sixteenth-century editor of *The praier and complaynte of the ploweman* or the extent of his involvement beyond the brief preface which we know for certain was not part of the original tract.[38] As I mentioned above, Foxe, Bale, Mozley, and Butterworth attribute the editorial involvement to William Tyndale. Hume disagrees and claims that George Joye was its editor. My own view, based on an examination of Tyndale's works, plus a number of the English Protestant tracts published on the continent between 1525 and 1532, is that the editor is indeed Tyndale, although I am aware that my evidence is not necessarily irrefutable.

I have already suggested why I believe that Hume's reasons for naming Joye are weak: her view that the anonymity of the tract is typical of Joye is not a strong argument in an era in which anonymity was often the rule rather than the exception. Furthermore, Hume questions her own evidence when she acknowledges that the printer of the tract, Martinus de Keyser, not only printed other works for Joye in bastard type – the face used for *The praier and complaynte* – but also printed works for Tyndale using the same type. Moreover, as mentioned earlier, although de Keyser printed works for Joye – four is my total count – he was printer of six for Tyndale.

There is nothing specific in the sixteenth-century preface of *The praier and complaynte* to connect it to any of Joye's known works. Joye, of course, was a dedicated reformer, and to the extent that both the preface and the tract itself attack what Joye himself attacked, the preface is generally consistent with Joye's reformist views, as it is with those of many other early sixteenth-century English reformers. But there are no clues in the preface to connect it specifically to Joye: no verbal echoes, no stylistic similarities. Moreover, as far as we know, Joye was not involved with other Lollard tracts of the period. Throughout his career he showed no explicit interest in Lollard writings or the dissemination of them, although probably some of his own views were influenced by Lollardy. In the preface to his 1534 edition of the New Testament Tyndale expresses displeasure with Joye for tampering with his (Tyndale's) translation of the New Testament. He states:

> But of this I challenge George Joye, that he did not put his own name thereto and call it rather his translation: and that he playeth boo peep, and in some of his books putteth in his name and title, and in some keepeth it out. It is lawful for who will to translate and show his mind, though a thousand had translated before him. But it is not lawful (thinketh me) nor yet expedient for the edifying of the unity of the faith of Christ, that whosoever will, shall by his own authority, take another man's translation and put out and in and change at pleasure, and call it a correction. (*Tyndale's New Testament* 13–14).[39]

Some might argue that Tyndale's claim – namely that Joye is unscrupulous or at least careless about attribution – makes Joye a likely candidate for the position of anonymous editor of *The praier and complaynte*. However, Tyndale is particularly annoyed with Joye because he distorts parts of the *translation* of the New Testament. Tyndale is not arguing against the use of others' works; rather he is arguing against their distortion by those who make changes without acknowledgment.

And now the case for Tyndale as editor of *The praier and complaynte*. Apart from the unproven claims of Foxe, Bale, Mozley, and Butterworth that Tyndale is the editor of the work, what more can be said in support of Tyndale's candidacy?[40] To begin, one can argue that Tyndale showed interest in other Lollard works reborn during the sixteenth century, perhaps going so far as introducing and editing some of them himself. Two works in particular, one with strong Lollard roots, the other with a possible Lollardy ancestry, that Tyndale may have edited are *The examinacion of Master William Thorpe* and *A compendious olde treatyse shewynge howe that we ought to haue the scripture in Englysshe* (*STC* 3021). As I mentioned earlier, many believe that Tyndale edited the Thorpe examination with a view to showing the continuity between Lollard and sixteenth-century English Protestant thought. In the preface to *The examinacion* the editor mentions one Thomas Hitton and appears perplexed by his death at the hands of church authorities: 'Who can tell wherfore that good preeste and holy martyr Syr Thomas hitton/ was brente/ now thys yere at maydstone yn Kent' (a2r). Reference to Hitton is also found in lines 84–7 of the preface to *The praier and complaynte.* This would not be a very compelling piece of evidence to suggest Tyndale's participation in either *The examinacion* or *The praier and complaynte* were it not that Tyndale, and Tyndale alone as far as I can see, also mentions Hitton on two occasions in works we know to be by him, once in *The Practice of Prelates* of 1530 (*Expositions and Notes* 340), and once again in his *Answer to Sir Thomas More's Dialogue* of 1531 (113). The dates of these two references, 1530 and 1531, are significant since they are the same as the publication dates of *The examinacion* and *The praier and complaynte* respectively, suggesting that Hitton may have been very much on Tyndale's mind at this particular time. In his *Answer to Sir Thomas More's Dialogue*, Tyndale implies that Hitton was a martyr for his beliefs, a claim that is also made explicitly in *The examinacion.* In the *Answer* he states, 'And when he saith that their church hath many martyrs, let him show me one, that died for pardons and purgatory, that the pope hath feigned' (113). The editor of *The praier and complaynte* also regards Hitton as a martyr and speaks of him as in a direct line of descent from St Stephen, traditionally seen as the first martyr of the Christian church: 'Euen as the olde phareses with the bischops and prestes presoned and persecuted Christe and his Apostles/ that al the rightuous bloude may fall on their heedes that hath ben shed from the bloude of Steuen the first martyr to the blode of that innocent man of God Thomas hitton whom willyam werham byschop of Canturbury and Iohn fyscher byschop of Rochestur morthered at maydeston in kente the last yere for the same trouth' (80–7).[41]

The other possible link between Thorpe's examination and *The praier and complaynte* that might tie Tyndale to the latter – assuming, that is, that he was involved with the former – is the statement made in both tracts about editorial care taken with the original material. Passages from both works that I cited above (Analogues and Sources 22–3) indicate that the editor was particularly concerned to make clear to the readers that he did not tamper with the text as such – an accusation that Tyndale brought against Joye, as we have seen – but only did his best to render each text in an English that would be comprehensible to his own readers. Indeed, the editor of the first edition of *The praier*, published on the continent, even added a glossary of thirty words and terms to help the reader better understand certain archaisms.

A further instance of Tyndale's possible interest in Lollard tracts is his unwitting participation in the hybrid final version of *A proper dyaloge betwene a Gentillman and an Husbandman*, published in 1530 (*STC* 1462.5). This work began its life in late 1529 or early 1530 as a dialogue written, I believe, by Barlowe and Roye, to which was added a reborn Lollard prose tract against clerical temporalities (*STC* 1462.3).[42] Following the publication in 1530 by Johannes Hoochstraten (Hans Luft) of a Lollard tract entitled *A compendious olde treatyse shewynge howe that we ought to haue the scripture in Englysshe* (*STC* 3021), *A proper dyaloge* was reissued with *A compendious olde treatyse* appended to it. In my critical edition of *A proper dyaloge* based on *STC* 1462.5, I argue that Tyndale was probably the sixteenth-century editor of *A compendious olde treatyse* and that it was his participation in this work that encouraged Barlowe and Roye (or their enterprising printer Hoochstraten) to append it to their first edition of *A proper dyaloge* (*STC* 1462.3), thereby creating the final version of the work (*STC* 1462.5). In my edition of *A proper dyaloge* I opt for Tyndale as the possible editor of *A compendious olde treatyse*, arguing on the basis of verifiable Tyndalian expressions in the work. In *A compendious olde treatyse* there is a gratuitous marginal reference to Robin Hood, a figure who seems to be a particular favourite of Tyndale's, given the five references to him in Tyndale's other writings. I also add that the editor's negative reference to Nicholas of Lyra in the marginal notes, next to a passage in the text itself which is positive about Nicholas, is consistent with Tyndale's other two negative references to him, one in the *Obedience of a Christian Man*, the second in his *Answer to Sir Thomas More's Dialogue*. Finally, a reference in *A compendious olde treatyse* to the church's perversion of truth as analogous to a tree with it roots turned upward is an echo of the same image that appears twice in Tyndale's *Obedience*. These linguistic parallels between *A compendious olde treatyse* and some of Tyndale's known works strongly point to Tyndale as editor of this reborn tract calling for a vernacular Bible.[43]

If we can assume that Tyndale was interested enough in Lollard thought to edit two of its tracts, it is altogether possible that he may also have been the editor of *The praier and complaynte of the ploweman*, a work that appeared within the same general time-frame as the others I have mentioned in this discussion.

Although the preface of *The praier and complaynte* does not provide conclusive evidence of Tyndale's involvement, there are clues which, when taken together, point in his direction. In true Pauline fashion the editor of the preface begins his four-page statement with a salutation wishing the 'Christen reader' 'grace' and 'peace' (11–13), a greeting not unlike those used by Tyndale in three of his works. In the Preface to his *Answer to Sir Thomas More's Dialogue* Tyndale wishes the reader 'The grace of the Lord' (5), and in the prefaces to *The Parable of the Wicked Mammon* (*Doctrinal Treatises* 37) and the *Obedience of a Christian Man* (131) he greets the readers with grace and peace, exactly the same salutation found in the preface to *The praier and complaynte*.

From the point of view of the content of the preface to *The praier and complaynte* I have detected two similiarities to Tyndalian thought. As the preface opens, the editor strives to make clear the continuity between Christ, who was persecuted for his teaching, and those presently persecuted by the contemporary church (16–75). The similarity between this view and one found near the beginning of the Preface to *The Practice of Prelates* is striking. The contemporary church officers, known as scribes and Pharisees in both works, have their pernicious method described in the following terms in *The Practice of Prelates*: 'O generation of serpents, how well declare ye that ye be the right sons of the father of all lies! For they, which ye call heretics, preach nothing save that which our Saviour Jesus Christ preached, and his apostles; adding nought thereto, nor plucking aught therefrom, as the scripture comandeth' (242). Additionally, the apparent anachronism in lines 21ff in *The praier and complaynte,* where the editor refers to the New Testament persecutors of Christ and his apostles as 'Byschops,' is no anachronism at all if one accepts Tyndale's explanation of the use of the word as a synonym for 'elder,' a legitimate biblical expression: 'Wherefore the apostles, following and obeying the rule, doctrine, and commandement of our Saviour Jesus Christ, their master, ordained in his kingdom and congregation two officers; one called, after the Greek word, *bishop,* in English an overseer: which same was called *priest* after the Greek, *elder* in English, because of his age, discretion and sadness' (253).

It would be stretching my argument if I were to list all of the similarities between Tyndale's various positions and the lines of thought expressed in *The praier and complaynte* with a view to determining complementarity, since many English reformers shared the same views, and since many of these positions were identical to Lutheran thought. But as my summary of Smeeton's claims and my frequent allusions to Tyndale's writings in the Commentary below make clear, there is compelling evidence to demonstrate a shared ideology between Tyndale and the author of *The praier,* a fact which would make Tyndale's editorship of *The praier* altogether natural and comprehensible. And the fact that *The praier and complaynte* is stridently antipapal *and,* it would seem, solidly opposed to divorce (1620–56) would make it particularly attractive to Tyndale, who not only saw the papacy as Antichrist, but was also enough his own man to stand against Henry VIII's tendentious arguments in favour of his divorce (see *The Practice of Prelates, Expositions and Notes* 323ff).

One further piece of internal evidence, minuscule in itself, but persuasive enough when taken together with the other echoes, has to do with the use of the word 'antiquate.' As the *OED* makes clear, the first recorded use of the word as a participial adjective occurs in Tyndale's *Exposition of the First Epistle of Saint John* (*Expositions and Notes* 136–225), published in 1531. However, near the very end of the preface to *The praier and complaynte* the word 'antiquate' appears in connection with the editor's comments on the archaic language of the tract. The editor's use of the word as a participial adjective in the same year that it appears in a work known to be by Tyndale helps to strengthen the view that the editor of this reborn Lollard tract might very well be Tyndale.

Finally, in 'A Proclamation for the abolishing of English Books, after the Death of Anne Askew, set forth by the King A.D. 1546, the eighth day of July,' *The praier and complaynte*, retitled *The Parable and Complaint of a Ploughman unto Christ*, appears in a list of books attributed to Tyndale (Foxe v 567). One might argue that the attribution is the handiwork of the sometimes inventive Foxe had not the editor made clear that he, rather than Foxe, made the attribution based on the original Bonner Register (Foxe v 583). We shall never know, of course, whether the compilers of the Bonner Register attributed the work to Tyndale, as Foxe may have done, because the initials 'W.T.' appear on the first sheet of the edition published in England in 1532, or whether they had a better reason for assigning it to him. Be that as it may, what we can say is that, if Tyndale did edit this work along with the Thorpe testament and *A compendious olde treatyse*, once thought by some to be a Lollard tract, he was not only influenced by Lollard thought as Smeeton demonstrates, but was also very much responsible for introducing it in the sixteenth century and disseminating it among both his reformist colleagues and those for whom his own work was intended. There could be no clearer evidence of the importance of Lollardy for the sixteenth-century reformers than the active involvement of one of their own – traditionally regarded as their most renowned figure – in the production of Lollard texts.

*The praier and complaynte of the ploweman* is an important tract if for no other reason than that its second edition, published in England in 1532, is the first of the English Protestant books published abroad to appear under the imprint of an English printer.[44] *The Short-Title Catalogue* supposes the printer to have been Thomas Godfray and there seems to be no reason to question that judgment.[45] Godfray's publishing career spans six years at least (1531–6), although the *STC* is careful to note that his work requires re-evaluation and that the dates assigned to his works are tentative, in fact 'more tentative that usual' (*STC* III 69).[46] If *STC*'s attributions to Godfray are accurate, one can see that he published a number of religious tracts characterized by various shades of reformist thought. Certainly *The praier and complaynte*, as we have seen, is stridently antipapal, as are *The Plowman's Tale* (1535–6; *STC* 5099.5) and *The triades or trinites of Rome* (1535; *STC* 14027.5). Godfray is associated with some of the works of the Protestant Joye – *The psalter of Dauid* (1534; *STC* 2371); *The prouerbes of Solomon* 1534; *STC* 2752) – and with certain of Tyndale's works – *The newe testamente* (1536; *STC* 2831); *A pathway into the holy scripture* (1536; *STC* 24462; 24463). In addition, Godfray's reformist tendencies are evident in his work on such tracts as *A treatise declaring and showing that images are not to be suffered in churches* (1535; *STC* 24238); William Marshall's translation of Martin Bucer's *Das einigerlei Bild* (1535; *STC* 24238); Christopher St German's *A tretyse concernynge the power of the clergye, and the lawes of the realme* (1535; *STC* 21588); *An epistell of the famous doctor Erasmus vnto Christofer bysshop of Basyle, concernyng the forbedynge of eatynge of flesshe* (1533; *STC* 10488.7); *A treatyse of the donation gyuen vnto Syluester pope of Rhome by Constantyne, emperour of Rome* (1534; *STC* 5641); Sir Francis Bygod's *A treatise concernynge impropriations of benefices* (1535; *STC* 4240; 4240.5); and *A panegyrie of Henry VIII as the abolisher of papal abuses* (1536; *STC* 13089a).

The list of titles above makes it clear why Andrew Wawn argues that Godfray 'was directly involved in the printing of Henrician propaganda' and 'an integral part of the Henrician propagandist organization' ('Chaucer, *The Plowman's Tale*' 177). It is Wawn's contention as well that Godfray may have worked closely with the king's official printer, Thomas Berthelet, and that the works that Godfray printed related 'directly to the polemics of the reformation controversy' and focused on values which were 'hostile to the papacy and favourable to the monarch' (179).

Concerning the English reaction to *The praier and complaynte*, no official prohibition specifically mentioning it appears until 8 July 1546 when it is listed against Tyndale's name in 'A Proclamation deuised by the kinges highnes, with the aduise of his most honorable counsell to auoide and abolish suche englishe bookes, as containe pernicious and detestable errours, and heresies' (Steele I, 30–1; Foxe v 567). This prohibition was no doubt occasioned by the resurgence of the conservative wing's attack on stridently Protestant thought during Catherine Parr's period of influence, a story eloquently retold by

McConica (*English Humanists and Reformation Politics* 213ff). During the 1530s *The praier and complaynte* is mentioned by Thomas More in *The Confutation of Tyndale's Answer* (1532), where in the process of listing books which he attacks as heretical he states, 'lest we shuld lakke prayours, we haue the prymer, and the ploughmnans prayour, and a boke of other, small deuocyons, and then the hole psalter to' (More VIII/1 11). A general prohibition against the importation of English books printed abroad appeared on 16 November 1538 (Steele I 19), by which time, according to my count, eleven English tracts had made their way from the continent to England, but no such prohibition was in effect when this work travelled from Antwerp to London sometime in 1531–2. Had this Lollard tract been written and known between 1528 and 1530, it doubtless would have fallen under the general interdiction issued in 1528–9 and again in 1530 (Steele I 13–14) when the climate was less accepting of reformist tracts than it seemed to be in the early 1530s. Indeed Stokesley's list of thirty condemned books, mentioned during his sermon on 3 December 1531, one day before the burning of the heretic and sometime monk Richard Bayfield, includes two Lollard tracts, *The A.B.C. agenste the Clergye* (a version of *A proper dyaloge betwene a Gentillman and an Husbandman*) and *A boke of thorpe or of John Oldecastelle* (see Aston 'Lollardy and the Reformation,' 150). There is no reason to think that *The praier and complaynte*, had it been generally available, would not have made it onto Stokesley's list.[47]

Despite the use made of Godfray, probably by Cromwell, in the service of the king's dispute with the papacy, it is still hard to explain the appearance of *The praier and complaynte* in 1532 as a propaganda tool. As I have shown, the work is clearly antipapal and from this point of view would have well served the propaganda campaign undertaken against the papacy in 1532. What makes this particular Godfray tract hard to fit into the neat category established by Wawn for Godfray's work as a whole is that, although it is antipapal and ferociously attacks the church's worldliness, it is also, strictly speaking, heretical, and, more important, clearly anti-Henrician in its position on marriage and divorce. If it is indeed true that throughout his dispute with the papacy Henry maintained and enforced doctrinal orthodoxy, it is difficult to understand how, as early as 1532, a work that is so obviously heterodox and calls into question such hallowed doctrines as auricular confession, the Eucharist, the mass, among others, would be allowed to be published by an English printer. Is it possible that the antipapal theme of *The praier and complaynte* was compelling enough to override the clear heterodoxy of the work? And might the addition of 'W.T.' on the first sheet of the 1532 edition give the impression that Tyndale was working on behalf of Henry's cause, thereby giving the cause the support that Cromwell at least wanted it to have?[48] More perplexing still, given its publication in England at a time when Henry was struggling with the papacy over his own divorce, are *The praier and complaynte*'s comments on the sanctity of marriage. Tyndale's comments on Henry's divorce in *The Practice of Prelates* are candidly opposed to the king's cause.[49] Despite being less pointed and less personal than Tyndale, the author of *The praier and complaynte* makes clear his objections to divorce, as the following excerpts make clear:

> Ne thou ne ordeynedist that a man schulde desyre the company of a woman/ and maken her his wife/ to lyuen with her in his lustys/ as a swyne doth or a horse. And hys wife ne lyked hym nat to hys lustes/ Lorde thou ne gaue not a man leue to departen hym from his wife and taken hym a nother. (1623–8)
>
> But Lorde thy maryage ys a commune acorde betwene man and woman to lyuen togeder to her lyues ende/ and in thy seruyse eyther the bettur for others helpe/ and thilke that ben thus ycome to geder ben ioyned by the/ and thilke that god ioyneth maye no man departe. (1629–33)

Although this discussion takes place within the context of the author's criticism of clerical celibacy, that context does not mitigate the full force of these statements against divorce. Such comments could not but work against the king's position on divorce, assuming that this tract received wide distribution, an assumption that seems likely given the presence of Tyndale's initials on the opening sheet.[50]

What can we make of the appearance of *The praier and complaynte* in England under the imprint of a London printer? The fact that the work has no colophon and no obvious indication of publisher may mean that Godfray knew that the work was controversial, if not positively subversive, but that he or Cromwell could not resist publishing it in any case because of its associations with Tyndale. Or it might also mean that the ideological confusion that resulted from the king's 'great matter' allowed works like *The praier and complaynte* to slip through the cracks and get published, whereas had it appeared between 1528 and 1530, even as a tract published only abroad, it undoubtedly would have been officially prohibited. An examination of the records of Henry VIII's reign shows that no offical proclamations against specific books appeared between 1530 and 1545–6; the only prohibition between these two dates was issued in 1538, and it specified only that English books printed abroad not be brought into the country. If one can generalize from this absence of official proclamations against books, one might say that the period between 1531 and 1538, when Henry was working to establish his new and self-proclaimed powers, was one of such ideological diversity, where the king fought heresy against the church and the church simultaneously, that the banning of specific books might have meant closing the door on resources that could serve a very valuable purpose at a later date. This absence of official prohibitions plus the possibility of somehow using Tyndale's name to support the king's cause may explain why the publication in England of the Lollard tract *The praier and complaynte of the ploweman vnto Christe* met little or no serious objection.

# The Ploughman Tradition of Complaint

In *The Arte of English Poesie* (1589), George Puttenham, commenting on William Langland's *The Vision of William Concerning Piers the Plowman*, makes a claim that the English reformers of the early and mid-sixteenth century would certainly have endorsed. He states: 'He that wrote the Satyr of Piers Ploughman seemed to haue bene a malcontent of that time, and therefore bent himselfe wholy to taxe the disorders of that age, and specially the pride of the Romane Clergy, of whose fall he seemeth to be a very true Prophet' (62).[51] A survey of ploughman and Piers literature in the sixteenth century proves that the English reformers were both very aware of the ploughman tradition of complaint which found its English literary origin probably in Langland's work, and also not reluctant to use, distort, or otherwise capitalize on it to suit their own politico-religious agenda.[52] The earliest printed edition of the B text of Langland's poem, printed by Richard Grafton for R. Crowley, appeared in 1550 (*STC* 19906). The popularity and importance of the work are attested to by the fact that it was reprinted twice in the same year (*STC* 19907 and 19907a). Another edition appeared in 1561 (*STC* 19908) to which was added an additional ploughman tract, *The Crede of Pierce Plowman*, a reprint of a work originally entitled *Pierce the Ploughman Crede*, published first by R. Wolfe in 1553 (*STC* 19904). Three other ploughman tracts appeared in the 1550s: first, *A godly dyalogue and dysputacion betwene Pyers plowman and apopysh [*sic*] preest concernyng the supper of the lorde*, published twice in 1550 by W. Copland (*STC* 19903 and 19903.5); second, *I playne Piers which can not flatter*, published possibly by N. Hill in 1550 (19903a), and again later in the century (*STC* guesses 1589) under a new and longer title, *O read me; for I am of great antiquite. I plaine Piers ... I am the gransier of Marten marprelette* (*STC* 19903a.5); and third, *Pyers Plowmans exhortation, vnto the lordes, knightes and burgoysses of the Parlyamenthouse* (1550?) (*STC* 19905). Further evidence of the popularity of the ploughman is evident in other printed examples of the figure. In his edition of *Pierce the Plowman's Crede* Skeat appends an undated short poem entitled *God spede the plough. The Short-Title Catalogue* lists another work, published possibly as early as 1510 by Wynkyn de Worde, entitled *Here begynneth a lytell geste how the plowman lerned his pater noster*, still in circulation in 1560 and 1582. Another Protestant tract published in 1579 (*STC* 24062) – the same year as Spenser's *The Shepheardes Calender*, a work that also makes use of the ploughman motif – and concerned almost entirely with secular, especially legal, subjects is *Newes from the North. Otherwise called the Conference between Simon Certain and Pierce Plowman*. An additional ploughman tract, *The Plowman's Tale*, whose tangled bibliographic history is unravelled in two important essays by Wawn, first appeared in print around 1536 bearing Thomas Godfray's imprint. Often falsely attributed to Chaucer in order to give it an authority it might not otherwise possess, the date of first publication of this work is wrongly given as 1606 by *STC*.[53] And finally Hugh Latimer's important 'Sermon on the Plowers' was delivered in January 1548 and published in the same year.

As this survey of titles and dates shows, with the possible exception of the anomalous *A lytell geste* (*STC* 20034), the work which forms the basis of this critical edition was, as far as we know, the first of the ploughman tales to appear in print in the sixteenth century, and perhaps the first since the appearance in manuscript of Langland's influential *The Vision of William Concerning Piers the Plowman*.[54] As the first such work, it, along with the Langland archetype and *A proper dyaloge*, may have served as partial inspiration for the spate of reformist ploughman tracts that followed in the 1550s and for *The Plowman's Tale* of the mid-1530s.

In his edition of all three Langland texts of *The Vision* Skeat dates the appearance of texts A, B, and C as 1362–3, 1377, and c.1393 respectively. Throughout my brief commentary on the complaint nature of Langland's poem I shall be referring to the B text since this was the one most often referred to in the sixteenth century and printed by Crowley three times in 1550 (*The Vision of William Concerning Piers the Plowman* EETS).

If Puttenham, writing in 1589, had been aware of the number of ploughman tracts *The Vision* unwittingly spawned in the sixteenth century – and perhaps he was – it would make his claim that Langland 'is a very true Prophet' because of his attacks on 'the pride of the Roman clergy' entirely understandable. However, it would be wrong to assume that Langland's poem necessarily reflects a strident fourteenth-century early Protestant or Lollard ideology despite what later Protestant propagandists might have made it into by appropriating elements from it to suit their own agendas. *The Vision of William Concerning Piers the Plowman* is clearly critical of aspects of the church and the clergy, but the work itself is not, strictly speaking, heretical, as its later manifestations in the sixteenth century were taken – or meant – to be.[55] For the sake of convenience, and with no regard for the complex allegorical dimension of the work,[56] one can divide the criticism against the church in *The Vision* into four categories: criticisms directed against the clergy; those specifically directed against the papacy; attacks on the friars; and incidental attacks on other abuses in the church that Langland alludes to in the course of his long poem.

In his attacks on the clergy Langland takes aim at its greed and avarice (I 188, 195); he associates some of the clerics with his allegorical figure Lady Meed or lucre (III 26ff), and claims that lawless priests live with concubines and mistresses (III 149). Priests often exact money for masses (III 251; XI 282), do not practise what they preach (IV 122; V 42–3; X 270–1), and prove their ignorance when they are unable to sing or read lessons or instruct the ignorant (V 422–3; XI 289–90; XII 184–5).

Langland's attacks on the papacy are no less severe: Lady Meed has been known to be familiar with popes (II 23) and has poisoned them with her influence (III 127); papal bulls and pardons are attacked when they are abused (VII *passim*); popes who do not carry out Christ's commands are upbraided (XV 483); papal indulgences are of no value to the recipients if charity towards their neighbours is absent (XVII 252–6); and popes who engage in wars are not being faithful to their spiritual calling (XIX 442).

Langland reserves his most sustained attack for the friars, a not surprising phenomenon given the general opprobrium in which they were held, even by fellow members of the church hierarchy.[57] According to Langland some friars are liars (II 181–2); others are prone to anger (v 136); dishonest friars spend other people's money on costly vestments and needless repairs to churches (v 268–9). Friars are imposters of holiness who ponder abstruse theological questions and preach falsehoods (x 71–2; xv 68–70); they are fickle and selfishly selective, associating only with those blessed by good fortune (XI 55–6); they deliberately seek out the rich and shun the poor (XIII 7–8); they are gourmands and eat only the best food (XIII 40–2); since St Francis's time many of them have abandoned charity (xv 225–7); they are shameless beggars who spend all they receive on themselves (xv 321–4); they are lecherous and seduce women (xx 341–5); and finally, reflecting a common concern in Langland's own era as well as in the sixteenth century, there are far too many of them (xx 264–7).[58]

Langland's fourth category of complaint, as I have called it, comprises incidental and sporadic criticisms which, along with the more sustained attacks already mentioned, add to the general impression that *Piers Plowman* is an unrelenting attack on church abuses. A brief sampler of these incidental criticisms indicates their orientation and scope: Langland objects to simoniacal and unlearned bishops (III 147–8); exhorts abbots, among others, to teach and by so doing correct men's faults (xv 267–8); attacks avaricious bishops and archbishops (xv 239–43); and chastises monks – a category of religious that Langland, for some reason, treats less harshly than others – who steal alms from noblemen and live outside their cloisters (x 295–9). Additionally, Langland's extended discussion of the figure of Antichrist in Passus xx of the poem would have well served both Lollards and sixteenth-century reformers who saw Antichrist as the church itself rather than, as Langland did, a manifestation of major corruption in the church.[59]

Finally, on at least three occasions in *The Vision*, Langland criticizes a church practice that the Lollards were to attack vigorously from the fifteenth century onwards, finding the source for their complaint perhaps in the influential early fourteenth-century tract *Defensor Pacis* by Marsilius of Padua. The practice, most clearly articulated in the sixteenth century in Barlowe and Roye's *A proper dyaloge betwene a Gentillman and an Husbandman*, concerns the impropriation of lands by the church and the transfer of secular property away from its rightful heirs to the church itself.[60] Langland attacks this practice once in Passus x (312–13) and twice in Passus xv (313–19 and 524–9). The fact that this same concern was still much in evidence in the minds of early sixteenth-century reformers, as *A proper dyaloge* attests, indicates both the continuity between Lollard thought and early reformist literature and also the possible influence that Langland's work – itself derivative, as Owst and others have shown[61] – may have had for sixteenth-century reformers and polemicists.

Despite its numerous complaints, only some of which I have discussed above, *The Vision* is still an orthodox tract, critical of an institution to which Langland continues to adhere even though he recognizes and expresses some of its major weaknesses. To the extent that Langland is a faithful, if critical, member of the church, he is an ancestor, not of Wycliffe and the Lollards or their sixteenth-century reforming descendants whose borrowings of the ploughman image and the Piers name would seem to suggest a direct line of descent, but rather of people like Thomas More or Erasmus, conservative reformers who wished to purge the church of its abuses while remaining within its pale from the point of view of doctrinal orthodoxy.[62] Ironically, however, as the number of sixteenth-century ploughman tracts indicates, Langland became at least a partial inspiration for radical English reformers who took from him both the name and profession of Langland's famous narrator as well as much of the criticism he directed against the Church.[63] Focusing on Langland's attacks, which admittedly are manifold and everywhere apparent in *The Vision*, these sixteenth-century reformers ignored his allegiance to and belief in aspects of the church which they regarded as anathema. Langland, for instance, supports the mass and attacks only the abuses associated with it (III 250–1); he views auricular confession as necessary and efficacious (XIV 89–92); he subscribes to the doctrine of purgatory (VI 42–5); and he believes in the value of the spiritual hierarchy from priest to pope, even though he is not blind to the various weaknesses inherent within it. In short, had the sixteenth-century reformers and their Lollard forefathers paid attention to the entire Langland poem, they would have had some difficulty in justifying their use of Langland as a exemplar of proto-Protestant thought. However, by radical decontextualization they were able to transform a devout and conservative critic into a valuable source of reformist thought, a not uncommon tactic of the era.[64]

Selective in their choice of content, the English reformers also ignored the complexity – the sometimes confusing complexity – of the Piers figure himself in Langland's poem. Generally speaking, all of the Piers and ploughman tales mentioned above focus on Piers as ploughman, that is, on the humble and simple figure who appears in the poem up to the end of Passus VII and does not reappear again in this form until he hooks up his allegorical plough in Passus XIX, although by this time he has lost somewhat his simple status and has come to represent the figure of Christ himself. The simple peasant Piers, who actually appears as a ploughman only in the first part of the poem from Passus V to VII, is the most appealing manifestation of the figure for Lollards and sixteenth-century reformers alike, probably because both groups believed that Christianity was not the preserve of an intellectually elite spiritual hierarchy which jealously appropriated the arcane mysteries of Christianity to itself, but rather the property of all simple Christians imbued with a feeling faith and an open heart. Indeed, the fact that Lollardy itself appealed to the lower orders of society would suggest why Piers the ploughman *qua* ploughman would serve as the perfect exemplar for the reformers.

In Passus V of *the Vision* Piers is associated with the allegorical figure of Divine Truth and tells pilgrims in quest of Truth how to reach his abode. In Passus VI Piers volunteers to guide the pilgrims to Truth if they, in turn, will help him sow his fields. In this guise Piers is a simple farmer, honestly employed in his labours, but clearly aware of Truth's home and prepared to lead the less enlightened to it with no wish for reward for his labour. The fact that Piers is closely associated with Truth – the goal to which all devout Christians aspire – makes him an altogether appropriate choice as the protagonist of later Lollard and Protestant prose tracts where he speaks out against abuses in the church. Because he is aligned with Christian truth in Langland's version, his credibility is already established when he is used by reformist writers as a spokesman for their cause and as a critic of the elitist, established church.

Not only is Piers as ploughman the *persona* focused on by subsequent writers who tend to ignore his complex allegorical significance as a type of Christ in the 'Do-wel, Do-bet, et Do best' sections of the poem, but frequent references throughout Langland's poem that laud the simple Christian would also have served the ends of later reformist writers well and drawn them to *The Vision*. For instance, in Passus VII, lines 62–5, Piers receives a papal indulgence releasing him from the temporal punishment due to his sins. With no intention of attacking the practice of indulgences itself – something that radical reformist writers could never resist doing – the narrator makes clear that a labourer who lives an honest and humble life would receive the same absolution that Piers did by virtue of his indulgence:

Alle lybbyng laboreres that lyuen with her hondes,
That trewlich taken and trewlich wynnen,
And lyuen in loue and in lawe for her lowe hertes,
Haueth the same absolucioun that sent was to Peres

Again, in a later passage the narrator compares the simple life of the peasant to that of the scholar, with the spiritual advantage going to the former:

Aren none rather yrauysshed fro the righte byleue
Than are this cunnynge clerkes that conne many bokes;
Ne none sonner saued ne sadder of bileue,
Than plowman and pastoures and pore comune laboreres.
Souteres and shepherdes suche lewed Iottes
Percen with a *pater-noster* the paleys of heuene,
And passen purgatorie penaunceles at her hennes-partynge,
In-to the blisses of paradys for her pure byleue,
That inparfitly here knewe and eke lyued.
Yee men knowe clerkes that han cursed the tyme,
That euere thei couth or knewe more than *credo in deum patrem*;
And pryncipaly her *pater-noster* many a persone hath wisshed.[65] (x, 456–67)

Even when speaking figuratively, Langland's narrator pays tribute to the simple labourer by employing metaphors borrowed from the labourer's own life experiences to explain difficult concepts, as in the following example:

Lele loue other lyf that owre lorde shapte.
And as glowande gledes gladieth nought this werkmen,
That worchen and waken in wyntres nightes,
As doth a kex or a candel that caughte hath fyre and blaseth,
Namore doth sire ne sone ne seynt spirit togyderes,
Graunteth no grace ne forgifnesse of synnes,
Til the holi goste gynne to glowe and to blase.
So that the holygoste gloweth but as a glede (XVII, 217–24)

And finally, when allegorizing Scripture and with a view to ensuring comprehension, the narrator employs texts appropriate to those whose interests in life do not extend far beyond the pleasures and comforts of home, hearth, and field:

Thre thinges there ben that doth a man by strengthe
Forto fleen his owne hous as holywryt sheweth.
That one is a wikked wyf that wil nought be chasted;
Her fiere fleeth from hyr for fere of her tonge.
And if his hous be vnhiled and reyne on his bedde,
He seketh and seketh til he slepe drye.
And whan smoke and smolder smyt in his syghte,
It doth hym worse than his wyf or wete to slepe.
For smoke and smolder smyteth in his eyen,
Til he be blere-nyed or blynde and hors in the throte,
Cougheth, and curseth.
...
Thise thre that I telle of ben thus to vnderstonde;
The wyf is owre wikked flesshe that will bought bwe chasted,
For kynde cleueth on hym euere to contrarie the soule.
...
The reyne that reyneth there we reste sholde
Ben sikenesses and sorwes that we suffren oft,
...
Ac the smoke and the smolder that smyt in owre eyghen,
That is coueityse and vnkyndenesse that quencheth goddes
mercy. (XVII, 315–42)

In all of these examples, as well as in the figure of Piers himself, the simple life of the humble Christian is lauded by the author. Langland's genuine admiration for such humble virtue would play nicely into the hands of the sixteenth-century reformers who pitted themselves against a legitimized and privileged church made up, in their view, of those who cared for little but their own aggrandizement.

Given the emphasis on the figure of Piers the ploughman and on the need for reform within the church, it is not surprising to discover that all three of Crowley's 1550 editions of the printed text of Langland appeared during the reign of the Protestant King Edward VI. In general, all three editions are faithful to the original's content and tone, but the distortion of Langland's orthodox, if critical, work is evident in an interesting tract entitled 'The Printer to the Reader' which precedes the poem. The document begins innocently enough by identifying the author of *The Vision* as one 'Roberte [*sic*] langelande, a Shropshire man borne in Cleybirie, about .viii. myles from Malverne hilles' (sig. *iir). The printer then goes on to explain how he came across the 'auncient copye' and how he determined its original date of composition. Then follows the rebaptism of the work as a Lollard tract as the printer identifies its goals with those of John Wycliffe, Lollardy's putative founder. Speaking of its initial appearance the printer states:

> In whose tyme it pleased God to open the eyes of many to se hys truth, geuing them boldenes of herte, to open their mouthes and crye oute agaynste the worckes of darckenes, as did John wicklefe, who also in those dayes translated the holye Bible into the Englisshe tonge, and this writer who in reportynge certaine visions and dreames, that he fayned him selfe to haue dreamed: doeth moste christianlye entrust the weake, and sharply rebuke the obstinate blynde. There is no maner of vice, that reigneth in anye estate of men, whiche this wryter hath not godly, learnedlye, and wittilye rebuked. (sig. *iir)

In addition to placing Langland's tract squarely in the Lollard camp, thereby making it a precursor, along with Wycliffe, of valuable reform, the printer also uses a negative reference in the work to 'Abbaies' to help explain and justify the suppression of the monasteries carried out with frightening efficiency and dispatch during Henry VIII's reign.[66] The printer shows no embarrassment in using a work written some

140 years before the suppression to validate Henry's actions against monasticism in England. He states: 'Nowe for that whiche is written in the .l. leafe, concerning the suppression of Abbaies: the scripture there alledged, declareth it to be gathered of the iuste iudgment of god, whoe wyll not suffer abomination to raigne vnpunished' (sig. *iiv). Finally, the printer 'contemporizes' Langland's poem by exhorting readers not to regard it as a work which talks 'of wonders paste or to come, but to amende thyne owne misse, which thou shalt fynd here most charitably rebuked' (sig. *iiv).

If Langland's work strikes the contemporary reader as quaint and antiquated, it certainly did not make the same impression on sixteenth-century reformers devoted to advancing radical views. Although Crowley acknowledges that 'the sence' of Langland's *The Vision* is 'somewhat darcke' because of 'The Englisshe' of 'the time it was written in,' it was, nevertheless, seen as a work ahead of its time which later reformers could use both to corroborate their own critical views of the church and to demonstrate that such views have a noble and hallowed ancestry.

In the following brief survey of the principal features of the English ploughman tradition, I focus on five aspects of the tradition: the general orientation of the tracts; the importance of the name of Piers; the various distortions introduced into reborn Lollard tracts in the sixteenth century in order to make them fit new historical and religious contexts; the focus and subject matter of the tracts, and the various personae of the Piers figure.

Of the several works within the ploughman tradition, a large number are of a radical reformist or complaint nature, although the specific issues complained about differ from tract to tract.[67] Some of the works, however, are neither complaint nor necessarily reformist in nature. For instance, the undated 'Tale of the Ploughman,' which at some time in its not altogether clear history seems to have been added to Hoccleve's poem 'The story of the Monk who clad the Virgin by singing Ave Maria,' since there are versions of this poem both with and without an addition entitled 'The Prologe of the Ploughman,'[68] is a pietistic, unpolemical, and altogether orthodox piece about a devout monk encouraged by the Virgin to recite her psalter on a daily basis. Similarly, the 1510 tract *Here begynneth a lytell geste,* a 208-line poem in rhyming couplets, brings a wealthy ploughman – an exception in the ploughman tradition – into contact with his confessor, who teaches the ploughman his *pater noster*.[69] The lesson involves the ploughman's giving away his various manifestations of wealth to worthy and impoverished suppliants, all of whom, preposterously, are named after the Latin terms which make up the *pater noster*. By the end of this exercise the ploughman has been rendered poor, but is now in far better spiritual shape than he was at the beginning of the poem with his wealth. Although he is unlike the majority of the ploughmen within this tradition at the poem's beginning, the financially impoverished but spiritually enriched ploughman is very much like his colleagues by the poem's end. A third undated tract, an excerpt in fact, which stands outside the tradition of radical reform despite the presence of a ploughman named Piers, is the undated fragment *The Banckett of Iohan the Reve vnto Peirs* [sic] *ploughman ...*' Uncharacteristically, as Hudson makes clear, this tract, which is a discussion of the Eucharist carried on by a number of members of the working class – Laurens laborer, Thomlyn tailyer, and Hob of the hille – sees Piers as the defender of the orthodox position on the Eucharist. Moreover, unlike most of the other ploughman tracts in this tradition, Piers is not the major figure in this work. Perhaps reflecting the importance of social hierarchy in this discussion – something which is absent, indeed even violated, in many other Piers tracts – the major defender of the orthodox position on the Eucharist is John the Reve.[70]

The name of Piers itself seems to have been an important part of the sixteenth-century ploughman tradition. Evidently this name conjured up memories of Langland's great Piers figure and made the connection between the archetype and its latter-day manifestations crystal clear. Of the fourteen ploughman tracts known to have been published in the sixteenth century (excluding number 9 in the list on page 203, below, which is Crowley's edition of Langland's poem), seven name their protagonist Piers or some variation of it (tracts 8, 10, 11, 12, 13, 14, 15), and five include the word 'plough' or 'ploughman' in their titles as if to signal the link with Langland's poem (tracts 1, 2, 3, 5, 6). Only two make no reference to either Piers or the ploughman in their titles (tracts 4 and 7), but both of these are clearly within the tradition of sixteenth-century radical reform since one introduces a ploughman, John Bon, who attacks the iniquitous doctrine of transubstantiation, and the other, largely through the eloquence of a farmer, focuses on economic injustices brought about by an unscrupulous and greedy clergy.

In connection with Langland's *The Vision* I have already mentioned the attempts made by Crowley to render his reborn versions of the poem suitable for the political-religious climate of the 1550s through the inclusion of a distorting preface. By mentioning Wycliffe's reforming zeal in the same breath as Langland's poem, and by using Langland's poem to justify the suppression of the monasteries, Crowley updates Langland's Piers, making him an appropriate figure for the fight against papistry or vestiges of it in the England of Edward VI. I have also discussed how the sixteenth-century editor of *The praier and complaynte*, originally a Lollard tract, focuses on the continuity between the past efforts at reform evident in the tract and the present iniquities against which reformers are obliged to struggle. Similar distortions and uses of historical material within new contexts are evident in tracts 4, 5, 6, and 13. The sixteenth-century version of the anonymous *The Plowman's Tale*, written probably in the late fourteenth or early fifteenth century, turns attribution and distortion into a fine art. Not only was this dialogue between a Pelican and a Griffon at one time attributed to Chaucer and associated with *The Canterbury Tales*, thereby simultaneously transforming Chaucer into a supporter of Lollardy and assigning to the work a significant pedigree it did not deserve, but also its own contents were changed in the sixteenth century to make it appear more antipapal than the original.[71] In Wawn's view there are two clear sixteenth-century additions to the poem: the fifty-two-line prologue which, significantly, highlights the figure of the ploughman, and a twenty-three-line section in the body of the tract itelf which attacks the papacy in more strident terms than the original.[72]

*Pierce the Ploughmans Crede*, a late-fourteenth-century Lollard tract, also shows signs of sixteenth-century tampering with original material.[73] Although the alteration is slight and easily overlooked, it is, nevertheless, a crucial indication of the length to which reforming writers would go to update helpful, if historically fixed, material. The first change in this Piers tract occurs in lines 748 and 756 where in the manuscripts the author laments the fact that the children of beggars are sometimes unjustly catapulted into positions of authority to which they have no right. The position mentioned in the two manuscript versions is a bishopric. However, in the 1553 printed edition the two references to bishop are changed to the word 'abbot' so that the insult is directed away from bishops and towards the head of monastic houses. Skeat is critical of this 'clumsy alteration' on aesthetic grounds because it ruins the alliteration of the lines (*Pierce the Ploughmans Crede* xvii), but he fails to see the ideological reason for the change. By 1553 Henry VIII's dissolution policy had done its work effectively and these uncomplimentary references to abbots receiving positions that they did not rightly deserve would have served to justify Henry's policy on moral grounds. In 1553 Henry's earlier policy would have been seen as an effective way of doing away with one manifestation of corruption in the church. The fact that enormous wealth reverted to the government coffers because of dissolution could not, of course, be ignored, but the moral justification for the decision might have gone some way to minimize the financial motive.[74]

The second change to this tract is more extensive and possibly even more crucial to the reformed church in the early 1550s since it involves a contentious doctrinal issue that had been in the air in England for many years and had served to divide the reformers themselves both in England and on the continent. It occurs near the very end of the tract and concerns five lines, all of which focus on the vexed question of transubstantiation. The lines that the 1553 edition suppresses are as follows:

> And in the [sacrament] also that sothfate God is,
> (Fullich his fleche and his blod that for vs dethe tholede.
> ...
> For Crist seyde it is so so mote it nede worthe;
> Therfore studye thou nought theron ne stere thy wittes,
> It is his blisdsede body so bad he vs beleuen. (823–4; 828–30)

These lines, which conjure up the image of the Catholic doctrine of transubstantiation, are excised in the 1553 text for obvious reasons: since the doctrine itself was associated with a church that had been suppressed in Henry VIII's and Edward's reigns, any work that seemed to support the doctrine would appear to undermine Protestant belief.[75] This would be particularly regrettable and inconsistent in a tract devoted to exposing enormities within the Roman Catholic Church. Hence, even though this late-fourteenth-century Lollard work well served the purposes of the Edwardian church, it could not simply be reproduced and disseminated without careful editing of possibly subversive material. If Peres's creed was to make its presence felt in the sixteenth century, it would have to be a revised and laundered version of that creed that Peres would be forced to articulate whether or not he, or his creator, subscribed to it.

The final sixteenth-century ploughman tract that manipulates history in order to render it answerable to contemporary religious agendas is *A proper dyaloge betwene a Gentillman and an Husbandman*.[76] In this work the husbandman and his gentleman interlocutor lament their dreadful economic states and, by implication, the economic condition of England as a whole by blaming their poverty on clerical greed, especially greed associated with the impropriation of secular lands. In order to justify his argument that such complaints are not the newfangled ravings of disaffected Lutheran heretics, the husbandman invokes and cites at length an anonymous Lollard tract, 'made aboute the tyme of kinge Rycharde the seconde' (145; 685–7), calling for clerical disendowment. In addition to dragging a document written in the Lollard past into the sixteenth century, the husbandman supports his argument for a vernacular Bible by citing a long treatise arguing for the translation of the Bible into the vernacular. If Hudson is indeed correct in claiming that this document was the work of the orthodox Richard Ullerston (*Selections from English Wycliffite Writings* 145), the use of this tract by a sixteenth-century reformist radical shows that the reformists would go to any lengths, and ransack any work despite its provenance, to support their own religious agendas, even if those agendas were diametrically opposed to the borrowed source.

As a general rule the subject matter broached and discussed in these sixteenth-century ploughman tracts is diverse and multifaceted, although there is often a good deal of overlap among subjects of interest to reformist writers. Certain works have essentially a single focus (tracts 1, 7, 10, 13). *God spede the plough*, the earliest of them, is a poem whose refrain, 'I pray to God, spede wele the plough,' underlines the 'husbondys' complaint that he seems to work for almost everyone but himself. This ploughman's lament about his poverty, the subject of complaint here, becomes, in later ploughman tracts, a mark of distinction and a badge of honour, as we saw it to be in *The praier and complaynte.* Despite their overwhelming poverty other ploughmen in almost all instances are spiritually and often intellectually wealthy, aware of the true Christian life and penetrating enough to see through the tendentious obfuscations and guile of the traditional church. Indeed, the central condition for spiritual enlightenment in most of these tracts would seem to be poverty, if the hard but efficacious lesson learned by the wealthy ploughman in *Here begynneth a lytell geste how the plowman lerned his pater noster* is anything to go by.

Two works focus attention solely on the complex question of the Eucharist, an issue that divided not only reformer from traditionalist but also reformer from reformer.[77] *John Bon and mast Parson* (tract 7) is a work designed to attack the feast of Corpus Christi in particular and the orthodox position on the Eucharist in general.[78] Throughout the tract the ploughman, John Bon himself, gets the better of the 'enlightened' priest, and through the use of humour, irony, and sarcasm defeats the priest's arguments in support of the doctrines of transubstantiation and the real presence. In the brief but popular dialogue *A godly dyalogue and dysputacion betwene Pyers plowman and apopysh [*sic*] preest* (tract 10) Piers takes on a priest who supports the church's doctrine of transubstantiation, and undermines his anaemic arguments in support of the traditional view.[79] The priest in this dialogue, who appears to know neither his Augustine nor his Bible, but who, in any case, seems proud of his own ignorance which he regards as truth, is an easy target for the much more skilful Piers who makes use of *reductio ad absurdum* argumentative techniques to unsettle his ideological opponent.

The final Piers tract with a central focus is *Pierce the Ploughmans Crede* (13). This 855-line alliterative poem is the most sustained, lengthy, and vitriolic attack on the mendicant orders to appear in sixteenth-century England, even going beyond, in length and intensity, the excoriation of the friars found in Barlowe and Roye's *Rede Me and and Be Nott Wrothe,* published in 1528.[80] Structurally, *Pierce* is divided almost exactly into two equal parts. The first part is given over to an exercise in ironic self-indictment as representatives from the four orders of friars – Franciscans, Carmelites, Augustinians, and Dominicans – outdo each other in vilifying their mendicant colleagues.[81] In the second part the narrator of the tract, who is in search of someone to teach him his creed, meets Peres, an impoverished ploughman who confirms through statement and illustration what the friars, unwittingly, have already told us about themselves. As might be expected, it is finally from the learned and poor ploughman that the traveller learns his creed in the last sixty lines of the poem. Unable to receive spiritual instruction from those who, nominally at least, are in the best position to provide it, the traveller gets it from one of his own sort, an impoverished ploughman in whose meek heart the wisdom of the Holy Ghost has found a congenial home.

Other works are less focused on a single subject than the four just discussed. Still others within this reformist tradition, perhaps more concerned with content than form or structure, seem to be without focus at all, apart from their general interest attacking the church as a whole. In the former category is *A proper dyaloge betwene a Gentillman and an Husbandman* (4) which manages, not without difficulty, to level complaints in two areas: clerical greed that results in the unscrupulous taking over of land from naive lay people frightened by the fraudulent doctrine of purgatory; and the reluctance of the traditional Church to allow a vernacular Bible. Two noteworthy examples of unfocused discussion are *The Plowman's Tale* (6) and *I playne Piers which can not flatter* (11).

The dialogue between the Pelican and the Griffon which forms the essence of *The Plowman's Tale* pits humility against arrogance, poverty against wealth, simplicity against obfuscation, Lollard against traditional church. The Pelican, the feathered spokesman for reform, is outstanding for his loquacity: in this 1380-line alliterative poem he speaks directly to the Griffon in 1072 lines, he addresses the ploughman in 34 lines, and speaks to himself briefly in 5 lines. The Griffon, the representative of the traditional church, is given a total of 98 lines and is not allowed to speak at all until he has heard the Pelican go on for some 620 lines, scarcely drawing a breath. Although we are told by the ploughman-narrator near the beginning of the tract that the Griffon is 'of a grim stature' (86) and shows himself 'as sharp as fyre' (91), his remarkable taciturnity belies this description of a formidable adversary. He is verbally overwhelmed by the Pelican, himself somewhat unbelievably described as 'withouten pryde' (87) and as one who pursues 'his matter in mesure' (89). Wawn's description of this poem as 'anti-papal, anti-curial, anti-monastic, anti-mendicant, anti-clerical' ('Chaucer, *The Plowman's Tale*' 77) indicates the shot-gun approach that the Pelican uses to hit his many targets.

The second unfocused tract, *I playne Piers which can not flatter*, seems to have so much to say that its eighty-nine pages cannot contain it all or hold it together. Its frenetic quality and lack of central focus are evident in its mercurial form: although the entire piece is written in prose, it breaks into poetical doggerel at three points, even though the doggerel, with a specific rhyme pattern and rhythm, is set in prose.

From the various attacks against the Roman Catholic Church – the pope, bishops, transubstantiation, pilgrimages and shrines, clerical celibacy – and against anything that smacks of residual Catholic doctrine or practice in a church evolving towards Protestantism, it is clear that this work was written by one of the strong and enthusiastic Protestant reformers in evidence during Edward VI's reign when controversy between those holding extreme theological positions was rampant.[82]

The various personae of the Piers or ploughman figure in many of these tracts is worthy of comment. In almost every work within this tradition the ploughman, like Langland's protagonist, is wretchedly poor. In *God spede the plough* (1) the ploughman bewails his social and economic condition and lists the various forces – only one of which is the church – that keep him downtrodden and overworked. The husbandman in *A proper dyaloge* (4) complains about his poverty at length and competes with the gentleman to determine which of the two is less well off. Although not an integral part of *The Plowman's Tale* (6), the ploughman in this revived Lollard tract is poor too. When we first meet him, he is finishing his ploughing and complaining about the miserable state of his livestock: 'They ben feble, both oxe and cow, / Of hem nis left but boon and skin' (5–6). The ploughman himself is 'forswonke and all forswat; / Men might have sen through both his chekes' (14–15). As well as being sunburnt from working out of doors, 'his clothes ... were to-rent' (20). The fact that this prologue introducing and describing the ploughman is a sixteenth-century addition to the original tale indicates the importance of a *poor* ploughman to the tradition and the sixteenth-century editor's awareness of this central aspect of the ploughman's character.

Perhaps no Piers figure outside of Langland's is more graphically depicted as impoverished than the Peres of *Pierce the Ploughmans Crede* (13). The pathos created as a result of his impoverished state is enhanced by the presence of his downtrodden wife and children. The entire family is an unprepossessing sight, standing in stark contrast to the wealthy mendicants described in the first part of the tract by the narrator-traveller. The author of this work describes Peres and his family as follows:

And as y wente be the waie wepynge for sorowe,
I seith a sely man me by opon the plow hongen.
His cote was of a cloute that cary was y-called,
His hod was full of holes & his heer oute,
With his knopped schon clouted fulle thykke;
His ton toteden out as he the londe treddede,
His hosen ouerhongen his hokschynes on eueriche a side,
Al beslombred in fen as he the plow folwede;
Twey myteynes, as mete maad all of cloutes;
The fyngers weren for-werd & ful of fen honged.
This whit waselede in the [fen] almost to the ancle,
Foure rotheren hym by-forn that feble were [worthen];
Men myghte reken ich a ryb so reufull they weren.
His wijf walked him with a longe gode,
In a cutted cote cutted full heythe,
Wrapped in a wynwe schete to weren hire from weders,
Barfote on the bare ijs that the blod folwede.
And at the londes ende laye a litell crom-bolle,
And theron lay a litell childe lapped in cloutes,
And tweyne of tweie yeres olde opon a nother syde,
And alle they songen o songe that sorwe was to heren;
They crieden alle o cry a carefull note. (420–41)

The skilled ploughman-debater of *A godly dyalogue and dysputacion betwene Pyers plowman and apopysh preest* ... (10) is also poor and written off by those whom he defeats in argument as one of 'these hobbes and rusticals' who busy themselves 'readynge of Englysh heresy' (B3r). John Bon describes himself as a 'plain man' and, disingenuously one feels, given the skill of his argumentation, calls himself and his fellow ploughmen 'blind' (162). The narrator of *Pyers plowmans exhortation* ... (12), aware of his socioeconomic status, apologizes to his social superiors in Parliament for his 'rude boldnes' (A7v) and his 'rude language' (A8r) and claims that he is altogether 'ignoraunt/ of the arte of rethorycke' (B2r).[83]

The poverty and simplicity of these ploughman figures stand in stark contrast to their remarkable knowledge, or perhaps, as I suggested earlier, the former is a prerequisite of the latter. Indeed, throughout these tracts poverty and deprivation seem to be the true signs not only of unpretentious common sense but also of intelligence, Christian wisdom, and the ability to penetrate beneath the false wisdom of the traditional church in order to expose its rank hypocrisy. The ploughman of Rastell's *Of Gentylnes and Nobylyte* (3), essentially a work devoted to a secular, non-reformist subject, shows his wisdom by taking control of the debate from the 'marchaunt' and 'knyght' on what constitutes nobility. The ploughman of this tract is not intimidated by the wealthy and aristocratic company he keeps and argues compellingly on a subject which, as Axton tells us, occupied the thoughts of such worthies as Chaucer, Guillaume de Lorris, Jean de Meun, and Dante (*Three Rastell Plays* 21).

Peres of *Pierce the Ploughmans Crede* is a remarkably knowledgeable farmer whose attacks on all four mendicant orders we are prepared to credit because the author has skilfully allowed the friars to expose themselves in the first part of the poem. This Peres also shows his knowledge of history: he is aware of how the friars attacked Wycliffe (528ff) and comments on their persecution of Walter Brut (657ff). Peres's knowledge of the Bible is also impressive, as one might expect of a Lollard. In the course of his 400 lines, 60 of which are given over to a list of the creed's various terms, he alludes to biblical passages eight times and once invokes the name of St Hildegarde.

John Bon defeats his interlocutor, the frustrated parson, through common sense, reason, and irony. Totally demoralized by Bon's simple yet devastating criticisms of the Eucharist, the parson states, as if to dismiss Bon by attacking his social group, 'I had leaver with a Doctor of Divinity to reason, / Than with a stubble cur that eateth beans and peason' (163).

Bon's colleague, the redoutable 'Pyers plowman' of *A godly dyalogue ... betwene Pyers plowman and apopysh preest,'* combines common sense and reason with impressive scholarly credentials in defeating the priest in their discussion of the Eucharist. For instance, when the priest claims that Piers is a heretic for not believing that Christ's body and blood inhere in the bread and wine, Piers retorts that, if he is a heretic, so is St Augustine whose position on the Eucharist he cites in Latin and English. The priest acknowledges his ignorance of Augustine by claiming that he is 'not greatly occupyed ... in redyng of hys workes' (A4v). Piers adds that the priest does not seem to know his Bible either since, in Piers's view, the Catholic position on the Eucharist has no biblical authority. The author of this tract, perhaps thinking that the reader might find it preposterous to believe that a simple farmer could debate with and defeat a priest, or perhaps believing that the Bible itself validates the wisdom of the poor and marginalized, cites St Paul's first Epistle to the Corinthians to justify the ploughman's knowledge and success in debate: 'God hath chosen the weake thinges of the worlde to confounde thynges whyche are myghtye. yea thynges of no reputacyon for to bryng to nought thynges of reputacion, that no flesh shuld presume in his sight.'

The author of *A proper dyaloge betwene a Gentillman and an Husbandman* acknowledges the farmer's intellectual acumen – and perhaps the tradition of which he is a part – by allowing him to hold his own in an enlightened reformist discussion with a like-minded gentleman. It is the husbandman, for example, who explains to the gentleman the church's persecution of the Gospel during the reign of Henry V; in addition, he knows the rumours about the peculiar circumstances surrounding King John's death. He is also aware of the supposed pristine state of England prior to the onset of contaminating spiritual jurisdiction, a subject dear to the heart of William Tyndale, a far more obvious intellectual figure than our simple farmer.[84] Additionally, it is the farmer who first suggests the importance of a vernacular Bible, which leads to the inclusion of the third part of the tract in the revised version of *A proper dyaloge*.[85] But perhaps the most significant indication of the farmer's intelligence is his knowledge of the old Lollard prose tract on the injustice of clerical impropriation, a tract which forms the first of the two additions in *A proper dyaloge*. The fact that the husbandman knows this work and draws it to the gentleman's attention must also mean that he has read and understood it, a tribute not only to his literary skills but more importantly to the astonishing depth and breadth of his knowledge. For to have read this work means that the husbandman is familiar not only with large sections of the Old and New Testaments – as we would expect given the tradition of which he forms a part – but also with Robert Grosseteste, St Augustine, St Cyprian, St Gregory, and St Bernard of Clairvaux, the legends of St Hugh and St Swithun, and the *Polychronicon* of Ranulphi Higden.

Pyers, the narrator of *Pyers plowmans exhortation* (12), is an enlightened and concerned economic historian and social critic intent upon drawing contemporary social evils to the attention of English Parliamentarians.[86] He is, as well, not reluctant to offer solutions to these problems, some of which resulted in the 1549 rebellions throughout England, carried out, in large part, by the common people, who were concerned about economic injustices associated especially but not exclusively with enclosures.[87] What is remarkable about the Pyers of this work is his familiarity with economics, taxation policy, and the general demeanour of the country. In addition, he has a good sense of church history since he demonstrates his knowledge of the tyranny of the Roman Catholic Church under which the country once toiled, as it now appears to be toiling under the disastrous economic policies of the Protector, Somerset.

The Piers of *I playne Piers* (11) demonstrates his knowledge in the field of church history. Concerned about vestiges of papistry inherent in the Edwardian church, this radical reforming ploughman draws to his readers' attention a number of unscrupulous church practices from the past. For instance, he knows about the notorious Richard Hunne case (B1v) and the incidents surrounding the burning of William Tyndale's New Testament in 1526 (B2v). In addition, he attacks Thomas More, John Fisher, and Friar John Forest (B2v), the mildly conservative Six Articles promulgated during Henry VIII's reign (C2v), and John Massey, Bishop of Leeds (D8v), Cardinal Reginald Pole (E1r), Dr Edward Crome, Nicholas Shaxton, Bishop of Salisbury (E2v), 'the blynd byshope of norwyche,' Richard Nix (E2v–E3r), and Cardinal Wolsey's visitation officer, John Allen (E3v).[88] At least twice in the tract this ploughman shows his awareness of the importance of published material in disseminating reformist views: he condemns religiously conservative England under Henry VIII for its reluctance to allow honest works to be published in the country; the author states that documents detailing abuses within the church had to be published abroad, a clear reference to the activities of exiled English authors publishing their books on the continent, particularly between 1525 and 1535 (see Hume 'English Protestant Books').

The Piers of this tract is also aware of his reformist ancestors and even praises some near-contemporary reformist figures: William Tyndale and Miles Coverdale are lionized for their work on the English Bible (E2r); Thomas Bilney is praised and his martyrdom condemned (E3r); and Thomas Cramner is lauded for his stand against transubstantiation (F1r). Despite his humble calling the ploughman of *I playne Piers*, who emphasizes his plainess both in the title of the work and its body, is, in fact, a knowledgeable historian, albeit one bound to a radical reformist ideology which presents the past in the colours best suited to advance his cause.

One work in particular in the English ploughman tradition requires special attention because of its apparent popularity, but, more importantly, because of its altogether original use of the concept of the ploughman. Hugh Latimer's 'Sermon of the Plough,' more accurately entitled 'Sermon on the Plowers,' was preached 'in the Shrouds at paules churche in London, on the .xviii.daye of January. 1548' and published by John Day in the same year.[89] To what extent Latimer may have borrowed the pervasive ploughman metaphor of his sermon from Langland, or from Langland mediated through other English ploughman tracts already mentioned, is not clear and probably impossible to determine.[90] What is, clear, however, is that Latimer's sermon makes extensive and original use of the ploughman motif by turning it into a powerful trope that serves as the major structural device in the work, a work designed to remind prelates of their true calling and of the dangers in ignoring this calling.[91]

As I read it, Latimer's sermon is divided into two parts: the first part introduces the metaphor of the true prelate as ploughman, and the second part draws to his listeners' attention England's most formidable prelate-ploughman, the devil himself.

The sermon opens with Latimer explaining the metaphor and quickly apologizing for his use of figurative language. God's plough-land or God's field is 'the fathful congregation' (29). The one who sows this field with God's seed, that is, God's word as found in the Bible, is the preacher-ploughman, defined by Latimer as a 'man, whatsoever he be, that hath a flock to be taught of him, whosoever hath any spiritual charge in the faithful congregation, and whosoever he be that hath cure of soul' (30–1). Like all devout Protestants, Latimer justifies his use of this metaphor by pointing to its scriptural basis in Luke 8:5 and 9:62. He is keen to explain that his choice of imagery is grounded in Scripture because of an earlier incident in which his use of figurative language landed him in trouble, at least in some quarters. In the early part of this first section of the sermon Latimer is at pains to demonstrate the aptness of the agricultural imagery to the role of the preacher. Both dedicated ploughmen and true preachers must labour during 'all seasons of the year' (31) and can never rest from their tasks. He continues by listing parallels between the tenor and the vehicle of the comparison:

> And then they also may be likened together for the diversity of works and variety of offices that they have to do. For as the plowman first setteth forth his plow, and then tilleth his land and breaketh it in furrows, and sometime ridgeth it up again and at another time harroweth it and clotteth it, and sometime dungeth it and hedgeth it, diggeth it and weedeth it, purgeth and maketh it clean, so the prelate, the preacher, hath many diverse offices to do ... He hath then a busy work, I say, to bring forth his flock to a right faith and then to confirm them in the same faith; now casting them down with the law and with threatenings of God for sin; now ridging them up again with the gospel and with the promises of God's favor; now weeding them by telling them their faults and making them forsake sin; now clotting them by breaking their stony hearts and by making them supplehearted and making them to have hearts of flesh, that is, soft hearts and apt for doctrine to enter in; now teaching to know God rightly and to know their duty to God and their neighbors; now exhorting them, when they know their duty, that they do it and be diligent in it. (31–2)

Once having justified the appropriateness of the metaphor, Latimer turns his attention to prelates who neglect their ploughman duties. 'Lording loiters' (the alliteration here and elsewhere through the sermon is reminisicent of earlier alliterative ploughman tracts) and 'idle ministers' who hawk, hunt, card, and dice (36) set aside their plough and ignore the land because for them the land 'is too stony, too thorny, too hard to plow' (35). Others, described as 'unpreaching prelates' (35), are too involved in temporal affairs to carry out their spiritual duties as preachers. Neglect of spiritual ploughing is as life-threatening an an actual ploughman's refusal to plough his land: 'as it is necessary for to have this plowing for the sustenacion of the body, so must we have also the other for the satisfaction of the soul, or else we cannot live long ghostly. For as the body wasteth and consumeth away for lack of bodily meat, so doth the soul pine away for default of ghostly meat' (36).

Capitalizing on the unhappy economic implications of the dreaded practice of land enclosure, a practice severely criticized, for example, in *Pyers plowmans exhortation vnto the lordes, knightes and burgoysses of the Parlyamenthouse,* Latimer shows how the term can apply both to 'bodily plowings' and to 'the holy day plowing, the church plowing' (37). In both cases land is left unploughed, given over to some other use, so that both physical and spiritual sustenance of the members of the commonwealth is jeopardized.[92]

The second part of the sermon is devoted to explaining the diligence and goals of England's most formidable ploughman, the devil himself. Introducing the devil as an adversarial ploughman explains why the essence of this work is best captured in the title 'Sermon on the Plowers' rather than 'Sermon of the Plough,' as it is designated in Corrie's edition for the Parker Society. This sermon is about two categories of ploughers, those who should work on behalf of God – the prelates charged with planting God's seed in the ploughland that is God's 'faithful congregation' – and that tireless plougher, the devil himself, who works to undo the labour of true prelatical ploughmen. Latimer compares the devil's awareness of his labour to those prelates who refuse to show the same dedication to their tasks: 'He is the most diligent preacher of all other; he is never out of his diocese; he is never from his cure; ye shall never find him unoccupied; he is ever in his parish; he keepeth residence at all times; ye shall never find him out of the way; call for him when you will, he is ever at home. The diligentest preacher in all the realm, he is ever at his plow' (41).

Latimer makes it perfectly clear throughout the remainder of this work that the dedicated ploughman-devil works on behalf of the Roman Catholic Church under the leadership of the 'Italian bishop' (45), an interesting designation which attacks the pope of two fronts by emphasizing his purely local authority and his foreignness. The pope's ploughman is intent on deceiving people by encouraging them to place their faith in such inessential, distracting, and positively harmful things as candles, images, palms, ashes, holy water, purgatory, stocks, and stones, and the traditions of men rather than God. Moreover, he makes them believe that all must be communicated in Latin rather than English, an interesting commentary on the importance of the vernacular to the reformers, a notion developed at length by the farmer in *A proper dyaloge betwene a Gentillman and an Husbandman.* Throughout the tract, but especially in this second part where the real threat to Protestant England is openly expressed, Latimer is concerned about the possible resurgence of Roman Catholicism in England and the steps needed to be taken by prelate-ploughmen to ensure that their field is carefully ploughed in order to frustrate the endeavours of the Roman Catholic Church's principal ploughman, the devil.

Latimer's sermon is a brilliant piece, not only for his skilful use of the metaphor of the ploughers, but also because, by preaching a sermon on the value and importance of efficacious preaching, Latimer shows himself to be the kind of ideal plougher he sets out to define through the course of this tract, thereby justifying Kelly's designation of him as a Piers ploughman figure.

And finally a word or two on Edmund Spenser's use of the ploughman tradition. Norbrook has made us aware of Spenser's knowledge of both 'reforming, prophetic poetry' in general as well as *The Plowman's Tale* in particular, to which there seems to be an allusion in Spenser's translation of van der Noot's sonnets (59). In addition, in the April eclogue of *The Shepheardes Calender,* he uses the expression 'forswonke and all forswat,' a term almost identical to the one that appears in *The Plowman's Tale* (87).

What is especially important as a sign of Spenser's possible awareness and use of this tradition, however, is the presence of the character Piers in the May eclogue. Piers is important not only for his criticism of a clergy devoted to worldly values and luxury, a criticism which immediately associates him with both the radical reformist Piers and ploughman figures of the tradition we have already seen, but also for the nature of the poetic context in which he is situated. For although he bears the name of the ploughman of tradition, Spenser's Piers is in fact a shepherd and not a ploughman. Norbrook is doubtless correct when he claims that 'in the Middle Ages the two figures had similar associations' (59), but one does not have to look as far back as the Middle Ages – whatever its approximate time span might be – to see a dovetailing of the two traditions of shepherd and ploughman.[93] In fact, there is some indication of the coalescence of these figures in the work which is the subject of this book, *The praier and complaynte of the ploweman vnto Christe.* As I mentioned earlier in my analysis of the contents and structure of *The praier and complaynte,* the author often has his ploughman-narrator invoke the metaphor of the careful shepherd who tends his sheep and the irresponsible shepherd who has no concern for the welfare of his flock. Furthermore, Latimer in his 'Sermon on the Plowers' is not embarrassed to mix metaphors: his dedicated spiritual ploughman is a prelate, an individual described as one who 'hath a flock to be taught of him' (30). In the May eclogue Spenser makes Piers express his concern about the spiritual welfare of the Christian flock in similar terms. Although it is impossible to say whether Spenser may have known *The praier and complaynte* or Latimer's sermon, it is at least interesting to notice that he had no difficulty transforming a traditional ploughman figure into a shepherd in much the same way as the authors of *The praier and complaynte* and the 'Sermon on the Plowers' brought the two figures together within the same contexts. Additionally, if Cullen is correct when he states that 'Pier's ideal [in *The Shepheardes Calender*] like that of many Puritans and of Protestants in general, is that of primitive Christianity' (43), no ploughman tract that we have examined in this survey is clearer on the importance of the continuity between primitive Christianity and the ideology of present-day English reformers than *The praier and complaynte of the ploweman vnto Christe.*[94] In short, although we shall probably never be able to know precisely how much of the English literary ploughman tradition Spenser was aware of apart from his knowledge of Langland and *The Plowman's Tale*, it is altogether possible, based on the similarities I have briefly listed, that his knowledge may have extended beyond the range that Norbrook convincingly mentions.

# Editorial Method

This text is an old-spelling edition of the first edition of *The praier and complaynte of the ploweman vnto Christe*, published in Antwerp in 1531 by Martinus de Keyser. There are two extant copies of this edition, one at the Huntington Library, San Marino, California, the other at the Pierpont Morgan Library, New York City.[95] My choice of copy text is the Huntington Library copy. There is no indication of the author of this work, although the sixteenth-century preface (1–119) and the glossary of words and phrases (120–50) to the original Lollard tract (151–1679) may have been written by William Tyndale. I have collated my control text with the Pierpont Morgan copy for both substantive and accidental variants and have recorded these in Press Variants in the Copy Text, below.[96] I have also collated my control text with the only extant copy of the second edition (*STC* 20036), held by the Bodleian Library (Bodleian Tanner 23), for substantive variants, and have recorded these below in Variants and Emendations where appropriate.

Both John Foxe (II 728–47) and *The Harleian Miscellany* (VI 92–117) reprint a version of the first edition of *The praier and complaynte* which I have collated for substantive variants. Foxe updates certain spellings, adds his own side-notes (which I have included in the Commentary), and omits both the sixteenth-century preface and the glossary. *The Harleian Miscellany* updates punctuation, adds quotation marks and capitalization, and sometimes ignores the original's paragraphing. The editor also supplements the original glossary by adding a few meanings of difficult words and phrases and identifying a few of the very many biblical citations in the text.

The first edition is, in general, in a good state. I have emended conservatively and only when the Huntington text is obviously in error. For the most part I have taken my emended readings from the second edition (Bodleian Tanner 23) wherever possible. I have used readings from Foxe and Harleian exclusively only three times, once where both the first and second editions included a superfluous word which rendered the meaning of a passage nonsense (854), and twice where the first and second editions have the reading 'This' when it clearly should be 'Thus' as in Foxe and Harleian (1066 and 1242). The corrections I have taken from the second edition are in four areas: turned letters in Huntington (38, 422, 1200, 1450, 1462, 1520); dropped letters (1142, 1658); obvious misspellings (46, 54, 184, 197, 217, 292, 295, 342, 375, 378, 641, 751, 758, 771, 780, 828, 961, 969, 1148, 1298, 1351, 1374, 1386, 1396, 1439, 1467, 1486); and missing terminal punctuation, frequently at the end of a paragraph (40, 98, 292, 384, 400, 413, 456, 510, 536, 627, 630, 724, 787, 862, 1089). The section on Variants shows that, despite these emendations, the readings of my copy text are frequently correct and override variant readings from the other editions.

Since our knowledge of early punctuation practices is not entirely complete, I have retained the original punctuation throughout the tract, emending when necessary and wherever possible with 'correct' punctuation from the Bodleian second edition. I have also followed the paragraphing of the first edition.

Although I have retained the original spelling of the text, I have made some changes in orthography. I have silently changed the thorn into the current *th*, and the yogh into *y*, or *g*, or *gh*, or omitted it altogether where appropriate. I have expanded some standard sixteenth-century abbreviations, adding an *n* or *m* following a letter with a line above it (e.g., *ād*, *thē*) and expanding yͤ to *the*, yͭ to *that*, *yre* to *there*, and *yse* to *these*. A superscript form similar to the number 2 has been expanded to *er*, *ur*, or *re*. Another superscript form similar to the figure 9 has been expanded to *us*. An abbreviated form similar to a *p* with a double loop on the stem has been expanded to *ser*. I have normalized the long *s* throughout and expanded all ampersands. Black-letter type of the sixteenth century appears in this edition as roman. I have not tried to reproduce the original type sizes, nor have I included pilcrows (paragraph marks) that appear in the original printed text.

# Bibliographical Descriptions

Black-letter type in the original appears here in bold face.

**1531 *STC* 20036**

*Title Page* **The praierand | complaynte of the ploweman vnto | Chriſte:writtē not longe after | the yere of oure Lorde A | thouſande and thre | hundred.** [The words **The praier and** are about three times as big as the rest of the type on the title page.] **Chriſtus Matth. 10. | If they haue called the Lorde of the ho= | wſeBeelzebub: how moch mo² ſhal they | ſo call them of hys howſhold?**

*Collation* 8°, A–F$^8$ ($5) [B3r missigned A3r] 95 unnumbered leaves

*Contents* A1r title page; A1v ☙ **To the Chri= | ſten reader.** [The words **To the Chri=** are about three times the size of the rest of the expression.] **Grace be with the and peace be multi= | plied in the knowlege of god the father/ and | of oure Lorde Ieſus Chriſt Amen.** A3r **AMEN. The laſt daye of February.Anno.1531.** A3v **Here floweth the table.** A4r **The plowmans prayer.** [The size of the type from A1v to A3v is about half as big as the type in the complaint itself.]
F8r ❧ ❦ ☙
This edition has no colophon or catch-words.

*Running Titles* A4v–A6r **The prayer or complainte.** [on verso leaves] **Of the Plowman** [on recto leaves] A6v–A8r **The prayer or complainte.** [on verso leaves] **Of the Plowman.** [on recto leaves] A8v–B1r **The**

**prayer or complainte.** [on verso leaf] **Of the plowman.** [on recto leaf] B1v–B4r **The prayer or complaynte.** [on verso leaves] **Of the plowman.** [on recto leaves] B4v–B5r **The prayer or complaynte.** [on verso leaf] **Of the Plowman** [on recto leaf] B5v–B6r **The prayer or complainte.** [on verso leaf] **Of the Plowman** [on recto leaf] B6v–B8r **The prayer or complainte.** [on verso leaves] **Of the Plowman.** [on recto leaves] B8v–C1r **The prayer or complainte.** [on verso leaf] **of the plowman.** [on recto leaf] C1v–C4r **The prayer or complaynte.** [on verso leaves] **Of the plowman.** [on recto leaves] C4v–C6r **The prayer or complaynte.** [on verso leaves] **Of the Plowman** [on recto leaves] C6v–C8r **The prayer or complainte.** [on verso leaves] **Of the Plowman.** [on recto leaves] C8v–D1r **The prayer or complainte.** [on verso leaf] **Of the plowman.** [on recto leaf] D1v–D4r **The prayer or complaynte.** [on verso leaves] **Of the plowman.** [on recto leaves] D4v–D5r **The prayer or complaynte.** [on verso leaf] **Of the plowman** [on recto leaf] D5v–D6r **The prayer or complainte.** [on verso leaf] **Of the Plowman** [on recto leaf] D6v–D8r **The prayer or complainte.** [on verso leaves] **Of the Plowman.** [on recto leaves] D8v–E1r **The prayer or complainte.** [on verso leaf] **Of the plowman.** [on recto leaf] E1v–E4r **The prayer or complaynte.** [on verso leaves] **Of the plowman.** [on recto leaves] E4v–E5r **The prayer or complaynte.** [on verso leaf] **Of the Plowman** [on recto leaf] E5v–E6r **The prayer or complainte.** [on verso leaf] **Of the Plowman** [on recto leaf] E6v–E8r **The prayer or complainte.** [on verso leaves] **Of the Plowman.** [on recto leaves] E8v–F1r **The prayer or complainte.** [on verso leaf] **Of the plowman.** [on recto leaf] F1v–F4r **The prayer or complaynte.** [on verso leaves] **Of the plowman.** [on recto leaves] F4v–F5r **The prayer or complaynte.** [on verso leaf] **Of the Plowman** [on recto leaf] F5v–F6r **The prayer or complainte.** [on verso leaf] **Of the Plowman** [on recto leaf] F6v–F8r **The prayer or complainte.** [on verso leaves] **Of the Plowman.** [on recto leaves]

*Copies Collated* Huntington Library, California; Pierpont Morgan Library, New York

**1532 *STC* 20036.5**

*Title Page:* [Within a border of floral designs and vines on the left; with flowers, vines, and an animal (cat?) on the right; with a wider border at the top and bottom; in the top border floral designs with two animals (griffon and lion?) at either end; in the bottom border floral designs with two birds, an owl and an unidentified bird, perhaps a pelican, in the centre and on the right respectively] **The pra= yer and complaynt of | the Ploweman vnto | Chriſt: writtē nat lon | ge after the yere of | our Lorde. M. ⁊ | thre hūdered.** [The words **The pra=** are about twice the size of the type in the rest of this section.] **Christus Matth. 10 | ✗ If they haue called the | lorde of the houſe Beel= | zebub/ howe moch more | ſhall they ſo call them of his houſ holde?** [The size of the type in this section is about half as large as the preceding.]

*Collation* 8° A–D$^8$ E$^4$ F$^8$ ($2; F$3) 83 unnumbered leaves

*Contents* A1r title page; A2r **w. T. to the reder. | ¶Grace be with the and peace be multiplyed | in the knowlege of god the father/ and of our | lorde Ieſus Chriſt. Amen,** A4r **The plowmans prayer.** F6v [The type size of A2r–A3v is about half the size of the type in A4r–F6v.] This edition has no colophon.

*Running Titles* A2r–A3v **w. T. to the reder.** A4r **The plowmans prayer.** A4v–A6r **The prayer or complaynte** [on verso leaves] **of the plowman.** [on recto leaves] A6v–A7r **The prayer or complaynte.** [on verso leaf] **of the plowman.** [on recto leaf] A7v–B2r **The prayer or complaynte** [on verso leaves] **of the plowman.** [on recto leaves] B2v–B3r **The prayer or complaynte.** [on verso leaf] **of the plowman.** [on recto leaf] B3v–B7r **The prayer or complaynte** [on verso leaves] **of the plowman.** [on recto leaves] B7v–B8r **The prayer or complaynte.** [on verso leaf] **of the plowman.** [on recto leaf] B8v–C1r **The prayer or complaynte** [on verso leaf] **of the plowman.** [on recto leaf] C1v–C2r **The prayer or complayute** [on verso leaf] **of the plowman.** [on recto leaf] C2v–C5r **The prayer or complaynte** [on verso leaves] **of the plowman.** [on recto leaves] C5v–C7r **The prayer or complaynte.** [on verso leaves] **of the plowman.** [on recto leaves] C7v–D2r **The prayer or complaynte** [on verso leaves] **of the plowman.** [on recto leaves] D2v–D4r **The prayer or complaynte.** [on verso leaves] **of the plowman.** [on recto leaves] D4v–D8r **The prayer or complaynte** [on verso leaves] **of the plowman.** [on recto leaves] D8v–E1r **The prayer or complaynte** [on verso leaf] **of the plowman** [on recto leaf] E1v–E4r **The prayer or complaynte** [on verso leaves] **of the plowman.** [on recto leaves] E5v–F1r **The prayer or complaynte** [on verso leaf] **of the plowman** [on recto leaf] F1v–F6r **The prayer or complaynte** [on verso leaves] **of the plowman.** [on recto leaves] F6v **The prayer or complaynte**

*Catchwords* A2r–A3v **that** B4r–B4v **lepre: [lepre/]** C4r–C4v **plen= [plentuous]** D4r–D4v **the [keth]** E4r–E4v **wer= [werkes]**

*Copies Collated* Bodleian, Tanner 23 (only known copy)

# Notes

1 Along with *The praier and complaynte* de Keyser may have been responsible for printing some or all of the following: *The Psalter of Dauid* 1530 (*STC* 2370); *Ortulus anime. The garden of the soule* 1530 (*STC* 13828.4); *The prophete Ionas* 1531 (*STC* 2788); *The letters which Ihan Ashwel Printer of Newnham Abbey besids Bedforde sente secretely to the Bishope of Lyncolne* 1531 (*STC* 845); *A disputacion of purgatorye made by Iohan Frith* 1531 (*STC* 11388); *An answere vnto Sir Thomas Mores dialoge made by Vvillyam Tindale* 1531 (*STC* 24437); *The exposition of the fyrste Epistle of seynt Ihon with a Prologge before it: by W.T.* 1531 (*STC* 24443); *A supplicatyon made by Robert Barnes ... vnto the most excellent and redoubted prince kinge henry the eyght* 1531 (*STC* 1470); *The firste Boke of Moses called genesis ... by W.T.* 1534 (*STC* 2351); *Ieremy the Prophete translated into Englisshe* 1534 (*STC* 2778); *Dauids Psalter* 1534 (*STC* 2372); *The newe Testament* 1534 (*STC* 2826); *The newe testament yet once agayne corrected by Willyam Tindale* 1535 (*STC* 2830). Hume 'English Protestant Books Printed Abroad, 1525–1535' 1073–89.

2 John Foxe in *Acts and Monuments* reprints the tract but omits the important sixteenth-century preface while adding a large number of marginal notes. I have recorded these in the Commentary (Foxe II 728–47). The work also appears in *The Harleian Miscellany* VI 92–117).

3 The editor of *The Harleian Miscellany* seems to fall for the fraudulent date. He states: 'The author, who was a reformer before Wickliffe, is unknown by name' (92 note 1).

4 Margaret Aston states: 'Quite apart from the possibility of active proselytizing by the sixteenth-century inheritors of the old Lollard school, it was likely that the new reformers would be interested in the views of their protesting predecessors, both for the chance of adding vernacular

arguments to their own armoury, and to show that they themselves were not the founders of a new tradition' ('Lollardy and the Reformation' 150).

5 Foxe states: 'This book, as it was faithfully set forth by William Tindal, so I have as truly distributed the same abroad to the readers hands' (II 727). John Bale ascribes it to Tyndale in *Illustrium Maioris Britanniae scriptorum summarium* 1548 fol 221; J.F. Mozley claims that Tyndale is the editor, arguing that the reference to Thomas Hitton in the preface 'settles the matter' (*William Tyndale* 346). Charles C. Butterworth also supports Tyndale's candidacy (*The English Primers* 12 note 1). It is possible, of course, that all these supporters of Tyndale as editor were swayed by the appearance of the letters w. T. [*sic*] in the preface to the second edition.

6 Hume's view that Joye was the editor is not particularly strong, nor for that matter is the case made for Tyndale by Foxe, Bale, and Mozley. Hume's argument that de Keyser printed works for Joye is undoubtedly true since four of them are listed in her bibliography. However, de Keyser was also the printer for six of Tyndale's works.

7 As I make clear in the Commentary to this section of the tract, Tyndale for one saw no essential difference between biblical persecutors and their contemporary counterparts, and tried to produce linguistic evidence to establish the identity.

8 Kathryn Kerby-Fulton claims that within the medieval tradition of reformist apocalypticism the 'highest level of perfection ... was the imitation of the life of the apostles or of the early Church' (*Reformist Apocalypticism and Piers Plowman* 19). There is something of this sentiment throughout this preface.

9 Reference is also made to Hitton in the preface of a tract often attributed to William Tyndale, *The examinacion of Master William Thorpe* (*STC* 24045): Hitton 'was brente/ now thys yere/ at maydstone in Kent.'

10 A.G. Dickens states: 'Our sources afford much information on the social status of the Lollards. All save a few belonged to the common people – weavers, wheelwrights, smiths, carpenters, shoemakers, tailors and other tradesmen, "of whom", writes Foxe, "few or none were learned, being simple labourers and artificers, but as it pleased the Lord to work in them knowledge and understanding by reading a few books, such as they could get in corner"' (*The English Reformation* 53). Dickens goes on to add that 'Craftsmen and town-workers bulk larger than mere husbandmen' (53). In fact, this may have been the case, but within the context of the literary tradition, it seems clear that husbandmen, ie farmers, a group which would have included ploughmen, bulk much larger than either craftsmen or town-workers or, for that matter, any other occupational category into which 'common people' usually fell. *The praier and complaynte*, as well

as the number of ploughman tales I mention in The Ploughman Tradition of Complaint, below, would seem to validate this viewpoint.

11 In *Christian Plain Style* Peter Auksi has this to say about the moral implications of the notion of simplicity: 'To be simple implies sincerity, a lack of guile. In biblical terms the simple are innocent and harmless, and praised as such, but to the world the same may appear simple-minded or be called simpletons, ignorant, credulous, and unsuspecting. To the worldly, simplicity typically signifies a defect of knowledge, skill, or cunning, a defect useful only, if at all, for the disarming or charming of the suspicious' (4).

12 An expression taken from Jerome Barlowe and William Roye's *A proper dyaloge betwene a Gentillman and an Husbandman*, a tract which in part argues the same point being made here by the author of *A praier and complaynte*, namely that contemporary reformers are working within a well-established tradition of complaint. See Aston's comments quoted in note 4.

13 In this relatively short tract the Ploweman alludes to or cites in whole or in part approximately 165 biblical passages from both Testaments.

14 A complaint which is nowhere more dramatically recreated than in *Pierce the Plowmans Crede*.

15 Although the *OED* gives this term as current in c1380 and lists the first recorded usage – significantly – in Wycliffe's work, it became common linguistic currency in England only after Henry VIII's promulgation of the Acts of Succession and Supremacy. Hence, for example, in the 1533 and 1534 editions of Erasmus's English *Enchiridion Militis Christiani*, an extremely popular work in England in the sixteenth century, going through some eleven editions between 1533 and 1576 (E.J. Devereux *Renaissance English Translations of Erasmus* 104–13), all editions after 1534, ie after the Act of Supremacy, replace the word 'pope' found in the 1533 and 1534 editions with the phrase 'bishop of Rome.'

16 The word 'lewed' means, of course, 'lay,' that is those not ordained as priests or religious by the church. And as one reads this work, one notices the nature of the war between laity and clergy and the various manifestations of oppression that the latter imposes on the former. But the word 'lewed' also means 'unlearned,' 'ignorant,' and 'simple,' an equally apt meaning in this tract which pits the simplicity of ordinary, labouring Christians against a tendentiously knowledgeable and wealthy church.

17 About *The praier and complaynte* Helen C. White states: 'This work must be pretty nearly the most searching of its genre in its challenge to the common acceptances of contemporary secular society' (*Social Criticism in Popular Religious Literature of the Sixteenth Century* 26).

18 I find it hard to credit Anne Hudson's view that in *The praier and complaynte* 'the ploughman hardly exists outside the title' ('Epilogue: The Legacy of Piers Plowman' 257). As I have shown, the presence of the ploughman and the socio-economic group he represents is pervasive in this work.

19 As I stated above, the tract is ostensibly a prayer and complaint directed to God. In fact, however, it is a hortatory piece meant to appeal to all like-minded people under threat from a monolithic and uncaring church.

20 Because of the relatively few reformist ideas shared by sixteenth-century reformers and the compatibility between much of Lutheran and Lollard thought, it is unwise to assume that simply because one work follows another with similar ideas, the later one is somehow indebted to the earlier. Unless there is clear and irrefutable indebtedness between works, it is imprudent to create such indebtedness based solely on shared ideology.

21 I discuss the somewhat tangled bibliographical history of this work in my edition of *A proper dyaloge*. Here it is sufficient to say that the work was first published with dialogue and Lollard tract alone (*STC* 1462.3). Shortly after there appeared *STC* 3021; later in 1530 *STC* 3021 was appended to *STC* 1462.3 to create the final version, *STC* 1462.5, the basis of my edition.

22 There is by no means agreement on the issue of the identity of the editor. Foxe believes Tyndale to be the editor of this work. He states in part: 'To the text of the story we have neither added nor diminished, but, as we have received it copied out, and corrected by Master William Tindal (who had his own hand writing), so we have here sent it, and set it out abroad ... Furthermore, the said Master Tindal (albeit he did somewhat alter and amend the English thereof, and frame it after our manner), yet not fully in all words but that something doth remain, savouring of the old speech of that time' (Foxe III 249). More recently William A. Clebsch has also accepted Tyndale as editor of this work (*England's Earliest Protestants* 265).

23 Foxe claims that Hitton's martyrdom occurred on 20 February 1529. Tyndale mentions Hitton twice, once in *The Practice of Prelates* (*Expositions and Notes* 340), and again in *Answer to Sir Thomas More's Dialogue* (113). The fact that Hitton is mentioned twice by Tyndale may have been one of the reasons why his name was tied to both Thorpe's examination and *The praier and complaynte*.

24 Aston comments on the sixteenth-century reformers' awareness of the importance of tradition to support their causes and reformist ideologies. She states that with certain texts from past eras 'the work of recovery was openly acknowledged. Antiquity, since it was valuable, was avowed.

But other Reformation editors proceeded on different principles. It was one thing to publish a text, more or less as it stood, archaisms and all, to prove that new reformers were but old reformers writ large, with the right of precedent on their side. It was another to take over an old text, and rewrite it (without acknowledgement) to serve a new purpose, or alter it sufficiently to obscure its origin' (*Lollards and Reformers* 227).

25 John A.F. Thomson indicates the difficulties involved in trying to establish a clear and consistent set of doctrinal beliefs for Lollards. He states that 'one cannot talk of a single Lollard creed but must always remember that beliefs varied, not only from group to group, but even from individual to individual within the same group.' He continues: 'it is perhaps more accurate to consider Lollardy as a set of more or less consistent attitudes than as a set of carefully worked-out doctrines' (*The Later Lollards* 239).

26 That Thorpe had to show some restraint in front of his judges is evident when one compares his Testament to the examination. In the former he has nothing to lose by expressing himself candidly and, as a result, he pulls out all the stops, showing himself a strong opponent to both pope and church hierarchy in general. He states in part: 'from the highest priest to the lowest, all, as they say, study, that is, they imagine and travail busily, how they may please this world and their flesh. This sentence with many such others dependeth upon them, if it be well considered: either God the Father of heaven, hath deceived all mankind by the living and teaching of Jesus Christ, and by the living and teaching of his apostles and prophets; or else all the popes that have been since I had any knowledge or discretion, with all the college of cardinals, archbishops and bishops, monks, canons, and friars, with all the contagious flock of the commonalty of priesthood, who have, all my life time, and mickle longer, reigned and yet reign, and increase damnably from sin to sin, have been, and yet be, proud, obstinate heretics, covetous sinners, and defouled adulterers in the ministering of the sacraments, and specially in the ministering of the sacrament of the altar' (Foxe III 283)

27 Clebsch states that '*A Brefe Dialoge* [i.e., *A Lytle treatous*] first stated in English the viewpoint of the Reformation radicals' (234).

28 In a letter dated 4 October 1528 Herman Rynck, Wolsey's ambassador in Europe, tells of his efforts to buy up all copies of books printed in Cologne in English. In the letter he mentions trying to buy all copies of *Rede Me and Be Nott Wrothe* (letter reprinted in *English Reprints* ed Arber XIV 12–13). For Tyndale's comments see his 'The Parable of the Wicked Mammon' (*Doctrinal Treatises* 37ff). See my edition of *Rede Me and Be Nott Wrothe*.

29 These sentiments expressed near the conclusion of both works indicate the reformers' desire not only to spread the reformist message but also not to shy away from any material, original or otherwise, that might advance the cause. Roye expresses a similar view in *A Lytle treatous or dialoge*: But seynge that we can do nothynge of oure selves/ I beseche you all/ der bretheren/ to praye vnto the lorde for me/ that I maye have both mynde and strengthe wother soche bokes to translate' (A4v).

30 Dickens states: 'for decades after the coming of Lutheranism, numerous prosecutions took place in the ecclesiastical courts, during which the accused exhibited a whole group of very characteristic Lollard beliefs and showed no sign whatsoever of the justificatory and sacramental teachings peculiar to Luther or Zwingli' (58).

31 With the exception of *Rede Me and Be Nott Wrothe*, where monasticism is strenuously attacked in the second part, I have found no other work of this period which attacks monks as strongly as *The summe*. Normally, as we shall see in The Plowman Tradition of Complaint, below, mendicants are the religious orders which serve as the *bête noire* of both reformers and conservative critics alike.

32 The colophon for *The Lanterne* reads as follows: 'Imprynted at London in Fletestrete/ by me Robert Redman/ dwellynge at the sygne of the George/ newxte [*sic*] to Saynt Dunstones church.' Redman flourished as a printer between 1524 and 1540.

33 This quotation from *The Lanterne* is reminiscent of Oldcastle's comment on the hierarchy in his *examinacion*: 'Rome is the very nest of Antichrist; and out of that nest come all the disciples of him; of whom prelates, priests, and monks, are the body, these pilled friars are the tail behind.'

34 A more recent study, Carl R. Trueman's *Luther's Legacy*, addresses this issue by focusing on the importance of Lutheran thought for the early English reformers.

35 In his biography of Tyndale David Daniell seems sceptical about the claims Smeeton makes. He states: 'Smeeton in his interesting book detaches Tyndale far too eagerly from Luther; it is not for nothing that Smeeton's book began as a thesis at Louvain, a university opposed to Luther since Luther's own time' (*William Tyndale* 393 note 24).

36 I shall deal with the question of the direct relationship between Tyndale's works and *The praier and complaynte* below in The Editor and Early English Editions, where I discuss the possibility that Tyndale was the editor of this work. Patrick Collinson seems hastily dismissive of Smeeton's claims about Tyndale's indebtedness to Lollardy. He states: 'there is no documented evidence whatsoever to sustain his thesis' ('William Tyndale

and the Course of the English Reformation' 80). Recently, however, a book by Andrew Brown (*William Tyndale on Priests and Preachers*), about which I have read only a review in the *Times Literary Supplement*, 4 October 1996, questions the conventional view that Tyndale was born near the Vale of Berkeley and claims that he was actually born in the 'long-standing Lollard area' of the Forest of Dean, a claim which, if true, might help support the views of those who believe that he was influenced by Lollard thought.

37 Further evidence of the prevalence of Lollardy and Lollards in England can be found in Foxe's narratives of many of the heresy hearings. A good summary of the 'Lollard Survival' is in Dickens 49–56. Dickens claims that the nature of heresy in Tudor England 'was overwhelmingly Wycliffe [*sic*], at least until 1530' (50), the approximate period we are dealing with in this study.

38 As to whether the entire tract might be a sixteenth-century production made to appear like an original Lollard tract, Hudson states: 'The balance of probability is against the likelihood that the strongly archaic language of the *Praier and complaynte* was composed by a sixteenth-century forger, but this cannot be formally proven ... In subject matter there seems to me nothing in the *Praier* that would be out of place in a Lollard tract of the early fifteenth century' ('"No Newe Thyng"' 172–3).

39 Joye's response to Tyndale is found in his *An Apology made by George Joy, to satisfy, if it may be, W. Tindale.* 1535 (reprinted in *The English Scholar's Library* III).

40 The most recent support for Tyndale as editor of *The praier and complaynte* is found in *The Complete Works of St. Thomas More*: 'In addition to his *Answer*, Tyndale had published two works earlier in 1531, *The Plowman's Prayer* and a translation of *Jonas*' (VIII/3 1237). This baldly stated claim is unverified.

41 For details of Hitton's life see my note on Hitton in the Commentary 84–7.

42 This tract is published separately and in its entirety in *The English Works of Wyclif Hitherto Unpublished* under the title 'The Clergy May Not Hold Property' (362–404).

43 There is no unanimity about the original author of this tract. Margaret Deansley sees it as a Lollard effort authored by William Purvey (*The Lollard Bible and Other Medieval Biblical Versions*). Hudson disagrees and argues that it was written by the orthodox, if critical, Richard Ullerston (*Selections from English Wycliffite Writings*).

44 Of the English Protestant books published abroad between 1525 and 1535 the dates of those which were first published in England are as follows: *A*

*compendious olde treatyse shewynge howe that we ought to haue the scripture in Englysshe* 1538 (*STC* 3022); *The practyse of Prelates* 1548 (*STC* 24466); *The prophete Ionas* 1537 (*STC* 2781); *The letters which Iohan Ashwel Priour of Newnham Abbey ... sente to the Bishope of Lyncolne* 1548? (*STC* 846); *A disputacion of purgatorye* 1537 (*STC* 11387); *The exposition of the fyrste Epistle of seynt Ihon* 1537? (*STC* 24443.5); *A supplicatyon made by Robert Barnes* 1534 (*STC* 1471); *An exposicion vppon the.v.vi.vii. chapters of Mathew* 1536? (*STC* 24441); *The Souper of the Lorde* 1546 (*STC* 24465); *A boke made by Iohn Frith prisoner in the tower of London* ... 1546 (*STC* 11382); *The Obedience of a Christen man* 1537? (*STC* 24447.7).

45 Godfray uses the same title-page border for his edition of *The praier and complaynte* as he did for *The forme and maner of subvention or helpyng for pore people deuysed and practysed in the cytie of Hypres* (*STC* 26119).

46 *STC* states that 'only two of Godfray's imprints have dates, the Chaucer, 1532 (5068), and the *Subvention in Ypres*, 1535 (26119), and neither of them has an address' (III 69).

47 That Lollard works reborn on the continent and smuggled into England could be officially condemned in 1531 (as they were in the Bayfield case) and yet in 1532 be allowed to be printed in England by someone with links to the King's Printer without condemnation (the situation of *The praier and complaynte*) seems preposterous. James K. McConica's explanation might be the one that solves the mystery. He argues that, after Wolsey's fall in 1529 and until Reginald Pole's departure from England in 1532 and Thomas More's resignation in the same year, there was a common mission among conservative reforming Erasmians. In 1532, however, the climate changed largely as a result of the king's 'great matter'; under the able stewardship of Thomas Cromwell more strident, less conservative, more politically motivated propaganda began to appear from the printing presses (*English Humanists and Reformation Politics* 106–49).

48 McConica, among others, summarizes the attempts made by Cromwell, through his Antwerp agent Stephen Vaughan, to get Tyndale to return to England to work on the king's behalf. The negotiations which took place through 1531–2, at approximately the time that *The praier and complaynte* appeared in England and was published there, were finally unsuccessful. McConica wonders if Vaughan might have sent Tyndale's translation of Erasmus's *Enchiridion Militis Christiani* to Cromwell 'in a final attempt to revive Tyndale's cause with a work which was sure to please the King' (145). An English translation of the *Enchiridion*, thought

by some to be by Tyndale, was published in England by John Byddell in 1533. If McConica's speculation about Vaughan sending the *Enchirdion* to Cromwell is correct, it might also explain how *The praier and complaynte* arrived in the country and why it appeared in 1532 with the initials W.T. on its first sheet.

49 Mozley, commenting on the reaction to Tyndale's *The Practice of Prelates*, states: 'The book ... gave great offence to the King's party, and provoked a speedy retort. On some day before December 4 [1530] ... a placard was put out by authority and posted in conspicuous places, recounting the opinions of the universities in favour of the divorce, and attacking the *Practice of Prelates* by name' (169–70).

50 If the conditions surrounding the publication of the 1532 edition of *The praier and complaynte* are as extraordinary as they appear to be, the relative scarcity of both the first and second editions might mean that the work was informally suppressed soon after it saw the light of day in England because of its anti-Henrician contents. But this is mere speculation.

51 Other comments by Puttenham show that he was less enamoured of Langland's poem than the Lollards and Protestant reformers who were indebted to *The Vision*. Puttenham, writing as a modern, claims that Langland's 'verse is but loose meetre, and his termes hard and obscure, so as in them is little pleasure to be taken' (62).

52 As important as it is within the context of a thorough historical survey of the ploughman figure, I have not discussed the Latin tradition as found, for example, in the works of Virgil or Theocritus, nor am I unaware, thanks to Kerby-Fulton, of Bridget of Sweden's (1303–73) honouring the ploughman as one of the symbolic figures chosen to 'take the clergy back to their pristine state of unworldliness' (106). Kerby-Fulton adds that both the ploughman and his plough recur in a number of Bridget's visions and are perhaps among her favourite images (107).

53 *STC* is unaware of a copy of *The Plowman's Tale* in the Huntington Library that indicates that Thomas Godfray, who flourished in the 1530s, was the printer (Andrew N. Wawn 'Chaucer, "The Plowman's Tale" and Reformation Propaganda' 175).

54 Strictly speaking, another work in which a tiller of the soil plays a major role was published in 1530, one year prior to the appearance of *The praier and complaynte of the ploweman*. This important work entitled *A proper dyaloge betwene a Gentillman and an Husbandman* is a hybrid text made up of three parts: an exchange in poetry between two supporters of radical reform within the church; an old Lollard tract speaking out against the clerical impropriation of secular land; and a

prose document probably of the late fourteenth century which argues for a vernacular Bible. The husbandman or farmer in this work is eloquent and outspoken in his attack on abuses within the church. As such, he is a descendant of Langland's Piers, the difference being that Langland's critic remains within the pale of the church while the husbandman, like many of his sixteenth-century colleagues, seeks its overthrow (see my edition of *A proper dyaloge* and *STC* 1462.5). In addition to *A proper dyaloge*, another ploughman work, which need not concern us in a major way here, appeared from John Rastell's press in 1525. This work by William Rastell, entitled *Of Gentylnes and Nobylyte: A dyaloge betwen the marchaunt the knyght and the plowman dysputyng who is a verey gentylman and who is a noble man and how men shuld come to auctoryte/ compiled in a maner of an enterlude ...* (*STC* 20723), pits the opinions of a merchant, a knight, and a ploughman against each other on the question of the importance of wealth, inheritance, and birth as they apply to the notions of gentility and nobility. The fact that the ploughman essentially takes control of the debate and argues that gentility and nobility reside in those who possess virtue rather than wealth suggests that the author's views are represented in this simple but eloquent figure; in addition, the tract's final lines, spoken by a 'phylosopher,' corroborate the ploughman's position. The ploughman, like many we shall see in the survey which follows, is not cowed by the wealthy and aristocratic company he keeps in this tract. His arguments are detailed, fetching, and confidently expressed, and he clearly bests his two more economically successful interlocutors. Richard Axton argues that the themes of Rastell's interlude 'are the subject of an immense literature in the later Middle Ages and early Renaissance' (*Three Rastell Plays* 21) and mentions Chaucer, Guillaume de Lorris, Jean de Meun, and Dante to prove his claim.

55 Dean Milman, arguing for Langland's orthodoxy, states: 'The Visionary is no disciple, no precursor of Wycliffe in his broader religious views ... he acquiesces seemingly with unquestioning faith in the Creed and in the usages of the Church. He is not profane but reverent as to the Virgin and the Saints. Pilgrimages, penances, oblations on the altar, absolution, he does not reject, though they are nought in comparison with holiness and charity; on Transubstantiation and the Real Presence and the sacraments he is almost silent, but his silence is that of submission, not of doubt' (quoted in *The Vision of William Concerning Piers the Plowman* ed Walter W. Skeat l–li). More recently, John N. King has stated that, 'Although it voiced an orthodox call for religious reform, *Piers Plowman* remained under the old ban against Wyclifite texts' (*English Reformation*

*Literature* 52). Recent studies of the work assume its essential orthodoxy; see, for instance, Steven Justice 'The Genres of Piers Plowman.'

56 For a much fuller discussion of this enormously complex poem, especially the ways in which its concepts, figures, and ideology relate to a rich medieval tradition of reformist literature, see Kerby-Fulton's learned and impressive study.

57 Of all the members of the church's spiritual hierarchy, the friars seemed to come under constant attack from all sides. Langland attacks them, as does the author of *Pierce the Ploughmans Crede*. They also served as the inspiration for a number of satiric poems. See, for instance, 'Song Against The Friars' and 'On the Minorite Friars,' both taken from the Cotton manuscript (*Rerum Britannicarum* 263–70), and two fifteenth-century pieces (*Reliquiae Antiquae*): 'A Poem Against the Friars and Their Miracle-Plays' (I 322–3) and 'A Song Against the Friars' (II 247). For a study of the various complaints against mendicants see Penn R. Szitta, *The Antifraternal Tradition in Medieval Literature*.

58 The *New Catholic Encyclopedia* states that 'during the 13th century there was a remarkable growth in the number of mendicant orders until the Second Council of Lyons issued a decree in July 17, 1274, directed at the suppression of all but the four major orders.' Wycliffe's claim that the English friars numbered 4000 in his day is countered by David Knowles, who states that Wycliffe's number would be 'roughly correct for 1348' (*The religious Orders in England* II 103), but should be halved for 1380 probably as a result of the Black Death which swept through the country in the middle of the century. He further adds that Wycliffe's estimate of 20,000 friars in the country mentioned in one of his sermons is a 'fantastic overstatement' (II 104). Knowles gives approximate figures for the number of friars in 1320: Preachers 1760; Minors 1700; Carmelites 800; Austin Friars 600 (II 258).

59 A term used by Protestant reformers from Wycliffe's day onwards to refer to the papacy and the pope. *OED* claims that the word in this particular sense dates from Wycliffe, although King claims that the identification of Antichrist with the papacy was first made by the twelfth-century writer Joachim de Fiore (198).

60 Kerby-Fulton sees disendowment as a perennial theme in the writings of the major medieval apocalyptic authors.

61 Despite the temptation to regard *The Vision* as an altogether original achievement, G.R. Owst, in his book *Preaching in Medieval England*, argues that the contents of Langland's poem are indebted finally to the strong tradition of medieval preaching. He states: 'Half a century and more of learned criticism has been expended on Langland's famous

Vision. But through modern contempt for a pulpit now shorn of its ancient glory, the one complete clue to the poem is still persistently ignored. In reality, it represents nothing more nor less than the quintessence of English mediaeval preaching gathered up into a single metrical piece of unusual charm and vivacity' (295). And in his *Literature and Pulpit in Medieval England* Owst traces the figure (if not the name) of the humble ploughman to medieval sermon literature as well, where he appears variously as 'simple working folk,' 'the humble poor,' 'patientes pauperes,' 'fideles simplices,' 'the trewe pore peple,' 'goddes knyghtes' (569). Not everyone agrees with Owst. J.F. Goodridge, for instance, in his translation of Langland's poem claims that 'in all the sermons Mr Owst quotes, there is scarcely a single close parallel to anything in Langland; the similarities are those which would exist in any age between the writings of men who shared the same training, spoke the same idiom, and were concerned about the same kind of problems' (*Piers the Ploughman* 10). Perhaps the most balanced view is Siegfried Wenzel's: 'to date no case has been made that shows that Langland drew from a specific source or preacher. Names like Brinton and Bromyard appear again and again in the critical literature because their works are in print and relatively familiar. But it has not been demonstrated that any specific passage in *Piers* is unmistakably derived from such sermon texts or handbooks ... We must therefore think of the poem's sermon background as a diffuse and widely dispersed influence, furnishing commonplaces and perhaps even structural patterns that floated from pulpit to pulpit and settled in many written texts' ('Medieval Sermons' 167–8). More recently, Kerby-Fulton has convincingly argued the influence on *The Vision* of such early apocalyptic figures as Hildegard of Bingen, Bridget of Sweden, and Joachim de Fiore. As important as these similarities, however, are her judicious assessments of where Langland and these predecessors part company.

62 If Owst's claims about the sermon tradition in which Langland was working are correct, the author of *The Vision* would doubtless have seen himself as a devout, if critical, commentator on abuses that others, with impeccable orthodox credentials, had also brought to public attention.

63 In addition they may have come to regard the figure of the ploughman as a significant reformed Christian leader because of Langland's privileging of Piers as a reformer of the church in the later books of *The Vision* (see Kerby-Fulton 54).

64 The case of the English editions of Erasmus's *Enchiridion Militis Christiani* provides a good example of how the sixteenth-century managed to metamorphose the work of one man to make it fit a reformist context. The eleven English editions of this work published between 1533 and

1576 make selective changes to reflect the various alterations in official religious positions. For instance, in certain editions the word 'pope' is changed to 'bishop of Rome.' In others references to monasticism are excised following dissolution. References to the doctrine of transubstantiation and the mass are altered in certain editions once these two related concepts of Roman Catholic doctrine are jettisoned by the English church. Erasmus's own various comments on having simultaneously to run with the hare and to hunt with the hounds reflect his frustration. He states that he has been 'thrown to the Furies and torn to pieces by both sides' (Collected Works of Erasmus x 213). Again he feels like the conciliator between 'a pair of armed and angry drunks' (xi 392), or like Ulysses trying to 'steer midway between Scylla and Charybdis' (xi 117), or like someone 'stuck ... between the altar and the sacrificial knife' (xi 185).

65 The contrast here between scholar and ploughman serves to accentuate a concept that makes its way through all of the ploughman tracts that follow. Not only is the ploughman seen as a legitimate part of the Christian community, but his frequent presence in these tracts as narrator serves to validate what King has called 'the Protestant plain style' (138ff). Regularly in these tracts the ploughman-narrator apologizes for his apparent lack of rhetorical skill. This apology is itself a rhetorical device since 'plain style' came to be seen and lauded among Protestants, not only as the appropriate response to the obfuscatory style associated with the Roman Church, but also as the linguistic trademark of all those committed to reformist views. See Auksi *Christian Plain Style.*

66 Dickens has a brief but helpful study of the process and effects of dissolution (167–91).

67 For ease of reference I have catalogued these works and given their approximate dates below, in Sixteenth-Century Ploughman Texts.

68 Frederick J. Furnivall and I. Gollancz have published Hoccleve's 'The story of the Monk who clad the Virgin by singing Ave Maria' without the ploughman prologue (*Hoccleve's Works* 290–3); versions with and without the prologue are found in *A New Ploughman's Tale* ed Arthur Beatty 12–21.

69 This work appears in *Reliquiae Antiquae* I 43–7. Eamon Duffy briefly discusses this tract in *The Stripping of the Altars.* He states that the poem derives from a story 'used by St Bernardino to illustrate the duty of a parish priest to teach his people' (84). He adds that 'We certainly should not take it as an indicator of the general educational level of wealthy plowmen, but its effect does depend on the audience's sense of the general plausibility of the situation, as well as the enormity of the plowman's ignorance' (85).

70 Regrettably, because of its rarity, I have not been able to examine this text at first hand. It exists in a single manuscript found in the British Library, MS Harley 207, and an excerpt only is published in *Bishop Percy's Folio Manuscript* ed. J.W. Hales and F.J. Furnivall. About this work Hudson states: 'The subject of the discussion is primarily the Eucharist, the spokesman of the reformed faith (that specified to be of Luther, Oecolampadius, Karlstadt, Melanchthon, Bucer, Joye, Bale, Turner, and Frith ff.2v, 11v) is one *Doctor Dawcock*. The Doctor get the worst of the argument, even though he is supported by *Jacke Jolie* and *Nicholas Newfangill'* (Hudson, 'Epilogue: The Legacy of *Piers Plowman'* 260).

71 Skeat points out that *The Plowman's Tale* occurs in the second edition of *The Canterbury Tales* published in 1542, 'where it is added at the end of the Canterbury Tales [*sic*], after the Parson's Tale. In the next ... edition ... it is placed *before* the Parson's tale [*sic*], as if it were really Chaucer's, and the same arrangement occurs in the fourth edition, that of 1561, by John Stowe' (*Supplement to the Works of Geoffrey Chaucer* xxxi). The text of *The Plowman's Tale* is also in *Six Ecclesiastical Satires* 58–114. Thomas Wright's edition in 'Political Poems and Songs' (304–46) is published without the important prologue (*Rerum Britannicarum Medii Aevi Scriptores*).

72 Despite attempts made by the sixteenth-century editor to render this work more suitable for the cause of reform in the 1530s, there is one anomaly near the end of the poem which seems to work against the editor's goal. After unmercifully attacking the traditional church throughout, the Pelican, uncharacteristically one feels, suddenly asks that every man 'Of my wryting have me excused' (1365). Stranger still, however, are the words of the ploughman, who, unlike his fellow ploughman in this tradition, distances himself from the Pelican's reformist views. The ploughman encourages readers to 'Wyteth [i.e., blame] the Pellican, and not me' (1373) for the views expressed in the tract. And, as if to capitulate to the *status quo*, adds: 'To holy churche, I will me bowe; / Ech man to amende him, Christ send space!' (1377–8). It is unclear why the sixteenth-century editor of this work, careful enough to add a Protestant prologue and to insert into the tract a small section attacking the papacy, would not show similar attention to a passage near the end of the poem which seems to subvert the tract's reformist ideology. What seems to be called for – but does not happen – is careful excision.

73 References to this poem are taken from Walter W. Skeat's edition, *Pierce the Ploughmans Crede*. An edition of the poem is also found in *Six Ecclesiastical Satires* 8–49. Critical commentary on this work is found in Derek Pearsall *Old English and Middle English Poetry* and Thorlac

Turville-Petre *The Alliterative Revival*. However, for the purposes of this survey the most important and most extensive commentary on *Pierce the Ploughmans Crede* is in Helen Barr *Signes and Sothe*, which demonstrates the way in which *Pierce* borrows from and echoes Langland's poem.

74 Dickens comments on a policy of dissolution during Edward's reign which extended the work initiated by his father: 'So far as ordinary Englishmen were concerned, the most important measure of Edward's first Parliament was the one which assigned to the Crown all chantries, free chapels, colleges, hospitals, fraternities, guilds, and similar institutions throughout England and Wales' (230).

75 Skeat makes a telling point about these suppressed lines. He states: 'it is quite easy to see why Reynold Wolfe did not print them; they savoured far too much of the doctrine of transubstantiation ... and therefore he purposely suppressed them. But he did it very clumsily, for he quite overlooked the fact that the omission of them took away the clue to the context and quite robbed it of its meaning ... But now that these lines are restored, the drift of this whole passage is clear enough, and we perceive that the author is attacking the friars on yet one more point, viz. for the subtlety of their arguments about the sacrament of the mass, and for their attempt to explain a mystery which had much better, in his opinion, be left unexplained. His belief is, he says that "God's body and blood are really in the sacrament; and though proud friars dispute about God's deity like dotards, the more the matter is stirred, the more confused they become"' (xvii–xviii). What Skeat seems not to realize in his attack on Wolfe's suppression of these lines is that Wolfe could not possibly leave them untouched and still regard the work as a Protestant document. Even if the doctrine of transubstantiation is mentioned so as to attack the friars on one more front, the very fact that it is mentioned and validated in the original would make it anathema to the Edwardian church. Better therefore to sacrifice another volley against the friars by excising the lines which refer to the validity of transubstantiation than to strike out at the friars once more and by so doing appear to be supporting transubstantiation.

76 Apparently – and interestingly for the purposes of this discussion – this work in its own day was often mistitled *Dialogue of the Gentleman and Plowman* (Clebsch 266–7).

77 Tyndale sums up what he sees as the three basic views of the Eucharist in *A Brief Declaration of the Sacraments* (*Doctrinal Treatises* 366–7), and in a letter to Frith expresses concern about the divisive effects that the various views of the Eucharist are having on the reformers and their cause (*Doctrinal Treatises* liii–liv).

78 David Norbrook claims that this work was actually published in 1547 and written by one Luke Shepherd. The author's name, he thinks, might be a pseudonym combining the name of one of the gospel authors and the profession of shepherd which, 'along with the ploughman, is a favourite persona of mid-century writers, who like to present themselves as speaking simple truths in the voice of the people' (*Poetry and Politics in the English Renaissance* 933).

79 The fact that this work was published twice in 1550 suggests its popularity.

80 Barlowe and Roye devote more than 700 lines to an attack on the mendicants in their 3700-line medley of complaint.

81 In *Rede Me and Be Nott Wrothe* one of the complaints that the authors bring against the orders of friars is their jealousy of each other. When Watkyn, one of the two speakers, asks, 'What is their communicacion?' (2140), his interlocutor, Ieffraye, responds, 'By my sothe murmuracion / One backbytynge another' (2141–2), and adds, 'I tell the they murmur more, / Then eny persons that I knowe. / Full of envious suspicion' (2144–6).

82 Dickens discusses the foreign influences on English religious thought during Edward VI's reign. He claims that there was a 'rising influence of foreign theologians and continental religious movements' making its influence felt in the country. He states: 'For some time Archbishop Cranmer had been attempting to link England with international Protestantism by consulting with governments and scholars abroad. His friendship with Osiander, his marriage, his many contacts with foreign Reformers, all disposed him to this end. The men he befriended display in their life-stories the whole range of European religious politics, yet amongst them one grievous omission remained. Cranmer failed to persuade Melanchthon or any other representative leader of the Lutherans to visit England. Though henceforth foreign influences upon the English Reformation steadily increased, they came not from Wittenberg but from Strassburg, Zurich and Geneva' (257–8). It is quite clear that the author of this tract has affinities with this continental group of reformers. His strong anti-episcopal views demonstrate this, as does his position on the doctrine of transubstantiation and the real presence. Although Lutheranism never gained much ground in England during Edward's reign, it would be unwise to suggest that it did not make its presence felt there, especially during the early days of reform in the mid 1520s and early 1530s. However, even then it was not universally accepted amongst the reformers, as Frith's anti-Lutheran view of the Eucharist demonstrates. See Frith's *A Book Made by John Frith* (*STC* 11381) and his *A Christian Sentence* (*STC* 5190).

83 The narrator's reference to his 'rude language' and especially John Bon's characterization of himself as a 'plain man' should be read in the context of Auksi's illuminating study of the Christian plain style.

84 See, for example, Tyndale's *The Practice of Prelates* (*Exposition and Notes* 249–344).

85 See my edition of this work for commentary on the bibliographical history and various forms of the text.

86 Although there appears to be no way of knowing for certain who wrote this tract, it might not be simply idle speculation to propose the name of Robert Crowley. As mentioned earlier, Crowley was the person responsible for producing three editions of Langland's *The Vision* in 1550. He may have taken Piers' name and his reputation as a critic of established views and applied them to this work with a view to drawing attention to it. Crowley was a well-known Protestant critic of social and economic abuses and was especially critical of rent-rackers, engrossers, and those who indulged their greed through enclosures. See, for instance, his *The Way to Wealth* and especially *An informacion and Peticion agaynst the oppressours of the pore Commons of this Realme*, which, like *Pyers Plowmans exhortation*, is addressed to Parliament (*The Select Works of Robert Crowley* 129–50; 151–76). King believes that *Pyers Plowmans exhortation* was written by Crowley (474).

87 Complaints about the enclosing of land and the use of such land for the pasturing of livestock were by no means peculiar to Edward VI's reign. As R.H. Tawney and Eileen Power have shown, complaints about enclosures in the Tudor period stretch back into the reign of Henry VII. In volume III of *Tudor Economic Documents* they list a sampling of twelve anti-enclosure tracts from 1496 to 1550. Another important anti-enclosure tract published during Edward's reign by Hugh Singleton is *Certayne causes gathered together, wherin is shewed the decaye of England*. This work is important if only for the author's remarkable detailing of precise statistics to indicate the seriousness of the enclosure problem (*Four Supplications* 93–102).

88 Some of these figures are better known than others but all of them are found in Foxe, passim. The Richard Hunne case is especially interesting because of the heated controversies it gave rise to. The reformist view is found in Foxe IV 183–205. A less impassioned essay on the issue is in More IX, 213ff.

89 The work is printed in *Sermons by Hugh Latimer* 59–78 and in *Selected Sermons of Hugh Latimer* 28–49. My references to the sermon are from the latter source.

90 Certainly Robert L. Kelly argues against the 'spontaneity' of Latimer's

sermon, and the title of his interesting article 'Hugh Latimer as Piers Plowman' implies his awareness of the tradition in which Latimer may have been working.

91 One has to wonder to what extent the appearance of this sermon by itself or in combination with other English ploughman tracts published before 1550 might have motivated Crowley to issue his editions of Langland's *The Vision* in 1550.

92 This emphasis on the deleterious economic effects of enclosures nicely highlights the point made by Chester in *Selected Sermons* that 'Latimer was able to bring religious reform and economic reform into a meaningful relationship' (xxiv), a relationship that we saw developed in two other ploughman tracts: *Pyers Plowmans exhortation vnto ... the Parlyament-house* and *A proper dyaloge betwene a Gentillman and an Husbandman*.

93 It is one thing to talk about the 'similar associations' of ploughman and shepherd but quite another to identify the name of Piers with shepherds as Paul E. McLane does in *Spenser's 'Shepheardes Calender'*. As far as I can determine, McLane is in error when he states that 'the name of Piers had long been accepted as the stock denomination of the godly and unworldly spiritual shepherd' (176). The error indicates how easy it is to identify shepherds and ploughmen and apply the name Piers to the former occupation. Although Spenser may not have been responsible for creating this identification, he surely contributed to it in *The Shepheardes Calender*. In addition, given the furore over the whole question of enclosures in the sixteenth century – see, for instance, *Pyers Plowmans exhortation vnto ... the Parlyamenthouse* – it is not altogether reasonable, outside of a literary tradition, to think of shepherds and ploughmen in the same terms or as allies, since the former, in fact, may very well have come into conflict with the latter.

94 In saying this I am aware of Kerby-Fulton's comments on the importance of Bridget of Sweden's view on the relationship between primitive Christianity and the ploughman's task. See note 52, above.

95 Despite the claim in *STC* that the British Library also holds a copy of this edition, I have been assured by the staff at the Library that they have no such edition and that their only holding of this tract is a microfilm of the Bodleian Library's copy of the second edition published in England, probably in 1532 by Thomas Godfray.

96 Based on my collation of the Huntington copy with the Pierpont Morgan copy I conclude that the sheets of Pierpont Morgan were printed after Huntington's: On the title page of Pierpont Morgan some attempt has been made to place a space between the words *praier* and *and* which appear as one word in Huntington. On line 1029 Pierpont Morgan

restores the final 'e' on *forsweringe* which is broken in Huntington. And, finally, the running title on F7v of Pierpont Morgan is fainter than in Huntington, perhaps suggesting that the type should have been re-inked before the impression was taken. Except for these three, Pierpont Morgan duplicates all other anomalies and errors found in the Huntington copy.

# The praier and complaynte of the ploweman vnto Christe

[A1r]

**The praier and complaynte of the ploweman vnto Christe: written not longe after the yere of oure Lorde A thousande and thre hundred.**

Christus Matth.10.

If they haue called the Lorde of the ho=wse Beelzebub: how moch more shal they so call them of hys howshold?

**To the Chri= sten reader.** [A1v]

Grace be with the and peace be multi= plied in the knowlege of god the father/ and of oure Lorde Iesus Christ Amen.

Christe oure sauioure and his Apostels after hym/ although they taught no thinge which was not taught in the law and the prophetes more then a thousande yeres before/ ever and in euery place desyringe the audience to serch the olde scriptures and proue whether they testified with hym or no. yet all this not withstandinge/ the scribes/ the Phareses/ the Byschops/ the prestes/ the lawyers/ and the elders of the people/ cryed alwayes: what new lerninge ys this? These fellowes teach new lerninge. These be they that trouble all the world with their new lerninge and cete. And so with a vayne name of new lerninge/ and with their autorite and opinion of olde lerninge and auncientnes of the church/ they so blinded the same people that herde Christes doctrine of his awne mouth/ sawe hys lyuynge and his miracles/ and thei that at his cominge to Hierusalem mette hym by the waye/ cast their clothes and grene bowes in his waye/ cryenge with an open voyce: Blessed ys he that cometh in the name of the Lorde: The same people/ I saye/ were so blinded and iugled with them/ that the sixt daye after they cryed: hange hym on the crosse: hange hym on the crosse. And quitte one Barabas a mortherer/ and delyuered innocente Christ vnto deth.

All this did their byschops prestes and lawyers [A2r] bringe to passe/ onely by that they made the people beleue it was new lerninge. And that the scripture there was no man that cowlde vnderstande but they. And that Christ and his disciples were men nother of authorite nor reputacion/ but laye men/ ydiotes fyschers/ carpenters and other of the rascall sorte. So that it was not possible that ever God wold open that vnto soch a rude sorte/ which the religiouse phareses/ the holy byschops/ the vertuous prestes/ the auncient doctours/ the gret lerned lawyers and the wise and sage elders knew not. But it must nedes be that Christe and al his disciples were heretiques scismatiques and disceauers of the people and well worthy to be put to some shamefull deth for it/ to the example of all other. As they were in dede afterwarde.

But yet for all this even apon the crosse Christ ouercame his enemies. And when they thought that they had layed hym to slepe for ever he rose agayne. And his disciples haue ever had the victory apon the crosse/ and testified vnto the world the wisdome of God in these pore ydiotes/ and veray folishnes and wisdome of the flesh in these gret lerned aunciente fathers.

Even now after the same maner/ that ye maye grope with youre fyngers/ that oure holy byshops with all their ragmans rolle/ be of the selfe same sorte/ and veraye childerne of their fathers the phareses/ Bischops and prestes/ which so accused Christ and his Apostles of new lerninge: ye do se how they defame sclaunder and persecute the same worde and preachers and folowers of it/ withe the selfe same names/ callinge it new lerninge/ and them new masters. And retayne the people in erroure with their fathers olde face of religiouse phareses: fryers/ I wolde saye/ and monkes/ of holy byschops/ of ver [A2v] tuous prestes/ of aunciente doctors/ of the gret lerned lawyers and of the wise and sage elders. And take awaye the autorite and estimacion of gods worde and the credence of the preacher/ with/ ye maye se there ys no man preches so but two or thre/ and they haue no lernynge/ and the folish people which hath no lernynge folowes them. But ye shall se no man of substance/ of reputacion of autorite or lerninge take parte with them.

And so with these olde clokes of their fathers the phereses byschops and prestes/ fyrst they persuade the people the worde of god to be heresye. And by that meanes they lyberally prison and persecute vnto the deeth all the professours of the same. Even as the old phareses with the bischops and prestes presoned and persecuted Christe and his Apostles/ that al the rightuous bloude maye fall on their heedes that hath ben shed from the bloude of Steuen the first martyr to the blode of that innocent man of God Thomas hitton whom willyam werham byschop of Canturbury and Iohn fyscher byschop of Rochestur morthered at maydeston in kente the last yere for the same trouth. I pray god that they maye be ones turned vnto the Lorde that he maye heale them/ and forgeue them that synne of ignorancy. For as for these malicious tyrauntes that persecute against their awn conscience I praye not/ but leaue them to the iudgemente of god as manyfest synners against the holy goost.

As for the treuth when they haue slayne and put to sylence al the preachers of the same and layed it to slepe/ doutles god after his old facion shall there/ by them and by those meanes that they doute leest reyse vp the trouth againe/ to the vttur confusion of al hys enemies/ whose iudgement doth not slepe.

Now good reader/ that thou maist se playnly [A3r] that it ys no new thinge/ but an olde practyse of oure prelates lerned of their fathers the byschops phareses and prestes of the olde law/ to defame the doctrine of Christe with the name of new lerninge and the teachers therof with the name of new masters. I haue put forth here in printe this prayer and complaynte of the plowman which was written not longe after the yere of oure Lorde a thousande and thre hundred/ in his awne olde english/ chaingynge there in nothinge as ferforth as I coulde obserue it other the english or ortographie/ addinge also there to a table of soch olde wordes as be now antiquate and worne out of knoulege by processe of tyme. I desyre the to reade it with descrecion and ernestly/ or ever thou iudge/ and if thou fynde anythinge in it when thou haste conferred it with the scripture to thy edificacion or lerninge geve god thankes. And if here after there shall chaunce to come into my handes any more soch holy reliques perceauinge this to be accepted. I shall spare nother laboure nor cost to destribute it in to as many partes as I haue done thys/ by the help of god to whome be all honoure/ glorye and prayse for ever. AMEN.

The last daye of February. Anno.1531.

Here foloweth the table. [A3v]

Apayed. contented or pleased.
Ar than. before that.
Behizte. promised.
Byhest. promyse.
Byhoten promised.
Bliue. quyckely.
Benemen take a waye.
Clepe call.
Cheueteyn. capitain.
Chepinge. market.
Dreynte. drowned.
Desert. wildernes.
Dome iudgement.
Fele. often.
Fullen. baptise.
Forwarde convenaunte or bargen.
Heryinge. worship or worshipinge.
Hired men. parish prestes.
Lewed man. laye man.
Lesewes pastures or feldes.
Mawmetis. Images.
Nele will not.
Sternship. cruelnes.
Schepherdes. byschops. persons or vicars.
Sweuens. dreames.
Seggen. saye.
Thralles. bonde men.
Thraldome. bondage.
wonniers. Inhabitauntes or dwellers.
gerners. Chapmen.

**The plowmans prayer.** [A4r]

Iesu Christ that was ybore of the mayde Marie/ haue on thy pore servantes mercye and Pitie/ and helpe hem in her gret nede to fighte agens synne/ and agens the deuele that is autor of synne/ and more nede nes ther neuer to crie to Christ for helpe/ then it ys right now. For it ys fulfilled that God sayde by Isaye the Prophete: ye ryseth vp erlich to folow dronkenes and to drinke to it be even/ the herpe and other mynstresies bith in your festes and wine. But the warke of God ye ne beholdeth not/ ne taketh no kepe to the warkes of his handes: And therfore my people ys take prisoner for they ne had no connynge: And the noble men of my people deyeden for honger and the multitide of my people weren drye for thyrst/ and therfore hell hath drawen abroade her sowle/ and hath yopened hys mouth withouten any ende. And eft sones sayeth Isaye the prophet. The word ys floten a waye/ and the hyghnes of the people ys ymade seek/ and the erth [A4v] ys infect of hys wonnyers for they haue broken my lawes/ and ychaunged my right and han distroyed myn everlastinge bonde and forwarde betwene hem and me. And therfore cursynge shall deuoure the erthe/ and they that wonneth on the ertly shullen don synne. And therfore the erth tilyars shullen waxe wood/ and few men shullen ben yleft apon the erth. And yet sayeth Isaye the prophet/ this sayeth God for as moch as this people nygheth me with her mouth/ and glorifiethe me with her lippys/ and her harte ys ferre from me. and they han ydrad more mennys commaundementes then myne and more draw to her doctrines then to myne. Therfore woll I make a gret wondringe vnto this puple/ wisdome shall perish awaye from wise men/ and vnderstandinge of readie men shall ben yhid. And so it semeth that an other sayenge of Isaye ys fulfilled/ there as god bade hym go teach the puple/ and sayed go forth and saye to this puple/ eres here ye and vnderstand ye not/ and eyes ye haue sight and ne [A5r] know ye not. Make blinde the hert of this puple/ and make her eres hevye/ and close her yeen/ lest he se with his yeen/ and yhere with his eres/ and vnderstand with his hert and be yturned/ and ych hele hym of his syckenes. And Isaye sayd to god how longe Lord shal this be? And God sayed. For to that cyties ben desolate with outen a wonnyer/ and an howse withouten a man.

Here ys mychel nede for to make sorow and to crye to owre Lorde Iesu Christ hertilich for help and for succoure that he wole forgeue vs oure synnes and geve vs grace and connynge to seruen hym bettur here after. And god of hys endeles mercy geue vs grace and connynge trulich to tellen which ys Christes law in helpinge of mennes sowles/ for we beth lewde men/ and synneful men/ and vnconnynge and yf he woll be owre helpe and owre succoure/ we shullen well perfourme owre purpose. And yblessed be owre Lorde god that hydeth his wisdome from wise men and fro redy men/ and teacheth it to small [A5v] childern/ as Christ teacheth in the gospell.

Christen men han a law to kepe/ the which law hath twee parties. Beleve in Christ that ys God/ and ys the foundement of her law/ and vpon thys foundemente as he sayd to Peter/ and the gospel bereth witnes/ he woll byelden hys church. And this ys the fyrst partie of Christes law. The seconde partie of his law beth Christes commaundementes that beth written in the gospell/ and more verilech in christen mennes hertes.

And as towchinge the beleve we beleuen that Christ ys God/ and that there ne ys no God but he. We beleven never the lesse that in the godhed ther ben thre parsones/ the father/ the sonne and the holy gost/ and all these thre parsones ben one god and not many goddes/ and all they beth ylich mighty/ ylich good/ and ylych wise/ and ever have ben/ and ever shullen ben. We beleven this god made the worlde of noght/ and man he made after his awne lykenesse in paradise that was a lande of blysse/ and gaue hym that lon= [A6r] de for his erytage/ and bad hym that he shuld not eate of the tre of kowenge good and evill/ that was amydde paradyse. Then the devell that was fallen out of heven for hys pride had envye to man/ and by a fals suggestion he made man eate of this tree/ and breake the commaundement of God/ and tho was man ouercomen of the devell/ and so he lost his heritage and was yput out there of into the worlde that was a londe of trauel and of sorowe vndre the fyndes thraldome to ben punysshed for his trespasse. There man folowed wyckednesse and synne/ and god for synne of man sente a flode in to this worlde and dreynte all mankynde saue eght sowles. And after this flode he late men multiplien in the worlde and so he assayed whether man drad hym or loued hym/ and amonge other he fonde a man that hyght Abraham: this man he proued wether he loued hym and drad hym/ and bade hym that he shulde offeren Isaac his sonne apon an hyll/ and Abraham as a trewe seruant fulfilled his Lordes com [A6v] maundement/ and for this buxumnes and treweth/ God sware vnto Abraham that he wold multiplie his sede as the gravell in the see/ and the sterres of heven/ and he behight to hym and to hys heyres the londe of beheest for eretage for ever/ yf they wolden ben his trewe seruantes and kepe hys heestes. And god helde him forwarde/ for Isaac Abrahams sonne begate Iacob and Esau/ and of Iacob that ys ycleped ysraell comen gods puple that he chose to be his seruantes/ and to whome he behight the londe of byhest/ this puple was in gret thraldom in Egipt vnder Pharao that was kynge of Egypt: and they cryeden to god that he shuld delyveren hem oute of that thraldom/ and so he dyd: for he sente to Pharao Moses and his brother Aaron and bade hym delyver his puple to don hym sacryfice/ and to fore Pharao he made Moses don many wondres or that Pharao wold delyver his puple and at the last by myght he delyvered his puple oute of thraldom and led hem thorowgh a desert toward the londe of by= [A7r] heste/ and there he gaue hem a law that they shulden lyuen after/ when they comen in to her contrey/ and in ther wey thiderwarde/ the ten commaundementes god wrote himselfe in two tables of stoon: the remnawnt of the lawe he tawght hem by Moses his servant/ how they shulden do euerichone to other/ and yif they trespased ageyn the law/ he ordened how they shulden be punished. Also he tawght hem what maner sacrifices they shulden do to hym/ and he chees hym a puple to be his prestes/ that was Aaron and his children to don sacryfices in the tabernacle/ and afterwarde in the temple also. He chees hym the remenaunt of the children of Leuy to ben seruantes in the tabernacle to the prestes/ and he sayde: When ye comen in to the londe of behest/ the children of Levy they shullen haue noon heritage amonges her bretherne/ for ych woll be here parte/ and her heritage/ and they shullen serue me in the tabernacle by dayes and by nyghtes/ and he ordened that prestes shulden haue a part of the sacry [A7v] fyses that weren offred in the tabernacle/ and the fyrst begooten beestes/ both of men and beestes and other thinges as the law telleth. And the other children of Leuy that serueden in the tabernacle shulden haue tythinges of the puple to her lyeulood/ of the which tythinges/ they shulden geven the prestes the tenth partie in forme of offeringe. The children of Levy both prestes and other shulden haue howses and croftes and lesuvoys for her beestes in the lande of byhest/ and non other eretage/ and so God gaue hem her londe of byhest/ and bade hem that they ne shuld worship no other God then hym. Also he bade that they shulden kepe hys commaundmentes/ and yif they dyden so all her enemyes a boute hem shulden drede hem and ben her seruantes/ and yif they worshippeden fals gods and so forsoken hys lawes he byhight hem that he wold bringen hem out of that londe and maken hem seruen her enemyes/ but yet he sayed he nolde not bynemen his mercy awaye from hem/ if they wolden crye mercye and amen [A8r] den her defautes/ and all this was ydone on Gods syde.

And here ys mychell love yshowed of god to man. And who so loketh the Byble he shall fynde that man showed him litle love agyenwarde/ for when they weren ycomen in to her eritage/ they for geyten her god/ and worshippeden fals goddes. And God sente to hem the Prophetes and hys seruantes foele tymes to bydden hem withdrawen hem from her synnes/ and other they slowen them or they beten hem or they leden hem in prison and ofte tymes God toke apon hem gret vengeaunce for her synnes/ and when they cryeden after help to God/ he sente hem help and succoure/ this ys the generall proces of the olde testamente that God gaue to his people by Moses his seruant. And all this testamente and this doinge ne was but a schadewe and a fygure of a new testamente that was geuen in by Christ. And it was byhoten by Ieremie the prophe/ as sainte Paul beareth witnesse in the pistle that he writeth to the Iewys. And [A8v] Ieremie saith in this wise: Lo dayes shall come/ God sayeth/ and ych woll make a new bande to the hous of Israel and to the hous of Iude/ not lyche the forwarde that I made withe her faders in the day that I toke her honde to leden hem out of the londe of Egypte/ the which forwarde they maden veyne/ and yche had lordshippe ouer hem. But this shalbe the forwarde that yche wold maken with hem after thilke dayes: yche wole geue my lawes with yn hem in her inwardnesse/ and yche wole writen hem in her hartes/ and yche wole ben her God and they shullen be my puple/ and after that a man ne shall not teach his neyghebore ne his brother. For all/ God sayeth/ from the leest to the mest shullen yknowe me/ for yche wole forgeuen hem her synnes/ and I nele no more thinken on her synnes.

This is the newe testamente that Christ both god and man yboren of the mayden Marye he taughte here in this worlde to bringe man oute of synne and oute of the deuels thraldome and seruice [B1r] to heuen/ that ys londe of blisse and heretage to all thoo that beleuen on hym/ and kepen hys commaundementes/ and for his teachinge he was done to the deth. But the thrydde daye arose agene from deth to lyfe/ and fette Adam and Eve and many other folke oute of helle/ and afterwarde he came to his disciples and conforted hem. After he steyed vp to heuen to hys fader/ and thoo he sente the holy gost amonges his disciples: and in tyme cominge he wole come and demen al mankynde after her werkes/ and after the wordes he spake apon erth/ some to blisse both in body and in sowle ever withouten ende/ and some to payne with outen ende/ both in body and in sowle.

This is oure beleue and all christen mennes/ and this beleue ys the fyrst poynte of the newe testamente that yche christen man is holde stedfastly to beleue/ and rather to suffer the deeth than forsaken this beleue/ and so this beleue ys the bred of spirituall lyfe/ in forsakinge synne/ that Christe brought vs to lyfe. [B1v]

But for as much as mannes lyuinge ne stondeth not al

onlych by breed/ he hath ygouen vs a draught of water of lyfe to drinke. And who that drinketh of that water/ he ne shall neuer afterwarde ben a thurst. For this water ys the clere teachinge of the gospel/ that encloseth seuen commaundementes.

The furst is this: thow shalt loue thy God ouer all other thinges/ and thy brother as thy self/ both enemye and frende.

The seconde commaundemente ys of mekenes/ in the which Christ chargeth vs to forsake lordeship vpon oure brethern and other worldly worshippes/ and so he did hym self.

The thridde commaundemet/ ys in stondinge stedfastlych in truth and forsakinge all falsnes.

The forth commaundement:ys to suffre in this world diseses and wronges withouten agenstondinges.

The fyfth commaundemente/ ys mercy to forgeuen oure brethern here trespas: as often tyme as they gylteth/ with= [B2r] out askinge of vengeaunce.

The syxth commaundemente ys poernesse in spirite/ but not to ben a beggeer.

The seuenth commaundemente/ ys chastyte/ that ys a forsakynge of fleshlych lykinges dyspleasinge to God. These commaundentes enclosen the ten commaundementes of the olde lawe and somewhat more.

This water ys a blessed drinke for christen mennes soule. But more harme ys moch folke wolde dronke of this water/ but they mow not come thereto: for god sayeth by Ezechiel the prophete: when ych geue to you the most clene water to drinke/ ye troubled that water with your fete/ and that water so defouled/ ye geue my shepe to drinke. But the clene water ys yhidde fro the shepe/ and but yif God cleare this/ it ys drede lest the shepe deyen for thurst. And Christ that is the wisdome of the father of heuen/ and welle of this wisdome that come from heuene to erth to tech man this wisdome/ thorow the which man shuld ouercome the sleygh= [B2v] thes of the deuyl that is principall enemy of mankinde/ haue mercy and pite of his puple/ and shewe/ if it be his will/ how this water ys troubled/ and by whom/ and sith clere this water that his shepe mown drinken here of: and kele the thurst of her sowles. Blessed mote oure Lorde ben for he hath ytaught vs in the gospell that ar than he wolde come to the vniuersel dome ther shuld come manye in his name and seyen that they weren Christ: and they shulden done many wondres and begilen many men. And many false prophetes shulden arysen and begylen moch folke.

A Lorde yblessed mote thou ben of euerich creature/ which ben they that haue yseyd that they weren Christ/ and haue begyled thus thy puple? Trulich Lorde I trowe thilke that seyn that they ben in thy stede and bynemen thy worship and maken the puple worshupen hem as God/ and haue hyd thy lawes from the puple. Lorde who durst sitte in thy stede and benemen the thy worshupe and thy sacrifice/ and durst maken the puple worsh= [B3r] upe hem as goddes? The sauter telles that God ne wole not in the daye of dome demen men for bodilich sacrifices and holocaustes. But God sayeth yelde to me sacrifice of heryinge/ and yelde to god thine avowes/ and clepe me in day of tribulacion/ and ych wole defende the/ and thow shalt worshupe me.

The heringe of god stondeth in .iii. thinges. In louynge god ouer all other thinges. In dredinge god ouer all other thinges. In trustinge in God ouer all other thynges.

These thre poyntes Christ teacheth in the gospell. But I trowe men louen hym but a lytle. For who so loueth Christ/ he wole kepen his wordes. But men holden hys wordes for heresye and folye/ and kepeth mennes wordes. Also men dreden more men and mennes lawes and her cursinges/ then Christ and his lawes and his cursinges. Also men hopen more in men and mennes helpes/ than they do in Christ and in his helpe. And thus hath he that sitteth in gods stede bynomen god [B3v] these thre heryinges/ and maketh men louen hym and his lawes/ more than Christ and Christes lawes and dreden hym also. And there as the puple schulden yelde to god her vowes/ he seyeth that he hath power to assoylen hem of her avowes/ and so this sacrifice he nemeth away from god. And there as the puple shuld crye to god in the daye of tribulacion/ he letteth hem of her crienge to God and bynemyth God that worshupe. This daye of tribulacion is whan man ys fallen thorow synne in to the deuels seruise/ and than we shulden crye to god after helpe/ and axen forgeuenesse of oure synne/ and make grete sorowe for oure synne/ and ben in full will to do so no more ne non other synne/ and than oure Lorde god wole forgeuen vs oure synne/ and maken oure soule clene. For his mercy ys endeles.

But Lorde here men haue bynomyn the muche worshupe: For men seyn that thow ne myght not clene assoylen vs of oure synne. But if we knowlegen ouur synnes to prestes/ and taken of hem a pena= [B4r] wnce for oure synne yif we mowen speke with hem.

A Lorde thou forgaue some tyme Peter hys synnes and also Marye magdaleyne/ and other many synfull men withouten schryuinge to prestes/ and takynge penaunce of prestes for her synnes. And Lorde thou art as mighty now as thou were that tyme/ but yif any man haue bynome the thy might. And we lewed men beleuen/ that there nys no man of so greate power/ and yif any man maketh himselfe of so gret power/ he heieth hym selfe above God/ and saint Poul speketh of one that sitteth in the temple of God and highen hym aboue God/ and yif any soch be he is a false Christe.

But hereto seyn prestes/ that when Christ made clene leprous men/ he bade hem goo and show hem to prestes. And therfore they seyn that it ys a commaundement of Christ/ that a man schuld shewen his synne to prestes. For as theye seyn/ lepre in the old lawe betokeneth synne in this new lawe. A Lorde God: wether thyne [B4v] Apostles knew nat thy meninge as well as men done now? And yif they hadden yknowe that thow haddest commaunded men to schryuen hem to pristes/ and they ne taught not that commaundement to the puple/ me thinketh they hadden ben to blame: But I trow they knewen wel that it was non of thy commaundementes ne nedeful to heale of mannes soule. And as me thinketh the lawe of lepre/ ys nothinge to the purpos of schriuinge: for prestes in the old law hadden certein pointes and tokenes to know whether a man weer leprous or not and yif they were leprous/ they hadden power to putten hem awaie from other clene men/ for to that they weren clene/ and then they hadden power to reysseyuen hym amonge his brethern/ and offeren for him a sacrifice to god.

This nys nothinge to the purpos of schriuinge. For ther nys but one preste that ys Christ that maye knowe in certen the lepre of the soule. Ne no prest maye make the soule clene of her synne/ but Christ that ys prest after Melchysedekes ordre/ ne no prest here beneth maye ywit [B5r] for certayn wether a man be clene of his synne or clene assoyled/ but yif God tell it hym by reuelacion. Ne god ordened not that his prestes schulde sette men a penaunce for her synne after the quantyte of the synne/ but this ys mans ordinaunce/ and it may welbe that there cometh good herof. But I wote well that God ys much vnworschuped thereby. For men trust more in his absolucions/ and in his yeres of grace/ than in Christis absolucions/ and therby ys the puple moch apayred. For now/ the sorow a man shuld make for hys synne/ ys put awaye by thys schrift/ and a man ys more bolde to do synne for trust of this schrift/ and of this bodylich penaunce.

A nother myschefe ys that the puple ys ybrought in to this belefe/ that one preste hath a gretter power to assoylen a man of hys synne and clennere then an other prest hath.

A nother myschefe ys this that some prest may assoylen hem both of synne and peyne/ and in this they taken hem a po= [B5v] wer that Christ graunted no man in erth/ ne he ne vsed it noght on erth him selfe.

A nother myschefe ys/ that these prestes sellen forgeuenes of mennes synnes and absolucions for money/ and this ys an heresye accursed that ys ycleped symonye: and all thilke prestes that axeth price for grauntinge of spirituall grace beth by holy lawes depriued of her presthode/ and thilke that assenteth to this heresye. And be they war/ for Helyse the prophet toke no money of Naaman when he was made clene of his lepre: But giesi his seruant and therfore the lepre of Naaman abode with hym and with his eyres ever more after.

Here ys muche mater of sorowe to se the puple thus far ylad awey from God and worshupen a fals god in erth/ that by myght and by strength hath ydone awey the gret sacrifice of

God out of his temple/ of which mischefe and discomfort Danyell maketh mencyon/ and Christ bereth therof wittnesse in the gospell. Who that redeth it vnderstande it. Thus we have ytold ap= [B6r] erty/ how he that sayeth he sitteth in Christes stede/ bynemeth Christ his worship and his sacrifice of his puple/ and maketh the puple worshupen hym as a god on erth.

Crye we to god/ and knowlege we oure synnes euerichone to other/ as seynt Iames techeth/ and praye we hertiliche to god everychone for other and than we shulen hopen forgeuenes of oure synnes. For god that ys endeles in mercy sayeth that he ne will not a synfull mannes dethe but that he be turned from his synne and lyuen. And therfore when he came doune to saue mankynd/ he gave vs a law of loue and of mercye/ and bade/ yif a man do a trespas amende hym priuilich/ and yif he leue not his synne/ amende hym before witnesse/ and yif he ne amendeth not/ men shulde tel to the church: and yif he ne amendeth not thanne men schuld schone his cumpanye as a publicane or a man that ys mysbeleued. and this lawe was yfigured in the lawe of lepre/ who that redeth it he maye se the soth.

But Lorde God he that sitteth in thy stede/ hath vndo thy law of mercy/ and of lo [B6v] ue. Lorde thou byddest louen enemies as oure selfe: as thou shewest in the gospell there as the Samaritane hadde mercye on the Iew. And thow biddist vs also preyen for hem that cursen vs/ and that defamen vs/ and pursuen vs to deth. And so Lorde thou didist and thyne apostles also. But he that clepeth hym self thi viker on erth and heed of thy church/ he hath ondone thy law of loue and of mercy. For yif we speken of louynge oure enemyes/ he techeth vs to fight with oure enemies that Christ hath forboden. He curseth and desireth vengeaunce to hem that so doth to hym. Yif any man pursueth hym/ he curseth hym/ that it ys a sorowe a christen man to heren the cursinges that they maken/ and blasphemyes in such cursinge. Of that thinge that I know I maye bere true witnesse.

But yif we speke of louinge of oure brethern/ this ys vndon by hym that sayeth he ys gods viker in erth. For Christ in the gospell byddeth vs that we shulden clepen vs no fader vpon erth: But clepen [B7r] god oure father/ to maken vs loue parfytlich together: And he clepeth hym self fadur of fadurs and maketh many religions/ and to everich a fadur. But wheder ys loue and charite encressed by thes fadurs and by her religions or els ymade lesse? For a frier ne loueth not a monke/ ne a seculer man neyther/ nor yet one freer a nother that is not of the order: and it ys agenward.

A Lorde me thinketh that there ys litell perfeccion in these religions. For Lorde what charite haven such men of religion/ that knowen how they mown ageynstande synne and fleen awaye from her brethern that ben more vnconnynge than they ben/ and sufferen hem to travelen in the world with outen her counsell as beestes? Trulich Lorde me thinketh that there ys litell charite/ and then ys there litell perfeccion. Lorde God when thow were on erth thou were amonge synfull men to drawen hem from synne/ and thy disciples also. And Lorde I trowe/ thou ne grauntest not o man more kunninge then an other all for hym selfe: and I wote well [B7v] that lewed men that ben laborers ne trauele not alonlych for hem selfe. Lorde oure belefe ys that thou ne were not of the world/ ne thy techinge neyther/ ne thy seruantes that lyuenden after thy techinge. But all they forsoken the worlde/ and so every christen man must. But Lorde wether thou taughtest men forsake her brethren cumpanye and traueyle of the world/ to lyuen in ese and in rest/ and out of defoul and anger of the world by her brethern traueyle and so forsaken the worlde?

A Lorde thou ne taughtest not a man forsaken a poore astaate and traueyle to ben afterwarde a lorde of hys brethern or ben a Lordes felaw and dwellinge with Lordes as doth men of these newe religions. Lorde thou ne taughtest not men of thy religion thus to forsake the worlde to lyuen in perfeccion by hem selfe in ease and by other mennes traueyle.

But lorde they seyen they ben ybounde to thy seruyse and seruen thee both nyght and daye in synginge her preyers both for hem self and for other men that done hem good [B8r] both quycke and deed/ and some of hem gone aboute to teche thy puple when they haven leysure.

A Lorde yif they ben thy seruantes: whose seruantes ben

we that can not preyen as they done? And when thou were here on erthe/ for oure nede thou taughtest thy seruantes to preyen thy fader priuylich and shortlych/ and yif there had yben a bettur maner of preynge. I trowe thow woldest haue taught it in helpe of thy puple. And Lorde thou reprouist ypocrites that prayen in longe prayer and in open places to ben yholden holy men. And thou seyst in the gospell/ woo to you pharyseis ypocriets. And Lorde thou ne chargedest not thy seruantes with soch maner seruyse: But thou seyst in the gospell that the pharyseis worshupen the with her lippes. and her herte ys fer frome the. For they chargen more mennes tradicions than thy commaundementes.

And Lorde we lewede men han a belefe that thy goodnes ys endles/ and yif we kepen thyne hestes than ben we thy trew [B8v] seruantes and though we preyen the but a litel and schortlych thou wilt thinken on vs/ and graunten vs that vs nedeth for so thou byhighted vs some tyme: and Lord I trow that praye a man neuer so many quaynte prayers/ yif he ne kepe not thyne hestes he ne ys not thy good seruant. But yif he kepe thyne hestes than he ys thy good seruant/ and so me thinketh Lorde that preynge of longe preyers ne ys not the seruyse that thou desirist. But kepinge of thyne hestes: and than a lewed man maye serue God as well as a man of religion. And so Lorde oure hope ys/ that thou wilt as sone yhere a plowmans prayer/ and he kepe thyne hestes/ as thou wilt do a mans of religion: though that the plowman ne maye nat haue so much syluer for his preyer as men of religion. For they kunnen not so wel preysen her preyers as these other chapmen: But Lorde oure hope ys that oure preyer be neuer the worse though it be not so well sold as other mens preyers.

Lorde: Ezechiel the prophete seyeth that [C1r] whan he spake to the puple thy wordes they turned in to songes[1] and in to tales. And so Lorde men don now: they syngyn myrilych thy wordes/ and that singinge they clepen thy seruyse. But Lorde I trow that the best syngers ne heryeth the not most: But he that fulfilleth thy wordes he heryeth thee ful well/ though he wepe

1 *side-note* Songes.

more than singe. And I trow that wepinge for brekyng of thy commaundementes be more plesinge seruyse to thee than the singinge of thy wordes. And wolde God that men wolde serue hym in sorrow for her synnes/ and they schulden afterwarde seruen the in myrth. For Christ seith yblessed ben they that maken sorowe/ for they schulen ben yconforted. And woo to hem that ben myrrye and haue her comfort in this world. And Christ seide that the world schulde ioyen/ and his seruantes schulden be sory/ but her sorowe shuld be turned in to ioie.

A Lorde he that clepeth hym selfe thy viker vpon erth hath yordayned an ordre of prestes to do thy seruyse in church to [c1v] fore thy lewed puple in singinge matens evensonge and masse. And therfore he chargeth lewed men in payne of cursinge to bringe to his prestes tythinges and offeringes to fynden his prestes/ and he clepeth that gods part/ and dew to prestes that seruen hym in church.

But/ Lorde/ in the olde lawe the tythinges of the lewed puple ne were not dewe to prestes but to that other childer of Levy that serueden the in the temple/ and the prestes hadden her part of sacrifices/ and the fyrst bygeten beestes and other thinges as the law telleth. And Lorde seynt Poule thy seruant seyth that the ordre of the presthode of Aaron cesede in Christes cominge and the lawe of that presthode. For Christ was ende of sacrifices yoffered vpon the crosse to the father of heuen to brynge man out of synne and bycome hymselfe a prest of Melchisedekes ordre. For he was both kynge and prest witheoute begynnynge and ende/ and both the presthode of Aaron and also the lawe of that presthode ben ychanged in the comin [c2r] ge of Christ. And seynt Poule seith it ys reproued/ for it brought no man to perfeccion: For bloode of gotes ne of other beestes ne might not done awaye synne/ for to that Christ schadde his blode.

A Lorde Iesu wether thow ordenest an ordre of prestes to offren in the auter thy flesh[2] and thy blode to bringen men out of synne/ and also out of peyne? And wether thou geue hem alonlych a power to eate thy flesch and thy blode/ and wether

2 *side-note* Thy flesch.

non other man maye eate thy flesch and thy blode with outen leue of prestes? Lorde we beleuen that thy flesch is verey meate and thy blode verey drinke/ and who eteth thy flesch and drinketh thy blode dwelleth in the and thou in hym/ and who that eteth this breed shall lyve withoute ende. But Lorde thyne disciples seyde/ this is an harde worde/ but thou answerest hem and seydest: When ye seeth mannes sone steyn vp there he was rather/ the spirit ys that maketh you lyve/ the wordes that yche haue spoken to you ben sprite and lyfe. Lorde/ yblessed mote thou [c2v] be/ for in this worde thou techest vs that he that kepeth thy wordes/ and doth after hem eteth thy flesch and drinketh thy blode/ and hath an everlastinge lyfe in thee. And for we schulden haue mynde of this lyuinge thou gauist vs the sacramente of thy flesch and thy blode in forme of breed and wyne at thy souper to fore that thou schuldest suffre thy deth/ and toke breed in thine honde/ and seydest take ye this and ete it for it is my body/ and thou tokest wine and blessedest it/ and seydest this ys the blode of a newe and an euerlastinge testamente that shalbe sched for many men in forgeuenesse of synnes. As oft as ye don this/ do ye this in minde of me.

A Lorde thou ne bede not thine disciples maken this a sacryfice to bringe men out of peynes yif a prest offered thy body in the auter: but thou bede hem go and fullen all the folke in the name of the father and the sone and the holy gost in forgeuenesse of her synnes/ and teche ye hem to kepe those thinges that ych haue com= [c3r] maunded you. And lorde thine disciples ne ordeyned not prestes principallich to make thy body in sacramente but for to tech the puple. And good husbande men that well gouern her housholdes/ both wiues and children and her meynye/ they ordened to be prestes to techen other men the law of Christ both in worde in dede and they lyvedeyn as trew Christen men every daye they eten Christes body and dronken hys blode to the sustenaunce of lyvynge of here soules/ and other whiles they token the sacramente of his body in forme of breed and wine/ in mynde of oure lorde Iesu Christ.

But all this ys turned vpso doune for now who so will

lyven as thou taughtest[3] he schalben holden a fole. And yif he speke thy techynge/ he shalben holden an heretyke and a cursed. Lorde y haue no lenger wonder here of/ for so they seyden to the when thou were here some tyme. And therfore we moten taken in pacyence her wordes of blasfemie as thou dedest thy selfe/ or els we were to blame. [c3v] And trulych lorde I trowe that yf thou were now in the worlde and taughtest as thou dedest some tyme/ thou shuldest ben done to deeth. For thy teachinge ys damned for heresye of wise men of the worlde/ and then moten they nedes ben heretykes that techen thy lore/ and all they also that trauelen to lyue there after.

And therfore lorde/ yif it be thy will helpe thyne vnkunnynge and lewed seruantes that wolen by her power and her kunnynge helpe to destroye synne. Leue lorde syth thou madist woman[4] in helpe of man/ and yn a more frele degre than man is to be gouerned by mans reson. what perfection of charite is in these prestes and in men of religion that haue forsaken spoushode that thou ordenest in paradis by twyx man and woman/ for perfection to forsaken traueyle and lyuen in ese by other mennes traueyle? For they mowe not do bodilich workes for defoulinge of her hondes with whome they touchen thy preciouse body in the auter.

Leue lorde yif good men forsaken the [c4r] companye of woman/ and nedes they moten haue the gouernayle of man then moten they ben ycoupled with schrewes/ and therfore thy spoushode that thou madest in clenesse from synne it ys now ychaunged in to lykynge of the flesch. And Lorde this ys a gret myschefe vnto thy puple. And younge prestes and men of religion for defaute of wives maken many wymen horen/ and drawen thorow her yuel ensample many other men to synne and the ese that they lyuen in and their welfare ys a gret cause of this myschefe. And lorde me thinketh that these ben quaynte orders of religion and none of thy secte/ that wolen taken horen/ whilke god forfendes/ and forsaken wyues that

3 *side-note* Taughest.

4 *side-note* Woman.

god ne forfendeth not. And forsaken traueyle[5] that god commaundes/ and gyuen her selfe to ydelenes that ys the moder of all noughtines.

And lorde/ Marie thy blessed mother and Iosef touched ofte tymes thy body and wroughten withe here hondes/ and lyueden in as moch clennesse of soule [c4v] as oure prestes done now/ and touched thy body/ and thou touchedest hem in her soules. And Lorde oure hope is that thou goist not out of a pore mannes soule that traueleth for hys lyuelode with his hondes. For Lorde oure belefe ys that thyne house ys mannes soule that thou madest after thyne awne lykenes.

But Lorde god/ men maketh now greet stonen houses full of glasene windowes/ and clepeth thylke thyne houses and chirches. And they sette in these houses mawmetys[6] of stockes and of stones/ and to fore hem they knelen priuylich and apert/ and maken her preyers/ and al this they seyen ys thy worschup/ and a gret heryenge to the. A Lorde thou forbedest some tyme to make such mawmetes/ and who that had yworschupped sych had be worthy to be deed.

Lorde in the gospell thou saist that true heryers of god ne heryeth hym not in that hill beside Samarie/ ne in Hierusalem nayther: but trew heryers of god heryeth hym yn spirite and in trewthe. [c5r] And lorde God what heryenge ys it to bylden the a church of deed stones/ and robben thy quycke cherches of her bodyliche lyuelode? Lorde god what heryenge ys it/ to cloth mawmettes of stockes and of stones yn syluer and in golde and in other good coloures? And lorde I se thyne ymage gone in colde and in hete in clothes all to broken with outen schone and hosen an hungred and a thurst. Lorde what heryenge ys yt to tende tapers and torches bytore blinde mawmetes that mowen not I seyen. And hyde the that art oure light and oure lanterne to warde heuen and put the vnder a bonsshell that for darkenes we ne maye nat sene oure weye toward blisse? Lorde what heryenge ys it to knele tofore mawmetes that mowe not yheren/ and worschupen hem with

5 *side-note* Workinge.

6 *side-note* Mawmetes

preyers/ and maken thyne quyck ymages knele before hem and asken of hem absolucions and blessinges and worschupen hem as goddes/ and putten thy quyke ymages in thraldome and in traueyle ever more as bee= [c5v] stes/ in colde and in heet and in feble fare to fynden hem in lykynge of the world? Lorde what heryenge ys it to fetch deed mennes bones out of the ground there as they schulden kyndelich roten/ and schrynen hem in gold and in siluer. And suffren thy quike bones of thyne ymages roten in prison for defaute of clothynge? And suffren also thy quyke ymages perish for defaute of sustenaunce and rooten in the hoore house in abominable lecherye? Some become theves/ and robbers/ and manquellers/ that myghten ben yholpen with the gold and syluer that hongeth aboute deed mennes bones and other blynde mawmetes of stockes and of stones.

Lorde here ben gret abhominacions that thou schewdist to Ezechiel thy prophete that prestes done in thy temple/ and yit they clepen that thyne heryenge. But leue lorde/ me thinketh that they louen the litle/ that thus defoulen thy quyke ymages and worschupen blynde mawmettes.

[c6r] And lorde[7] an other gret myschefe there ys now in the worlde/ an hunger that Amos thy profete speketh of/ that there shall comen an honger in the erth not of breed ne thurst of drinke/ but of heringe of goddes woorde. And thy scheepe wolden be refresshed/ but their scheepardes taken of thy scheepe her lyfloode as tythinges. etc. and lyuen hem self therby where hem lyketh.

Of soch schephardes thou spekest by Ezechiel thy prophete and seist: woo to the schepehardes of Israel that feden hemselfe/ for the flockes of schepe schulden ben yfed of her schepherdys: but ye eten the mylke and clothden you with her wolle and the fatte schepe ye slow/ and my flocke ye ne fed not/ the sycke scheepe ye ne heled nat/ thylke that weren to broken ye ne knyt not to geder/ thylke that perisshed ye ne brought not againe: but ye ruled hem with sternschip and with power. And so the schepe beth sprad a brode in deuouringe of

7 *side-note* Schepherdre

all the beestes of the feelde. And Ieremie the prophete sayeth: [c6v] woo to the schepherdes that disparpleth abrode and so terith the flocke of my lesew.

A lorde/ thou were a good schepherde for thou puttest thy soule for thy schepe: but lorde thou teldest that thilke that comen not in by the dore ben night thefes and daye thefes/ and a thefe as thou seist cometh not but for to stele/ to sleyne and to distroye. And Zacharie the prophete seith that thou woldist reren vp a scepherde vnkunnynge/ that ne wole not hele thy schepe that beth sycke/ ne sech thilke that beth loste. Apon his arme ys a swerde and vpon his right eye/ his arme schall waxe drye/ and his right eye shall lese his light. O Lorde helpe/ for thy shepe beth at gret mischefe in the schepherdes defaute.

But lorde/ there cometh hyred men[8] and they ne fedden not thy schepe in thy plentuous lesew/ but feden thy schepe with swevenes and false miracles and talys. But at thy trewth they ne comen nat. For lorde I trowe thou sendest hem never. For have they hyre of thy schepe [c7r] they ne chargeth but litle of the fedinge and the kepinge of thy schepe. Lorde of these hyred men speketh Ieremie thy prophete/ and thou seyst that worde by hym: I ne sende hem not/ and they ronne blyue: I ne speke vnto hem and they prophicieden. For yif they hadden stonden in my councell/ and they had made my wordes knowen to the puple/ ych wolde have turned hem awaye from her yvell weye and from her wicked thoughtes. For lorde thou seist that thy wordes ben as fuyre/ and as an hamer brekynge stones. And lorde thou saist: Lo I to these prophetes metinge swevenes of lesinge/ that haue ytold her swevens/ and haue begyled my puple in her lesinge and in her false miracles/ when ye nether sente ne bede hem. And these haue profitet no thinge to my puple. And as Ieremie saith from the leest to the mest all they studien couetise/ and from the prophete to the prest all they done gyle.

A Lorde here ys mych mischefe and matere of sorow/ and yet there ys more. [c7v] For yif a lewed man wold tech thy puple trewth of thy wordes as he ys yholde by thy

8 *side-note* hiered men.

commaundemente of charite he shalbe forboden and yput in prison yif he do it. And so lorde thilke that haue the keye of conning/ haue ylockt the trewth of thy techinge vnder many wardes/ and yhid it from thy childern. But lorde sith thy techinge ys ycome from heuen aboue/ oure hope ys that/ with thy grace it shal breken these wardys/ and schewe hym to thy puple/ to kele both the hunger and the thurst of the sowle. And then schall no schepharde/ ner no false hyridman begyle thy puple no more. For by thy lawe I write/ as thou yhightest some tyme/ that from the lest to the mest all they schullen knowen thy will/ and weten how they schullen plese the euer more incertayne.

And leue lorde yif it be thy will helpe at this nede/ for there ys none help but in thee. Thus lorde by hym that maketh hymselfe thy viker in erth ys thy commaundemente of loue to the and to oure [c8r] brothern ybroken both to hym and to thy puple. But lorde god/ mercye[9] and pacyence that beth tweyne of thy commaundementes beth distroyed/ and thy puple hath forsake mercy. For Lorde Dauid in the Souter saith: Blessed beth they that done dome and rightfullnes in everich tyme.

O Lorde thou hast ytaught vs as right fulnesse of heuen and hast ybeden vs for geuen oure brethern as oft as they trespasen agenst vs. And lorde thyne olde lawe of iustice was that such harme as a man did his brother/ such he schuld suffer by the law/ as eye for an eye/ a toth for a toth. But Christ made an ende of thys law/ that one brother shulde not desyre wrake of an nother/ but not that he wolde that synne schuld ben vnpunished/ for there to hath he yordened kinges and dukes and other lewed officers vnder hem whilke as sainte Poule saith ne carien not the swerde in vayne/ for they ben the ministres of god and wrakers to wrath/ to hem that evill done. And thus hath Christ ymade an ende of this old lawe that one brother [c8v] maye nat suen an other hym selfe for that to wreken with out synne for brekynge of charite. But this charite Lorde hath thy viker ybroke and sais that we synnen

9 *side-note* Mercye.

but yif we suen for oure right. And we se I wote that thou taughtest vs some tyme to geue oure mantell also euer that we schulden suen for oure cote. And so lorde beleuen we that we ben ybounden to done by thy law that ys all charite/ and officers dutie is to defenden vs from thilke theuery though we complaynen not. but lorde thi law ys turned vpso downe.

A lorde what dome ys it/ to slene a thefe that take a mannes cattell a wey from hym/ and suffren a spousebreker to lyue and a lechour that kylleth a womans soule? And yet thy law stoned the spousebrekers and leichours/ and lette the theues lyuen and haue other punishment.

A lorde what dome ys it/ to slene a thefe[10] for stelinge of a horse/ and to let hym lyue vnpuneshed and to mayntene hym that robbeth thy pore puple of here lyfelode and the soule of his fode?

[D1r] Lorde it was never thy dome to sayen that a man ys an heretike and cursed for brekinge of mans lawe/ and demyn hym for a good man that breketh thyne hestes.

Lorde what dome ys it to cursen a lewed man yif he smyte a prest/ and not cursen a prest that smiteth a lewed man and leseth his charite?

Lorde/ what dome ys it to cursen the lewed puple for tethynges/ and not curse the parson that robbeth the puple of tethinges/ and ne techeth hem not god lawe/ but fedeth hem with payntinge of stonen walles/ and songes of laten that the puple knowen not?

Lorde what dome ys it to punysch the pore man for his trespas/ and suffren the rich continuen in hys synne for a quantite of money?

Lorde what dome ys it to slene an vnkunninge lewed man for hys synne/ and suffren a prest other a clerke that doth the same synne scapen a lyve? Lorde the synne of the prest or of the clerke ys a gretter trespas then it ys of a lewed vn [D1v] kunnynge man and gretter ensample of wickednesse to the comune puple.

Lorde what maner puple be we that nother kepen thy

10 *side-note* Thef

domes and thy rightfulnesse of the olde testamente that was a law of drede/ ne thy domes and thy rightfulnesse of thy newe testamente that is a lawe of loue and of mercy: but han an other law and taken of both thy lawes that is lykynge to vs/ and the remenaunte of hethen mennes lawes? and lorde thys ys a gret mischefe.

O Lorde thou sayst in thy lawe/ ne deme ye nat and ye ne schulen not ben demed: for the same mesure that ye meten to other men/ men shall meten to you agenwarde. And lorde thou seist that by her werken we schulen knowen hem. And by that we knowen that thou ne commaunded vs to demen mennes thoughtes/ ner her werkes that ne weren not agenst thy lawe expressely. And yet Lorde he that seyth he ys thy vikar wil demen oure thoughtes and asken vs what we thynken/ nat of the [D2r] Lorde ne of thy hestes/ for they caren litle for hem/ but of him and of his whilke they setten aboue thyne/ and maken vs accusen oure selfe/ or els they willen acursen vs/ for oure accusers mowen we nat knowen. And lorde thou seidest in thyne olde lawe that vnder two witnesses at the lest or thre schulde stande every matter. And that the witnesses schulden ever be the first that schulden helpen to kyl hem.

And when the scribes and these phareses some tyme broughten before thee a woman[11] that was ytake in spousebrekynge and axeden of the a dome/ thou didest write on the erth/ and than thou gaue this dome: he that ys with outen synne throwe fyrst at her a stone/ and lorde they wenten forth awey from the and the woman/ and thou forgeue the woman her trespas/ and bede her goo forth and synne no more.

Swete lorde yf the prestes token kepe to thy dome/ they wolden ben agast to demen men as they done. O lorde yif one [D2v] of them breke a commaundement of thy lawe/ he wole axe mercy of the/ and not a peyne that ys dewe for the synne for peyne of deth were to litel. O lorde how doren they demen any man to the deth for brekynge of her lawes other assenten to such lawe? for brekynge of thy lawe they wolen setten men

11 *side-note* Ioan.viii.

penaunce or pardon hem and helpe and mainteynen hem as oft as they trespasen. But lorde yif a man ones breke her lawes or speke agenst hem he maie done penaunce but ones and aftur ben brunt. Trulich lorde thou seist/ but yif everich of vs forgeve other his trespas/ thy father ne wole nat forgeuen vs oure synnes. And lorde when thou henge on the crosse thou preydest to thy fader to haue mercy on thyne enemyes.

And yet they seyn Lorde that they ne demen no man to the deth/ for they seyn they ne mowen by her law demen any man to deth. A leue Lorde/ even so saiden her fornfaders the phareses that it ne was nat lefull for hem to kyllen any man. And yet they bidden Pilate to done the to the [D3r] deth agenst his own conscience/ for he wolde gladly haue yquitte thee/ but for that they thretned hym with the Emperoure/ and broughten agenst the false witnesse also. And he was an hethen man.

A lorde/ how moch trewer dome was therein Pilate that was an hethen iustice/ than in oure kynges and iustices that wolen demen to the deth and bern yn the fyre hym that the prestes delyueren vnto hem with outen witnesse or prefe? For Pilate ne wolde not demen thee for that the phareses seyden that yif thou ne haddest not ben a misdoer we ne wolde nat delyuer hym vnto thee/ for to they broughten in her false witnesses agenst the. But lorde as thou saidest some tyme that it schulde ben lighter at domes daye to Tyro and to Sydon and Gomorra than to the cities where thou wrought wondres and miracles/ so I drede/ it shalben more lighte to Pilate in the dome then to oure kynges and domes men that so demen withoute witnesse and prefe. For lorde to demen thy folke for heretikes ys to holden the an [D3v] heretike/ and to brennen hem ys to brennen the/ for thou seidest to Paule when he persecuted thy puple: Saul/Saul wherfore persecutest thou me/ and in the dome thou shalt seye/ that ye haue done to the lest of myne ye haue done to me.

Thus Lorde ys thy mercy and iustice fordone by hym that seith he is thy viker in erth: for he nether kepeth it hym selfe nor nille nor suffer other to do it.

The thridde commaundement that ys pacience[12] and

sufferaunce/ ys also ybroken by thys viker. Lorde thou byddist sufferen both wronges and strokes withouten ageinstandinge/ and so thou didist thy selfe to geuen vs ensample to sufferen of oure brethern. For sufferinge norissheth loue and ageinstondeth debate. And all thy lawe ys loue/ or else thinge that draweth to loue.

But Lorde[13] men techen that men schulden pleten for her right and fighten also therfore and els they seyn men ben in pereyle/ and thou bede in the old lawe men fight for her contrey. And thy selfe haddist [D4r] two swerdes in thy cumpanye when thou schuldest go to thy passion/ that/ as these clerkes seyn betokeneth a spirituall swerde and a temporall swerde/ that thou goue to thy viker to rule with thy church. Lorde this is a sligh speche: but lorde we beleuen that thou art kynge of blisse/ and that ys thyne heretage and mankyndes cuntrey/ and in this worlde we ne ben but straungers and pelgrimes. For thou lorde ne art not of this world/ ne thy law nether/ ne thy trew seruantes that kepen thy law. And Lorde/ thou were kynge of Iuda by enheritage yif thou woldest haue yhad it/ but thou forsoke it and pletedest not therfore/ ne foughte not therfore.

But Lorde for thy kynde heritage and mankyndes cuntrey/ that ys a londe of blisse/ thou foughtest mightelych: In bataile thou ouercome thy enemie/ and so thou wonne thyne herytage. For thou that were a lorde mightiest in bataile/ and also lorde of vertues art rightfullich kynge of blisse/ as Dauid seith in the Sauter. But lorde thyne enemie smote the dispiteful= [D4v] lych and had power of the and henge the vp on the crosse as thou haddist ben a thefe/ and bynomyn the all thy clothes/ and stekede the to the harte with a spere.

O Lorde this was an harde assaute of a batayle and here thou ouercome by pacyence mightylich thyne enemyes/ for thou ne woldest nat done agenst the will of thy fader. And thus lorde thou taughtest thy seruantes to fighte for here

12 *side-note* Pacience.

13 *side-note* Swerde.

cuntrey. And lorde this fightinge was in figure ytaughte in the olde lawe. But lorde men holden now the schadewe of the olde fightinge and leuen the lighte of thy fightinge that thou taughtest openlych both in worde and in dede.

Lorde thou goue vs a swerde[14] to fighte ageinst oure enemies for oure cuntrey/ that was thyne holy techinge/ and christen mennes law. But lorde they swerde ys put in a shethe and in prestes warde that haue forsake the fightinge that thou taughtist. For as they sein it ys ageyns her order to ben men of armes in thy bataile for it ys vnsemelich/ as they seyn/ that [D5r] thy viker in erth/ other his prestes schulden suffer of other men. And therfore yif any man smite hym/ other any of his clerkes he ne taketh it not in pacience/ but and he smiteth with hys swerde of cursinge/ and afterwarde with his bodylich swerde/ he doth hem to deth. O lorde me thinketh that this is a fightinge ageynst kynde and moch ageyns thy techinge.

O Lorde whether thou axsedist after swerdes in tyme of thy passion to ageynstonde thyne enemies? nay forsoth thou lorde. For Peter that smote for gret loue of the hadde no gret thonke of the for his smitinge. And Lorde thou were mighty ynow to haue ageynstonde thyne enemies. for thorowgh thy lokinge they fellen doune to grounde. Lorde yblessed mote thou be. Here thou techest vs that we schulden suffren. For thou were mighty ynow to haue ageinstande thine enemies and thou haddest wepen/ and thy men weren harty to haue smiten.

O swete Lorde how maye he for schame clepen hym selfe thy viker and heed [D5v] of thy church/ that maye not for schame suffere? Sith thou art a lorde and suffredist of thy sugestys to geuen vs ensample and so did thy trew seruantes.

O lorde whether thou geue to peter a spirituall swerde to curse and a temporall swerde to sle mennes bodyes? Lorde I trowe not for then Peter that loued the so moch wolde haue smite with thy swerdes. But lorde/ he taught vs to blessen hem that cursen vs/ and suffren and not smiten. And lorde he

14 *side-note* Christen mens swerde

fedde thy puple as thou bede hym/ and therefore he suffrede the deth as thou diddist.

O Lorde why clepeth any man hym Petrus successour/ that hath forsake pacience and fedeth thy puple/ with cursinge and with smytinge. Lorde thou seydest in thy gospell when thy disciples knewen well that thou were Christ/ that thou mostest go to Ierusalem and sufferen of the scribes and pharysees spitinges/ reprofes and also the deth. And Peter toke the a syde and said god for beede that. And lorde thou seydist to Peter/ go by hinde me Sathanas [D6r] thou sclaundrest me in Israel. For thou ne sauourest not thilke thinges that ben of god/ but thilke that ben of men. Lorde to mennes witte it ys vnresonable/ that thou or thy viker yif thou madist anny on erth schulden soffren of youre sugettes.

A Lorde whether thou ordenist an ordre of fighters to turne men to the beleue? other ordenist that knightes schulden swere to fight for thy wordes?

A lorde/ whether thou bede that yif a man turne to the feith that he schulde geue his goodes and catell to thy vikar that hath gret Lordschips and more then hym nedeth? Lorde ye wote well that in the begynnynge of the church men that weren converted threwen a doune her goodes before the aposteles fete. For all they weren in charite/ and non of them saide this ys myne ne Peter made hym selfe no lorde of these goodes.

But lorde now he that clepeth hym selfe thy viker apon erth and successoure to Peter hath ybroke thy commaundement of charite. For he ys becomen a Lorde. And he [D6v] hath broken also thy commaundemente of mercy/ and also of pacyence. Thus Lorde we ben fallen in to gret mischefe and thraldome/ for oure cheueteyn hath forsaken werre and armes and hath treted to haue peace with our enemies.

A Lorde yif it be thy will/ drawe oute thy swerde out of his scheth/ that thy seruantes maye fight there with agenst her enemies/ and put cowardise oute of oure hartes. And comfort vs in bataile/ ar than thou come with thy swerde in thy mouth to take vengeaunce on thyne enemies. For yif we ben acorded with oure enemies tyll that tyme come/ it ys drede lest thou take vengeaunce both of hem and of vs to gader. A lorde there nys no helpe now yn this gret mischefe but onlych in thee.

Lorde thou geue vs a commaundemente of treweth in byddinge vs saye ye ye/ nay nay/ and swere for no thinge.[15] Thou geue vs also a maundemente of mekenes and a nother of porenes. But Lorde he that clepeth hym selfe thy viker on erth/ hath ybroken these commaundementes/ for he [D7r] maketh a law to compell men to swere/ and by hys lawes he techeth that a man to saue hys lyfe maye forswere and lye. And so Lorde thorowgh comfort of hym and of his lawes/ the puple ne dredeth nat to swere and to lye/ ne oft tymes to forsweren hem. Lorde here ys litill treuth.

O Lorde thou hast ybroughte vs to a lyuinge of soule that staundes in beleuinge in the and kepinge thyne hestes and when we breken thyne hestes than we slen oure soule. And lesse harme it were to suffer bodylich deth.

Lorde kynge Saule brake thyne hestes/ and thou toke his kyngdome from his eyres ever more after hym/ and gaue it to Dauid thy seruante that kept thyne hestes. And thou saidest by Samuel thy prophet to Saul kynge that it ys a maner herienge of false goddes to breke thyne hestes. For who that loueth the ouer all thinges and dredeeh the also: he nole for nothinge breke thyne hestes.

O Lorde yif brekynge of thyne hestes be heryenge of false goddes. I trowe that [D7v] he that maketh the puple breke thyne hestes/ and commaundeth that his hestes ben kept of the puple maketh hymself a false god on erth/ as Nabugodonosor did some tyme that was kynge of Babylon.

But Lorde we forsaken such false goddes and beleuen that there ne ben no mo goddes than thou. And though thou suffre vs awhile to ben in disease for knowleginge of the: we thonken the with oure harte for it ys a token that thou louest vs to geuen vs in this worlde some penaunce for oure trespas.

Lorde in the olde lawe thy trewe seruantes token the

15 *side-note* Not swere.

deth/ for they wolde not eten swynes flesch that thou haddest forboden hem to ete. O Lorde what treweth ys in vs to eten vnclene mete of the soule: that thou hast forboden? Lorde thou saist he that doth synne ys seruaunte of synne/ and then he that lyeth in forsweringe hymselfe/ ys seruaunte of lesinge/ and than he ys a seruaunte to the deuell that ys a lyar and fader of lesinges. And lorde thou saist no man maye [D8r] serue two Lordes at ones. O Lorde then everich lyar for the tyme that he lyeth other forswereth hymselfe forsaketh thy seruyce for drede of hys bodilich deth and becometh the devils seruaunte.

O Lorde what treweth ys in hym that clepeth hymselfe seruaunte of thy seruantes/ and in hys doinge he maketh hym a Lorde[16] of thy seruauntes. Lorde thou were both Lorde and master and so thou saide thy selfe/ but yet in thy warkes thou were as a seruaunte. Lorde thys was a gret trueth and a gret mekenes: but Lorde thou bede thy seruauntes that they ne schulden haue Lordschip ouer her brethern. Lorde thou saidest kynges of the hethen men han Lordschupe ouer her suggetes/ and they that vsen her power ben ycleped well doers.

But Lorde thou saidest it schulde not be so amonges thy seruauntes: But he that were most schulde be as a seruaunte. Thus Lorde thou taughtest thy disciples to ben meke. Lorde in the old lawe thy seruauntes durst haue no lordschu [D8v] pe of her brethern/ but yif that thou bede hem. And yet they schulden not do her brethern as they diden to thralles that serueden hem. But they shulden do to her brethern that were her seruauntes as to her awn brethern. For all they were Abrahams childern. And at a certen tyme they schulden lettin her brethern passen from hem in fredom/ but yif they wolden wilfullych abyden stille in seruise.

O lorde thou gaue vs in thy cominge a lawe of parfite loue/ and in token of loue thou clepedest thy selfe oure brother. And to maken vs parfecte in loue thou bede that we schulden clepe to vs no fader vp on erth/ but thy fader of heuen we schulde clepen oure fader. Allas Lorde/ how

16 *side-note* A lorde

violentlych oure bredern and thy chyldren ben now yputte in bodilich thraldome/ and in dispite as beestes ever more in greuous traveill to fynde proude men in ease? But lorde yif we taken thys defoule and this dysease in pacience and in mekenes and kepen thyne hestes/ we hopen to be fre. And Lorde geue oure [E1r] brethren grace to comen oute of thraldome of synne that they ben fallen in thorowgh the desyringe and vsage of lordschupe vpon her brethren. And Lorde thyne prestes in the old law hadden no lordschupis amonge her brethern/ but houses and lesewes for her beestes: but Lorde oure prestes now have gret lordschupe and putten her brethren in gretter thraldome than lewed men that ben Lordes. Thus ys mekenesse forsake.

Lorde thou byddest in the gospell that when a man ys ybede to the feest he shulde sitte in the lowest place/ and then he maye be sette hyer with worshup when the Lorde of the feest beholdeth how his gestes sitteth. Lorde it ys drede that they that sitten now in the hyest place shullen ben beden in tyme to cominge sitte byneth. And that wole be schame and vileyne for hem. And it ys thy sayenge/ thilke that hyeth hym selfe schall ben ylowed/ and thilke that loweth hem selfe schulen ben an heyghed. O lorde thou byddest in thy gospell to ben ware of the ypocresye of phareses/ for it ys a pointe of [E1v] pride contrary to mekenes. And lorde thou saist that they louen the furst sittinges at the sopeer/ and also the principall chayres in churches/ and gretinges in chepinge/ and to be ycleped mastres of men. And Lorde thou saist ne be ye nat cleped masteres/ for one ys youre master and that ys Christ and all ye ben brethren. And ne clepe ye to yow no fader apon erth for one ys youre fader that ys in heven. O Lorde this ys a blessed lesson to teche men to ben meke.

But Lorde[17] he that clepeth hymself thy viker on erth he clepeth hym selfe fadur of fadours agens thy forbedinge. And all these worshupes thou hast forboden. He appreueth hem/ and maketh hem masters[18] to many/ that techen thy puple her

17 *side-note* Fader

18 *side-note* Master.

owne techinge/ and leuen thy techinge that ys medefull/ and hyden it by quaynte gloses from thy lewed puple/ and feden thy puple with sweuenes that they meten/ and tales that doth litell profite but moch harme to the puple. But Lorde these glosers seggeth that they ne desyren nat the state of mastrie to ben worschuped thereby/ but to profite the mo [E2r] re to thy puple when they prechen thy worde. For as they seggen the puple wolen leuen more the prechinge of a mayster that hath ytake a state of scole/ than the prechinge of a nother man that hath not ytake the state of mastrye.

Lorde whether it be any nede the maystres beren witnesse to thy techinge that it ys trewe and good? or Lorde whether maye any maystre mowe by his estate of maystrye/ that thou hast forboden/ drawe any man from hys synne rather then an other man that ys nat a maystre/ ne wole be non for it ys forboden hym in thy gospell? Lorde thou sendest no maystres to prech the puple/[19] and thou knowlegist in the gospell to thy fader that he hath yhid hys wisdome from wise men and redy men/ and schewed it to litle children. And Lorde maystres of the law hylden thy techinge folye/ and seiden that thou woldest destroye the puple with thy techinge. Trulych Lorde so these maystres seggeth now: for they haue ywritten many bokes ageyns thy techinge that ys treweth/ and so the pro [E2v] phesie of Hieremie ys fulfilled/ when he sayeth: Trulich the false poyntigh of the maysters of the law hath ywroughte lesinge. And now ys the tyme ycome that saynte Paule speketh of there he sayeth/ tyme schall come whan men schulle not susteine holsome techinge. But they schullen gadre to hepe maistres with hutchinge eares/ and from trueth they schullen turnen a waye her heringe/ and turnen hem to tales that maystres haue ymaked to schowen her maistrye and her wisdome.

And Lorde a man schall leue more a mannes werkes than hys wordes and the dede scheweth well of these maysters that they desyren more maystrye for her own worschupe than for profite of the puple. For when they be maystres they ne

19 *side-note* Thechinge.

prechen not so oft as they did before. And yif they prechen/ communlych it ys before rych men there as they mowen bere worschupe and also profite of her prechinge. but before pore men they prechen but selden when they ben maistres: and so by her workes we may sene that they ben false glosers.

[E3r] And lorde me thinketh that whoso wole kepen thyne hestes hym nedeth no gloses: but thilke that clepen hemselfe Christen men/ and lyuen agenst thy techinge and thyne hestes/ nedelych they mote glose thyne hestes after her lyuinge other else men schulden openlych yknow her ypocrisie and her falsheed.

But Lorde thou saist that there nys nothinge yhid that it schall not be schewed some tyme. And Lorde yblessed mote thou be. For some what thou schewest vs now of oure myscheues that we ben fallen in thorowgh the wisdome of maystres/ that haue by sleygthes ylad vs a waye from thee and thy techinge/ that thou that were mayster of heuen taught vs for loue/ when thou were here some tyme to hele of oure soules withouten errour or heresye. But maystres of the worldes wisdome and her founder haue ydamned it for heresye and for erroure.

O Lorde/ me thinketh it ys a gret pride thus to reproue thy wisdome and thy techinge.[20] And Lorde me thinketh that this [E3v] Nabugodonosor kynge of Babylon that thus hath reproued thy techinge and thine hestes/ and commaundeth on all wise to kepen hys hestes/ maken thy puple heryen hym as a god on erth/ and maketh hem his thralles and his seruauntes.

But Lorde we lewed men knowen no god but the/ and we with thyne helpe and thy grace forsaken Nabugodonosor and hys lawes. For he in his prowd astate wole haue all men onder hym/ and he nele be vnder no man. He ondoth thy lawes that thou ordenest to ben kept/ and maketh his owne lawes as hym lyketh/ and so he maketh hym kynge abouen all other kynges of the erth/ and maketh men to worschupen hym as a god/ and thy gret sacryfice he hath ydone awaye.

20 *side-note* To reproue.

O Lorde here ys thy commaundemente of mekenes mischeflych to broke/ and thy blessed commaundement of porenesse ys also to broken and yhid from thy puple. Lorde Zacharie thy prophet sayth that thou that schuldest ben oure kynge schuldest ben a pore man/ and so thou were/ for thou saidest [E4r] thy selfe/ foxes haue dennes[21] and briddes of heuen nestes/ and mannes sone hath nat where to legge hys heed on. And thou saidest yblessed ben pore men in spirite/ for the kyngdome of heuen ys hern. And woo to rych men for they han her comforte in this world. And thou bade thy disciples to ben ware of all couetyse for thou saidist in the abundance of a mannes hauynge ne ys nat his lyflode. And so thou techist that thilke that han more then hem nedeth to her lyuinge lyuen in couetyse. Also thou saist that but yif a man forsake all thinges that he oweth/ he ne maye not ben thy disciple. Lorde thou saist also that thy worde that ys ysowe in rych mennes hartes[22] bringeth forth no fruite. For rychesse and the businesse of this world maketh it withouten fruite.

O Lorde here ben many blessed techinges to tech men to ben pore and loue porenesse. But Lorde harme ys/ pore men and porenesse ben yhated/ and rych men ben yloued and honoured. And yif a man be a pore man/[23] men holden hym a man with out [E4v] grace/ and yif a man desyreth porenesse men holden hym but a fole. And yif a man be a rich man/ men clepen hym a gracyous man and thilke that ben bysye in getinge of rychesse ben yholde wise men and redy: but Lorde these rych men sayen that it is both lefull and medefull to hem to gadre richesse to geder. For they ne gadreth it not for hem selfe/ but for other men that ben nedy/ and Lorde her werkes schowen the trueth. For yif a pore nedy man wolde borowen of her rychesse/ he nole leue hym none of hys good/ but yif he mowe be seker to haue it againe by a certeyn daye.

But Lorde thou bede that a man schulde lene and nat hopinge yeldinge ageyne of hym that he leneth to: and thy

21 *side-note* Pore men.

22 *side-note* Rych men

23 *side-note* Nota.

fadur of heuen wole quyte hym hys mede. And yif a pore axe a rych man any good/ the rych man wole geue hym but a litell and yet it schalbe litell worth. And lorde me thinketh that here ys litell loue and charite/ both to god and to oure brethren.

For Lorde thou techest in thy gospell that what men do to thy seruauntes thy do [E5r] ne to thee. A Lorde yif a pore man axe good for thy loue/ men geueth hym a litle of the worst. For these rich men ordeynen both breed and ale for goddes men of the worst that they haue. O Lorde syth all the good that men haue cometh of thee. How dare any man geue thee of the worst/ and kepe to hymselfe the best? How mowe soch men saye that they gaderen rychesse for others nede as well as hem selfe/ syth her werkes ben contrary to her wordes? and that ys no gret treweth. And be ye seker these goodes that rych men han they ben gods goodes ytake to youre kepinge/ to loke how ye wolen by setten to the worshupe of god. And lorde thou saist in the gospell/ that who so is trewe in litell/ he ys trewe in that thinge that is more. And who that ys false in a litell thinge/ who wole taken hym towarde thinges of a gretter value? And therfore be ye ware than han gods goodes to kepe. Spende ye thilke trulych to the worschupe of god lest ye lesen the blisse of heuen for the vntrewe despendinge of gods goodes in this worlde.

[E5v] O Lorde these rych men seggen that they done moch for thy loue. For many pore laborers ben yfounde by hem/ that schulden fare febelich ne were not they and her redinesse for soth me thinketh that pore laborers geueth to these rych men more then they geuen hem ageyn warde. For the pore man mote gone to hys laboure in colde and in hete/ in wete and drye/ and spende his flesch and hys bloude in the rych mennes workes apon gods grounde to fynde the rych man in ese/ and in lykynge/ and in good fare of mete and of drinke and of clothinge. Here ys a gret gifte of the pore man. For he geueth his own body. But what geueth the rych man hym ageynwarde? Sertes febele mete/ and febele drinke/ and feble clothinge. What ever they seggen soch be her werkes/ and here ys litel loue. And who soever loketh wel a boute/ all the worlde fareth thus as we seggen. And all men stodyeth on every syde/ how they maye wexe rych. And everych man almest ys a schamed to ben holden a pore man.

And lorde I trowe for thou were a [E6r] pore man men token litell regarde to the and to thy techinge. But Lorde thou come to geue vs a new testamente of loue and therfore it was semelych that thou came in porenesse to proue who wolde loue thee and kepen thyne hestes. For yif thou haddist ycome in forme of a rych man and of a lorde/ men wolde rather for thy drede then for thy loue/ haue ykepte thyne hestes. And so lorde now thou mighte well ysee which louen thee as they schulde in kepynge thyne hestes. For who that loueth thee in thy porenesse and in thy lowenesse/ nedes he mote loue the in thy lordschupe and thy highenesse.

But Lorde the worlde ys turned vpsedowne/ and men louen pore men[24] but a litell ne porenesse nother. But men ben aschamed of porenesse/ and therefore lorde I trowe that thou arte a pore kynge. And therefore I trowe that he that clepeth hym selfe thy viker on erth hath forsake porenesse/ as he hath ydo the remenaunte of thy law and ys by come a rych man and a Lorde/ and maketh hys tresoure apon the [E6v] erth/ that thou forbedest in the gospell. And for his right and his rychesse he wole plete/ and feghte/ and curse. And yet Lorde he wole segge that he forsaketh all thinges that he oweth as thy trewe disciple mote done after thy techynge in the gospell.

But lorde/ thou ne taughtest not a man to forsaken hys goodes/ and pleten for hem and feghten/ and cursen. And Lorde he taketh on hym power to assoylen a man of all maner thinges/ but yif it be of dette. Trewelych Lorde/ me thinketh he knoweth litell of charite. For who that beth in charite possesseth thy goodes in comune and nat in propre at hys neghboures nede. And than schall there none of hem seggen thys ys myne/ but it is goodes that god graunteth to vs to spenden it to hys worschupe. And so yif any of hem boroweth a porcion of thilke goodes/ and dispendeth hem to gods worschupe. God ys apayed of this spendinge/ and aloweth hym

24 *side-note* Porenesse.

for his trew doinge. And yif god ys apayed of that dispendinge that ys the principall lorde of thilke goodes/ how darre any of his ser [E7r] uauntes axen there of acountes other chalengen it for dette? Serten of one thinge I am in certen/ that these that charge so moch dette of worldly catell they knowen litle of Christes law of charite. For yif ych am a bayly of gods goodes in the worlde/ yif I se my brother in nede/ ych am yholden by charite to parte with hym of these goodes to his nede/ and yif he spendeth hem well to the worschupe of god/ I mote be well a payed as though ych me selfe had spendid hem to the worschupe of god. And yif the principall Lorde ys well payed of my brothers doinge and the despendinge of hys goodes/ how maye I segge for schame that my brother ys dettoure to me of the goodes that I toke hym to spenden in gods worshupe at hys nede? And yif my brother spendeth amys the goodes that I take hym/ Ich am dyscharged of my delyueraunce of the goodes/ yif I take hym in charite thilke goodes at his nede. And ych am yholde to ben sory of hys yvell dispendinge ne I maye not axen the goodes/ that I toke hym to his nede [E7v] in forme of dette. For at hys nede they weren hys as well as myne. And thus ys my brother yholde to done to me yif he seith me in nede/ and yif we ben in charite/ lytell schulde we chargen of dette. And ne we schulde nat axen so dettes/ as men that knowen not god. And than be we pore in forsakynge all thinges that we owen. For yif we ben in charite/ we wolen nother fyghte nor curse ne plete for oure goodes with oure brethren.

O Lorde thus thou taughtest thy seruauntes to lyuen.[25] And so they lyueden while they hadden good schepherdes that fedden thy scheepe and ne robbed hem not of her lyfelode/ as Peter thy good schepherde and thy other Apostles. But Lorde he that clepeth hymselfe thy viker vpon erth and successoure to Peter/ he robbeth thy puple of her bodylich lyfelode for he ordeneth proude schepherdis to lyuen in ese by the tenth party of pore mennes traueyll. And he geueth hem leue to lyuen where hem lyketh. And yif men ne wolen nat wilfullych

25 *side-note* schepherdes

geuen hem these tythin [E8r] ges/ they wolen han hem ageyn her will by maystrye and by cursinge to maken hem rich.

Lorde how maye any man segge that sych schepherdes that louen more the wole then the scheep/ and feden not thy scheep in body ne in soule/ ne ben such rauenours and theves?[26] And who maye segge that the maintenoure of such schepherdes/ ne ys nat a maintenour of theves and robbers? How wole he assoyle schepherdes of her robbinge with out restitucion of her goodes that they robben thy scheep of ageinst her will? Lorde of all schepherdes blessed mote thou be. For thou louedest more the scheep then her wole. For thou fedest thy sheep both in body and in soule. And for loue of thy sheepe thou toke thy deeth to bringe thy scheep out of wolues mouthes. And the most charge that thou goue to Peter/ was to fede thy scheep. And so he did trewelich/ and toke the deth for thee and for thy schepe. For he come in to the folde of scheep by the that were the dore. And so I trowe a fewe other did as he dyd/ though they [E8v] clepen hemself Successours to Peter. For her workes schowen what they ben. For they robben and sleen and distroyen: they robben thy scheepe/ of the tenth parte of her traueyle and feden hem selfe in case. They sleen thy scheepe. For they pyenen hem for hunger of her soule to the deth. They distroyen thy schepe. For with mighte and with sternschipe they rulen thy scheep/ that for drede they ben disparpled a brode in mownteynes/ and there the wilde beestes of the felde distroyeth hem/ and deuoureth hem for defaute of a good schepherde.

O Lorde yif it be thy will delyuer thy scheep oute of such schepherdes warde that retcheth not of thy scheep/ han they her wole to make hem selfe rich. For thy scheepe ben in gret mischefe and foule accumbred with her schepherdes.

But for thy schepherdes[27] wolden ben excused they haue ygeten hem hyridmen to fede thy puple/ and these comen in schepes clothinge. But dredeles/ her werkes schewen that with in forth they ben but wolfes. For han they her hyre/ they ne

26 *side-note* Nota.
27 *side-note* hyrid men.

retch= [F1r] eth but a litell how sorrilich thy scheep ben kepte. For as they seggen hem selfe they ben but hirid men that han no charge of thy scheepe. And when they shulden feden thy scheepe in the plentuous lesewe of thy techinge/ they stonden betwene hem and her lesewe/ so that thy schepe ne han but a sighte of thy lesewe but eten they schullen nat thereof. But they feden hem in a sorry sowre lesewe of lesinges and of talys. And so thy schepe fallen in to greuous syckenesse thorowgh thys yuel lesew. And yif any scheepe breke ouer in to thy lesewe to tasten the swetnes therof/ anon these hyrid men dryue hym oute with houndes. And thus thy schepe by these hyrid men byn ykepte oute of her kyndlych lesew/ and ben yfed wyth soure grasse and sory baren lesewes. And yet they foden hem but selden/ and when they han sorylich fed hem/ they taken gret hyre/ and gone awaye from thy scheep and letten hem a worth. And for drede lest thy schepe wolden in her absence go to thy swete lesewe. They haue enclosed it all aboute so strong= [F1v] lich and so highe ther maye no scheep comen there with in. But yif it be a walisch leper of the mounteynes that maye with his longe legges lepen ouer the wallys. For the hyredmen ben full certen that yif thy scheepe hadden ones tasted the swetnesse of thy lesew. They ne wold no more ben yfed of these hyrid men in her soure lesewes/ and therfore these hyridmen kepen hem oute of that lesew. For hadden the scheepe ones ytasted wel of thy lesew. They wolden with oute a ledder go thider to her mete and than mote these hired men sechen hem a nother laboure to lyue by than kepinge of scheepe. And they ben fell and war ynowe therof/ and therfore they feden thy schepe with soure mete that naughte ys and hiden from thy schepe the swetnesse of thy lesewe. And so though these hyrid men gone in schepes clothinge/ in her workes they ben wolues/ that much harme done to thy scheep as we haue ytold.

O lorde/ they comen as schepe/ for they seggen that they ben pore and haue forsaken the world to lyuen parfetlych as [F2r] thou taughtest in the gospell. Lord this ys schepes clothinge. But Lorde thou ne taughtest not a man to forsaken the trauelouse lyuynge in porenesse in the worlde/ to lyuen in ese with rychesse by other mennes traueyle/ and haue lordshupe on her brethern. For Lorde this ys more to forsaken the and go to the worlde.

O Lorde thou ne taughtest not a man to forsake the worlde to lyuen in poreness of begginge[28] by other mennes traueyle that ben as feble as they ben. Ne Lorde thou ne taughtest not a man to lyuen in porenesse of begginge/ that were stronge ynough to traueyle for hys lyfelode. Ne Lorde thou ne taughtest not a man to ben a begger to beghen of men more then hym nedeth/ to bylden gret castels and maken gret festes to thilke than han no nede.

O Lorde thou ne taughtest not men this porenes/ for it ys oute of charite. But thy porenesse that thou taughtest norscheth cherite. Lorde syth poule saith that he that forsaketh the charge of thilke that ben homelich with hym hath forsaken his faith and [F2v] ys worse then a mysbeleued man. How than mowe these men seggen that they beleuen in Christ/ than han forsake her pore feble frendes/ and let hem lyue in traueyle and in disese/ that traueyled full sore for hem/ when they weren younge and vnmighty to helpen hem self? And they wolen lyue in ese by other mennes trauayle euer more in begginge with outen shame.

Lorde thou ne taughtest not this maner porenesse/ for it ys oute of charite. And all thy lawe ys charite other thinge that norscheth cherite. And these hyridmen these schepherdes sende aboute to kepe thy schepe/ and to feden hem other whiles in sorry bareyne lesewes. Lorde thou ne madest none such scheepherdes ne kepers of thy scheep that weren gerners aboute cuntreys/ and wolden ones oder twyes a yere fede sorylich thy schepe/ and for so litle traueyle taken a gret hyre/ and sythen all the yere afterward do what hem lyketh/ and let thy schepe perish for defaute of kepinge.

But thy schepherdes abyden still wi= [F3r] th her schepe/ and feden hem in thy plentuous lesewe of thy techinge/ and gone byfore thy schepe and techen hem the waye in to that plentuous and swete lesewe/ and kepen thy flocke from raueninge of the wilde beestes of the feelde.

28 *side-note* Begginge.

O Lorde delyuer thy scheepe out of the warde of these schepherdes and these hyred men that stonden more to kepe her riches that they robben of thy scheep/ than they stonden in kepinge of thy scheep.

O Lorde/ when thou come to Ierusalem some tyme thou droue out of the temple sellers of beestes and of other chaffre/ and saidest: Myne house schulden ben cleped an house of preyers: but they maden a den of theves of it. O Lorde/ thou art the temple in whom we schulden preyen thy fader of heuen. And Salomons temple that was ybelded at Ierusalem/ was fygure of this temple. But Lorde/ he that clepeth hym selfe thy viker vpon erth/ and saith that he occupieth thy place here on erth/ ys by come a chapman in the temple and hath his chapmen walkynge in [F3v] dyuerse contreys to sellen his chaffare and to maken hym rych. And he saith thou gave hym so gret a power aboven all other men/ that what ever he byndeth ether vnbyndeth in erth/ thou byndest other vnbyndist the same in heven. And so of grete power he selleth other men for geuenesse of her synne. And for moch money he will assoylen a man so clene of hys synne/ that he behoteth men the blisse of hevin withouten any peyne after that they be deed that geuen hym much money.

Byschopriches and cherches and such other chaffares he selleth also for money and maketh hym self rych. And thus he begileth the puple.

O Lorde Iesu/ here ys much vntrueth/ and myschefe/ and mater of sorow. Lorde thou saidest some tyme that thou woldest be with thy seruauntes in to the ende of the world.[29] And thou saidest also there as tweyne or thre ben ygadred togeder in thy name/ that thou art in the mydle of hem. A lorde/ then it was no nede to thee to maken a leftenaunte/ sith thou wol [F4r] te be evermore amonges thy seruauntes.

Lorde thou axedest of thy Disciples who they trowed that thou were. And Peter answered and saide that thou art Christe Gods sone. And thou saidest to Peter. Thou art yblessed Symon Bariona for flesch and bloude ne schowed not this to

29 *side-note* chirch

the/ but my fader that ys in heven. And I saye to the/ that thou are Peter/ and vpon this stone ych wole byld my church/ and the gates of hell ne schullen nat availen agenst it. And to the ych wole geve the keyes of heuen/ and what ever thou byndest vpon erth shall be bonde in heuen and what ever thou vnbyndest on erth schalbe vnbounden in heuen. This power also was graunted vnto the other disciples as well as to Peter as the gospel opunlych telleth. In this place men seggen that thou graunted to Petrus successours the selue power that thou gaue to Petre. And therfore the byschop of Rome/ that saith he ys Peters successour[30] taketh thys power to him to bynden and vnbinden in erth what hym lyketh. But [F4v] Lorde/ ych haue much wondre how he maye for schame clepen hymselfe Peters successour. For Peter knowleged that thou were Christ and god/ and kepte the hestes of thy law/ but these han forsaken the hestes of thy law/ and hath ymaked a law contrary to thyne hestes of thy lawe. And so he maked hym self a fals Christ and a false god in erth. And I trouwe thou gaue hym no power to vndo thy law. And so in takinge this power vp on hym he maketh hym a fals Christe and Antechrist. For who may be more agens christ than he that in his wordes maketh hymselfe Christes viker in erth. And in his werkes vndoth the ordinaunce of Christe/ and maketh men byleuen that it ys nede full to the heale of mennes soules to byleuen that he ys Christes viker in erth. And what ever he byndeth in erth ys ybounden in heuen/ and vnder this coloure he vndoth Christes lawe/ and maketh men on alwise to kepen his lawe/ and his hestes. And thus men maye yseen that he ys agens Christ/ and therfore he [F5r] ys Antechrist that maketh men worshupen hym as a god on erth/ as the proude kynge Nabugodonosor did sumtyme that was kynge of Babylone.

And therfore we lewed men that knowen no God but thee Iesu Christ/ beleuen in thee that art oure god/ and oure kynge/ and oure Christ/ and thy lawes. And forsaken Antechrist and Nabugodonosor that ys a false God/ and a false Christ and his lawes that ben contrary to thy techinge. And

30 *side-note* Viker

Lorde strength thou vs agenst oure enemies. For they ben aboute to maken vs forsake thee and thy lawe/ other ellis to putten vs to deeth. O Lorde onlych in the is oure trust to helpe vs in this mischefe for thy gret goodnesse that ys with outen ende.

Lorde/ thou ne taughtest not thy disciples to assoylen men of her synne/ and setten hem a penaunce for her synne/[31] in fastinge ne in preyenge/ ne othere almous dede/ ne thy selfe ne thy disciples vseden no such power here on erth. For Lorde thou forgeue men her synnes/ and bede hem synne no [F5v] more. And thy disciples fulleden men in thy name in forgeuenesse of her synnes. Nor they toke no such power apon hem as oure prestes dare now. And lorde thou ne assoyledest no man both of hys synne and of his peyne that was dewe for his synne/ ne thou grauntedst no man such power here on erth.

And lorde me thinketh/ that yif ther were a purgatorye/ and eny erthlyche man had power to delyueren synfull men from the peynes of purgatorye/ he schulde/ and he were in charite/ sauen everich man that were in waye of saluacion from thilke peynes/ syth they make hem gretter then any bodilych peynes of thys worlde. Also yif the bischop of Rome had such a power he him selfe schulde never comen in purgatorye ne in hell. And sith we se well that he ne hath no power to kepen hymselfe ne other men nother out of these bodilich peynes of the worlde: and he maye go to hell for hys synne as a nother man maye. I ne byleue nat that he hath so gret a po [F6r] wer to assoylen men of her synne as he taketh vpon hym abouen all other men. And I trowe that in thys he hyeth hym selfe aboue god.

As touchinge the sellinge of byschopryches and personages/ I trow it be a poynte of falshede. For agens gods ordinaunce he robbeth pore men of a porcion of ther sustinaunce and selleth it/[32] other geueth it to fynde proude men in ydlenesse that done the lewed puple litell

31 *side-note* Penaunce.

32 *side-note* Selleth

prophet and much harme as we tolde before. Thus ben thy commaundementes of treweth/ of mekenesse and of porenesse vndone by hym that clepeth hym self thy viker here vpon erth.

A Lorde thou goue vs a commaundemente of chastite that ys a forsakynge of fleschliche lustes. For thou broughtest vs to a lyuynge of soule that ys ygouerned by thy worde. For Lorde thou ordenedist woman more frele than man to ben ygouerned by mans rule and his helpe to plese the and kepe thyne hestes. Ne thou ne ordeynedist that a man [F6v] schuld desyre the company of a woman/ and maken her his wife/ to lyuen with her in his lustys/ as a swyne doth or a horse. And hys wife ne lyked hym nat to hys lustes/ Lorde thou ne gaue not a man leue to departen hym from his wife and taken hym a nother.

But Lorde thy maryage[33] ys a commune acorde betwene man and woman to lyuen togeder to her lyues ende/ and in thy seruyse eyther the bettur for others helpe/ and thilke that ben thus ycome to geder ben ioyned by the/ and thilke that god ioyneth maye no man departe. But Lorde thou saist that yif a man se a woman to coueten hyr/ than he doth with that woman letcherye in his herte. And so Lorde/ yif a man desyre his wife in couetyse of such lustes/ and not to flye from whordome/ his weddinge ys letcherye/ ne thou ne ioynest hem nat to geder. Thus was Raguels doughter ywedded to seven husbandes that the devell strangled. But Tobye toke hir to lyue with her in clennesse and bringinge vp of her childern to thy worschyp/ and on [F7r] hym the deuell ne had no power. For the weddinge was ymaked in god/ for god and thorough God.

O Lorde the puple ys ferre ygo from this maner of weddinge. For now men wedden her wives for fayrenesse/ other for rychesse or some such other fleschlych lustus. And lorde so it preueth by hem for the most parte. For a manne shall not fynde two wedded in a londe/ where the husbonde loues the wife/ and the wife ys buxum to the man/ as they shulden after thy law of mariage. But other the man loues not

33 *side-note* Maryage.

his wife/ or the wife ys not buxum to her man. And thus Lorde ys the rule of prefe that neuer faileth to preve whether it be done by thee or no. And Lorde all this mischefe ys comen amonge thy puple for that they knowe not thy worde/ but her schepherdes and hyrid men feden hem with her swevennes and lesynges. And Lorde/ where they schulden gon before vs in the felde/ they seggen that her order ys to holy for thy mariage. And Lorde he that calleth hymselfe thy vyker vp on erth will not suffren [F7v] prestes to taken hem wyues for that it ys ageins his law: But lorde he will dispensen with hem to kepen horen for a certen som of money. And Lorde/ all horedome ys forfended in thy law. And Lorde/ thou neuer forfendest prestes her wives ner thy Apostles nether. And well I wote in oure londe prestes hadden wiues vntill Anselmus dayes in the yere of oure Lorde god a leven hundert and twenty and nyne as huntindon writes. And Lorde this makes puple for the most parte leuen that lechery ys no sinne. Therfore we lewed men preyen the that thou wolt sende vs shepherdes of thyne owne that wolen feden thy flock in thy lesewe and gon before hem selfe and so writen thy law in oure hartes that from the leest to the mest all they mayen knowen the. And Lorde geue oure kynge and his Lordes harte to defenden thy trew schepherdes and thy shepe from oute of the wolues mouthes/ and grace to know the that art the trew Christ the sonne of thy heuenly father/ from the [F8r] Antechrist that ys the sonne of pride. And Lorde geve vs thy pore schepe pacience and strength to suffer for thy law the cruelnes of the mischeuous wolues. And Lorde as thou hast promysed shorten these dayes. Lorde we axen this now/ for more nede was there neuer.

# Commentary

The commentary is designed to gloss difficult readings, identify all biblical and secular allusions, and provide references to and analogues from Lollard writings and early English sixteenth-century reformation tracts. All New Testament citations in the section entitled 'To the Christen reader' are taken from David Daniell's modern-spelling edition of Tyndale's *New Testament*. Page references to Daniell's edition are given in parentheses immediately following the citation. All biblical citations in the text of *The praier and complaynte* itself are from the Forshall and Madden edition of the so-called Wycliffe Bible.

**7–10** Matthew 10:21. The suggestion is that the papacy and its adherents are members of Beelzebub's household. Beelzebub, made famous in English literature by Milton in books 1 and 2 of *Paradise Lost*, is called the prince of devils in Matthew 12:27 and the chief of the devils in Luke 11:15. The reference to Matthew 10:21 is designed to prepare the reader for the conflict between true believers and the papacy and its adherents which the tract itself explores at length. In Matthew 10:21 Christ addresses his twelve apostles preparing them for the hardships they will confront from their enemies. *The praier and complaynte* explores these hardships as they apply to contemporary disciples of Christ.
**16ff** This introduction to *The praier* in which the author draws a comparison between, on the one hand, the biblical Pharisees and the present-day church and, on the other, Christ and his apostles and present-day devout Christians, is not unlike the comparison Tyndale establishes in his 'Preface' to *The Practice of Prelates* (*Expositions and Notes* 242); see also his *Parable of the Wicked Mammon* (*Doctrinal Treatises* 42–3).
**18** *a thousande yeres before* This attempt to provide a chronology between the prophets and Christ's era may be based loosely on the time periods found in Revelation 20:4–7.

**19–20** John 5:39.
**21** *Byschops* An interesting anachronism to make the link clear (or to create a link) between the Old Testament adversaries of Christ and present-day ones. Tyndale seems to have no difficulty with the anachronism, indeed would not even acknowledge the existence of one, as in *The Practice of Prelates*: 'Wherefore the apostles, following and obeying the rule, doctrine, and commandment of our Saviour Jesus Christ, their master, ordained in his kingdom and congregation two officers; one called, after the Greek word, *bishop*, in English an overseer: which same was called *priest* after the Greek, *elder* in English, because of his age, discretion, and sadness; for he was, as nigh as could be, always an elderly man: as thou seest both in the new and old Testament also, how the officers of the Jews be called the elders of the people, because ... they were ever old men, as nigh as could be' (*Exposition and Notes* 153).
**21–5** For example, Matthew 15:1; Mark 7:5, 11:18, 11:28; Luke 5:21, 6:7, 11:53–54, 19:47–8.
**29–32** See Matthew 21:1–9; Mark 11:1–9; John 12:9–13.
**33–4** *sixt daye after they cryed* The time period seems roughly correct. John 12:1: 'Then Jesus six days before Easter, came to Bethany where Lazarus was, which was dead and whom Jesus raised from death' (151).
**34–5** Matthew 27:15–22; and also Mark 15:6–14; Luke 23:17–21; John 18:39.
**37–52** *All ... enemies* Cf *I playne piers* (*STC* 19903a): 'these poore knaues ... are so wood, trowe these harlotes pridye that Christe wolde with saue to dye, for such a prophane beggerly blode, but comforte ye ye plowman, fysshers, tylers, and coblers Christe our kynge was a poore man' (A7r).
**38–40** *onely ... they* Ie, only because they were able to make the people believe that (Christ's doctrine) was new learning, and that only they were able to understand the scriptures.
**42** *fyschers* See, for example, Matthew 4:18: 'As Jesus walked by the sea of Galilee, he saw two brethren: Simon which was called Peter, and Andrew his brother, casting a net into the sea, for they were fishers, and he said unto them, follow me, and I will make you fishers of men' (25). In Matthew 10:3 Matthew the apostle is called a publican or tax gatherer (32). In Mark 6:3 those in the synagogue call Christ 'that carpenter, Mary's son' (69).
**47–8** *Christe ... people* Cf Tyndale's ironic version of the argument used to deem Christ and his apostles heretics in his *An Answer to Sir Thomas More's Dialogue*: 'First, the right church was under Moses and Aaron, and so forth; in whose rooms sat the scribes and Pharisees and high priests in the time of Christ. And they were there before Christ. And Christ and his apostles came out of them, and departed from them, and left them. Wherefore the scribes, Pharisees, and high priests were the right church;

and Christ, and his apostles and disciples, heretics, and a damnable sect!' (42).

**53–7** *And ... fathers* Ie, Christ's simple disciples have profited from his death on the cross by manifesting both Christ's wisdom and the worldly wisdom (which is folly) of the learned doctors. Cf Paul 1 Corinthians 1:18–20.

**58–9** *grope with your fyngers* Cf John Frith 'Preface' to *A Disputation of Purgatory*: 'However we may now well taste at our finger's ends that we have long been in that miserable case' (86). See as well Roye's *An exhortation to the diligent studye of scripture'*: 'Verely all reason muste knowledge/ and every man ... must nedes fele at hys fyngers endes/ that what so ever thinge may be godly with pryste hode and after it/ the very same maye be well begunne in pristehode/ and before it' (*STC* 10493; D6v–D7r).

**59–60** *ragmans rolle* Barlowe and Roye's use of the word in *Rede Me* is not unlike *The praier*'s ironic use of it:

And so redynge a ragge mans roule,
He exhorteth to praye for the soule,
Of this persone and of that.
Which gave boke, bell, or challes,
To the fortheraunce of goddes serves,
Babblynge he wotteth neare what. (1265–70)

Frith (*A pistle to the christen reader:the revelation of antichrist*, *STC* 11394) uses the term 'ragmans roole' (B3r), and Skeat discusses the term with reference to Passus I line 73 of *Piers the Plowman* (Langland *The Vision of William* II 10).

**69–75** *And ... them* Ie, these new Pharisees undermine God's word and the authority of the true preacher by saying that only two or three ignorant preachers preach and only foolish, unlearned people follow them. Men of substance, reputation, authority, and learning, however, will have nothing to do with them.

**83–4** *Steuen the first martyr* St Stephen (died AD 36 in Jerusalem; feast day 26 December) is generally regarded as the first Christian martyr. His story is the subject of Acts 6–7. Acts 6 describes him as 'a man full of faith and of the holy ghost' and 'full of faith and power' (172; RSV Acts 6:5, 8). Stephen was stoned to death because his apology before the Sanhedrin in defence of primitive Christianity angered his hearers (see *The Penguin Dictionary of Saints*). The author of this introduction, like Stephen in an earlier time, opts for the purity of primitive Christianity.

**84–7** *Thomas hitton ... trouth* About Hitton Daniell states: 'In January or February [1529], a priest named Thomas Hitton, who had been on the Continent and was probably known personally to the English refugees at Antwerp, was seized in Kent for preaching heresy. At his examination he confessed that he had smuggled a New Testament and a Primer in from abroad. After imprisonment he was condemned by Archbishop Warham, and the Bishop Fisher of Rochester, and on 23 February burned alive at Maidstone. He was the reformers' first English martyr' (182). For contemporary views on Hitton see Tyndale's *The Practice of Prelates*: 'And [Thomas] More, among other blasphemies in his dialogue, saith, that none of us dare abide by our faith unto the death. But shortly thereafter God, to prove More that he hath ever been a false liar, gave strength unto his servant, Sir Thomas Hitton, to confess, and that unto the death, the faith of his holy Son Jesus; which Thomas the bishops of Canterbury and Rochester, after they had dieted and tormented him secretly, murdered at Maidstone most cruelly' (*Expositions and Notes* 340). Tyndale mentions the story again in his *Answer to Sir Thomas More's Dialogue* 113. Foxe narrates Hitton's story with his characteristic Protestant bias (VIII 712–5). According to Foxe, Hitton appeared before William Warham, archbishop of Canterbury, five times to answer charges brought against him. He was accused of owning and reading heretical books, claiming that the Catholic religion was idolatrous, stating that the pope was Antichrist, and refusing to swear an oath to tell the truth. More in 'The Apology' adds that Hitton 'rayled agaynst the blessed sacrament' (IX 113). In 'The Confutation of Tyndale's Answer' *The Complete Works* 8, I p 17) More refers to Hitton as 'the dyuyls stynkyng martyr' VIII/1 17. According to the editor of 'The Confutation,' More was concerned that 'the reformers were glorying in their first English martyr' (More VIII/3 1208). Hitton was put to death under orders from Warham after consultation with John Fisher, Bishop of Rochester, on 20 February 1529–30. Hitton's name also appears in the preface to *The examinacion of Master Thorpe* (*STC* 24045), a work sometimes ascribed to Tyndale: Hitton (sometimes spelled Hytton) 'was brente/ now thys yere/ at maydstone yn Kent.'

**93–8** Cf Jeremiah 20:11.

**104** The sentence beginning *I haue put forth* is clearer if the full stop preceding it is read as a comma.

**109** *antiquate OED* gives Tyndale's 'Exposition of the First Epistle of St. John' (1531?) (*Expositions and Notes*) as the first recorded usage of this word.

**111** *or ever thou iudge* Ie, before you judge it.

**114–17** *And ... thys* Cf the conclusion of the prefatory letter in Barlowe and Roye's *Rede Me and Be Nott Wrothe*: 'Wherfore dere brother, yf eny mo soche smale stickes come vnto youre hondes, which ye shall iudge apte vnto the augmentacion of this fyre, sende them vnto me [yf in englonde they maye not be publisshed] and by goddes grace with all my power and possibilite, I shall so endever my sylfe to kyndle theym, that as many as are of the sede of abraham shall se their light' (149–56).

**116** The sentence beginning *I shall spare* is clearer if the full-stop preceding it is read as a comma.
**120–50** *Here foloweth the table.* This 'table' or glossary of words preceding the text of *The praier* proper is a feature that I have not seen in any other reformist work of the period. It is designed, first, to provide readers with glosses on words or phrases from an earlier period with which they may not be familiar. In two instances, however, it works to ensure that the particular metaphorical meaning of words used in this text is not missed by the reader. 'Hired men' are defined as parish priests (138) and 'Schepherdes' as bishops, parsons, or vicars (144), transforming the literal sense of each into metaphorical ones.
**152 Foxe side-note** 'The complaynt of Esai applied to these times.'
**157–65** *ye ... ende* Isaiah 5:11–14.
**159–60** *But ... not* Here as elsewhere throughout this tract, and in Middle English in general, negatives are multiplied for emphasis.
**166–73** *The word ... erth* Isaiah 24:4–6.
**174–80** *this ... yhid* Isaiah 29:13–14.
**182–90** *go ... man* Isaiah 6:9–11.
**199–202** *And ... gospell* Cf Matthew 18:3–4.
**203–4 Foxe side-note** 'The law of Christ standeth on two parts.'
**205–7** *vpon ... church* Matthew 16:18.
**211–317** A prolix summary of God's love for humankind as manifested in his providential dealings with it in the Old Testament.
**213–15** *thre ... god* Cf 1 John 5:7.
**217–28** *We ... trespasse* Genesis 1–3.
**228–30** *There ... sowles* Genesis 6–8.
**230** *eght sowles* The eight souls are Noah, his wife, their three sons Sham, Ham, and Japheth, and their wives.
**233–6** *this ... commaundement* Genesis 22.
**233 Foxe side-note** 'Abraham.'
**237–41** *God ... heestes* Genesis 22:17–18.
**240** *Isaac ... Esau* Genesis 25:24–6.
**243** *Iacob that ys ycleped ysraell* Genesis 35:10.
**243** *this ... byheste* Exodus *passim*
**245–6** *this ... Egypt* Exodus 1:14.
**246–7** *and ... thraldom* Exodus 2:23.
**255–6** *the ... stoon* Exodus 34:1, 28.
**261–2** *Aaron and his children* Exodus 28:1.
**262** *the tabernacle* The construction of the tabernacle is dealt with at length in Exodus 25–7.
**265–72** Deuteronomy 18:1–4.

**272–5** *And ... offeringe* Numbers 18:21, 26.
**279–80** *and ... hym* Exodus 20:1–4.
**280–8** *Also ... syde* See, for example, Deuteronomy 11–12 and Leviticus 26.
**289 Foxe side-note** 'Gods love to man.'
**290–300** *man ... seruant* See Exodus 32; 2 Kings 17; 2 Kings 23.
**298** *this ys* This phrase is clearer if it is separated from the preceding word *succoure* by a full stop.
**302–3** *sainte ... Iewys* Hebrews 1:1–2.
**304–17** *Ieremie ... synnes* Jeremiah 31:31–3.
**324–5** *deth ... helle* Cf *How the plowman lerned his pater noster* (*STC* 20034): 'Syr I byleue in Jhesu cryste/ Whiche suffred deth and harrowed hell,' and *Pierce the Ploughmans Crede*:

With thorn y-crouned, crucified and on the crois dyede,
And sythen his blessed body was in a ston byried,
And descended a-doune to the dark helle,
And fet oute our formfaders. (805–8)

Christ's descent into hell is based on the apocryphal gospel of Nicodemus which Sisam claims dates 'from the fourth century, though the legend is referred to nearly two centuries earlier' (*Fourteenth Century Verse and Prose* 171). The harrowing was the subject of one of the York mystery plays. Sisam claims that there was 'a prose translation in late Anglo-Saxon, and a Middle English verse rendering' (171). The harrowing is dealt with eloquently in Passus xviii of Langland's *The Vision of William*.
**326–8** *he ... disciples* John 20:19, 22.
**329–32** *demen ... sowle* 2 Timothy 4:1. See also Acts 10:42.
**333** The issues raised in 318–32 essentially summarize the points of belief of the Nicene Creed.
**337–8** *bred ... lyfe* Cf John 6:33.
**339–40** *But ... breed* Cf Luke 4:4.
**340–2** *ygouen ... thurst* John 6:35.
**343–4** *seuen commaundementes* The seven commandments, which serve as the thirst-quenching water of life, are taken from various parts of the New Testament but are listed here as if they are found in one section. They seem to be a conflation of some of the eight beatitudes (Matthew 5:3–12) and the spiritual works of mercy. These seven commandments are not to be confused with *the ten commaundementes of the olde lawe* (362–3) which are contained by these seven commandments of the New Testament. Here, as elsewhere, the author attempts to demonstrate the continuity between the two testaments. I have not been able to locate other references to seven commandments which might suggest a tradition in which the author of this tract is working although Sloyan comments on 'the practice of teaching sacred

truths by sevens.' He states: 'St Augustine's *Sermon on the Mount* had given the lead to this technique, with its harmonization of the seven petitions of the Lord's Prayer and the beatitudes ... It is to Hugh of St. Victor (ca. 1119) that we owe it chiefly, in his four-page work *De quinque septenis seu septenariis*. Hugh lists as his "five sevens" catalogues of the capital sins ... the petitions of the Lord's Prayer, the gifts of the Holy Ghost ... the virtues ... and beatitudes' (31). In general, the whole question of the number of commandments is not clear. The *New Catholic Encyclopedia* (4, 5–8) suggests that the number ten for the commandments might simply be a 'round number' rather than an exact one. Further, no clear sense of a specific number originally adhered to what finally became known as the seven commandments of the church, although the thrust of the majority of these church-made commandments militates against reformist ideology.

**345 Foxe side-note** 'Speciall precepts or lessons of the gospell.'

**345–6** *The ... frende* Matthew 22:36–9. In Matthew 22:40 Christ states 'on these two commandments hang all the law and the prophets.' The author of *The praier* combines these two into one and, apparently, is unwilling to concede that 'on these two ... hang all the law' since he adds six more.

**347–50** *The ... self* Perhaps a reference to the beatitudes, Matthew 5:5: 'Blessid ben mylde men, for thei schulen welde the erthe' (IV 10).

**351–2** Cf John 1:17.

**353–4** *The ... agenstondinges* Perhaps another reference to one of the beatitudes, Matthew 5:10: 'Blessid ben thei that suffren persecusioun for rightfulnesse, for the kingdom of heuenes is herne' (IV 10).

**354 Foxe side-note** 'Christes sheepe stopped fro cleane water and compelled to drinke puddell.'

**355–7** *The ... vengeaunce* Perhaps a conflation of the beatitudes, Matthew 5:11: 'Ye schulen be blessid, whanne men schulen curse you, and schulen pursue you, and shulen seie al yuel agens you liynge, for me' (IV 10), and Matthew 6:14: 'For if ye forgyuen to men her synnes, youre heuenli fadir schal for gyue to you youre trespassis' (IV 14).

**358–9** *The ... beggeer* Matthew 5:3: 'Blessed ben pore men in spirit, for the kyngdom of heuenes is herne' (IV 10). Presumably the author does not want the reader to believe that he is validating the mendicant life of friars by lauding the poor in spirit. Hence his addition *but not to be a beggeer*. Friars from time immemorial were under constant attack for their unscrupulous mendicancy. See, for example, Tyndale in *The Practice of Prelates* (*Expositions and Notes* 277). For a more disinterested view of antifraternalism see Szitta *The Antifraternal Tradition*.

**360–3** *The ... more* References to lust throughout the New Testament are too frequent even to guess which one or ones the author of *The praier* may have in mind. See, for instance, 1 Peter 2:11; 1 Peter 4:2; 2 Peter 2:18; 2 Timothy 2:22; Galatians 5:24.

**365–6** *But ... therto* Ie, a great harm is that many people would drink of this water (of the seven commandments) but they cannot do so. What follows is the explanation from Ezekiel as to why those who might want to drink this clear water cannot.

**366–71** *Ezechiel ... thurst* Ezekiel 34:18–19.

**372** *wisdome ... wisdome* The reference to the well continues the metaphor of the clear water of the seven commandments. Cf John 4:3.

**380** *ar ... dome* Ie, before he would come in universal judgment (at the end of the world).

**381–4** *ther ... folke* Matthew 24:24. The *universal dome* in 380 is a reference to the end of the world, the second coming.

**385–7** *A ... puple* This sentence is clearer if the first phrase is seen as a declarative sentence in its own right. The question then begins with *which* on 356: who are they who have said they were like you and have, as a consequence, fooled or beguiled the people? The answer to the question is found in the next sentence: *Trulich ... puple* (387–90).

**392–7** *The ... me* Psalm 49.

**401 Foxe side-note** 'The honouring of God standeth in three things.'

**401** See, for example, Matthew 22:37 and Mark 9:23.

**422** Cf Deuteronomy 4:28–31 and Jeremiah 33:11.

**423 Foxe side-note** 'Against auricular confession.'

**423–7** Ie, for men say that you might not forgive entirely our sins unless we confess them to priests, speak to them in confession, and receive penance from them for our sins.

**428 Foxe side-note** 'Sinnes forgiue without shrift.'

**428–9** *Peter ... magdaleyne* Peter's sins refer to his well-known denial of Christ in the Gospel stories. See, for instance, Matthew 26:69–75. Both Mark 16:9 and Luke 8:2 report that Christ cast seven devils out of Mary Magdalene. Cf *I plaine piers*: 'Christ vnto Peter his sinnes forgaue, and Mari Magdelyn prest neuer shraue' (E7v). Cf 'Of Confession': 'Whenne crist forgaue marie magdeleyne hir synnes, he vsed not siche rowynge; and whenne he forgaue petir hise synnes, and poule his, and other men heren that he clensid, he vsed not sich rownyng in ere, ne siche asoylyng as prestis vsen nowe' (*The English Works of Wyclif* 328). See also 'Sixteen Points on which the Bishops accuse Lollards': 'schrift of mouthe is not nedeful to helthe of soule, but only sorowe of hert doth awey euery synne' (*Selections from English Wycliffite Writings* 19).

**435–7** *saint ... Christe* 2 Thessalonians 2:4.

**438 Foxe side-note** 'Obiection of the priestes to maintain shrift. Answer to the obiection.'

**438–9** *But ... preestes* Matthew 8:1–4. Tyndale also seems aware of the leper story cited by those who support auricular confession; see *Obedience of a Christian Man* (*Doctrinal Treatises* 264).
**438–53** *But ... men* Cf 'On Confession': 'But yitt argueth antecrist that this sentence is heresie, ... for crist bad ten leprouse men go and shewe hem to prestis, as it was boden in the olde lawe, but thise prestis in the oolde lawe assoileden not rownyngly, as we don nowe, but bi signes of goodis lawe thei sheweden wheche men weren leprouse, and which weren not leprouse, and to her iugement shuld stonde' (*The English Works of Wyclif* 342–3).
**438–56** The sense of the passage is as follows: present-day priests assume that Christ's cleansing of the lepers is a sign that Christ's followers, the priests themselves, have the power to cleanse sinners of their sins, thereby justifying the practice of auricular confession. The author argues that Christ's apostles surely know the meaning of Christ's cleansing of the lepers at least as well as present-day priests. And had they kept hidden from men the fact that priests have power to cleanse sin, they would have been to blame. However, they knew that Christ never gave such power to priests. The only power priests in the old law possessed was to determine who might be a leper and to isolate lepers from their brethren until they were cleansed of their disease.
**460–1** *prest ... ordre* Psalm 109:4.
**463 Foxe side-note** 'Penance for sin, is mans ordinance, not Gods.'
**463** *his* Ie, man's.
**468** *yeres of grace* Indulgences: the removal for a certain number of days, months, or years of the temporal punishment due to sin. A plenary indulgence removed a lifetime's worth of temporal punishment due to sin which otherwise would have to be expiated after death in purgatory.
**473 Foxe side-note** 'Mischiefes that come by auricular confession.'
**476–7** *assoylen ... peyne* The suggestion is that one of the evils of auricular confession is that some priests may attribute to themselves the power to forgive both sin and the temporal punishment that the sinner is supposed to endure as a result of sin. Temporal punishment not suffered in this life is purged from the soul after death in purgatory. About this 'pain' and purgatory see Frith's *A Disputation of Purgatory* (*The Work of John Frith* 102).
**480 Foxe side-note** 'Popish priestes charged with simony.'
**480–2** *A ... symonye* In *Pierce the Ploughmans Crede* (117–32) the Franciscan friar agrees to absolve the traveller of his sins in return for money. The traveller is encouraged to contribute so that he might be painted in the church's west window. Compare *Piers Plowman* III 84; XIV 210. Tyndale is everywhere critical of auricular confession and the abuses associated with it. The following passage from *Answer to Sir Thomas More's Dialogue* captures the extent of his vituperation and also his concern, expressed here, that confession

encourages a form of simony: 'As ye fashion it, mean I, and of that filthy, Priapish confession, which ye spew in the ear; wherewith ye exclude the forgiveness that is in Christ's blood, for all that repent and believe therein, and make the people believe that their sins be never forgiven until they be shriven unto the priest; and then for no other cause save that they have there told them, and for the holy deeds to come, which the confessor hath enjoined them, more profitable oft-times for himself than any man else' (172). See also the Lollard tract 'Of Servants and Lords': 'In confessouris regneth moche gile for thei conforten and norischen grete men of this world in ere synnys for to gete a benefice, worldly wynnynge ... and vnder colour of holynesse leden men to the gatis of helle and sellen soulis to sathanas' (*The English Works of Wyclif* 237).

**485–8** *Helyse ... after* 2 Kings 5 *passim.* Cf 'The Clergy May Not Hold Property': 'criste commendid and confermyd the dede of the blessid prophete helyse, that refusid the giftis proferid to hym of Naaman after the miracle and grace that god had done by hym to Naaman ... And oo grete cause whi helize wold not assent to Naaman to take eny giftis of hym in this case was for that helize had been a symonient, sith his man giezi, that ran aftir naaman and toke giftis of hym thorow occasion of that grace so minystred, was a symoonyent, notwithstondynge that that grace was not geuen by hym in eny wise to Naaman, but that he toke tho giftis bi occasion of that grace' (*The English Works of Wyclif* 378). See also *The Lanterne of Light* (*STC* 15225): 'This couetyse styred Giezi to take mede of Naaman for a spiritual benefyce that god him selfe hathe wrought by his seruaunt Helysy in clensynge of his mesebry/ and therfore Giezi with his generacyon were smyten for ever with the leper of Naaman' (H7v–H8r).

**491–3** *gret ... mencyon* Daniel 5:2–3.

**493–4** *Christ ... gospell* Perhaps a reference to Matthew 21:12–13 where Christ casts the merchants out of the temple for profaning it. The entire section of the tract which attacks auricular confession, simony, and the distortion of Christ's message is, in fact, an attack on the papacy and the traditional church, although neither has yet been mentioned openly.

**498–501** *Crye ... synnes* James 5:16.

**501–2** See 422.

**502** *he ne will not a synfull mannes dethe* Ie, he will not will a sinful man's death.

**505–10** Matthew 18:15–17.

**510** *this ... lepre* Ie, just as Christ was the only one able to cleanse lepers, so he is the only one able to forgive and cleanse sins.

**512 Foxe side-note** 'The pope breaketh the law of loue, and mercy.'

**513–14** *loue ... oure selfe* Matthew 5:44. See also Luke 6:27 and 6:35.

**515** *Samaritane ... Iew* Luke 10:30–4.
**523–5** *Yif ... cursinge* Cf John Frith *Antithesis Wherein are Compared Together Christ's Acts and the Pope's*: 'The Pope saith, They that be enemies to me and my cardinals be cursed with the great excommunication, and cannot be absolved without much money; this is evident enough' (*The Work of John Frith* 309). See also 'Sixteen Points on which the Bishops accuse Lollards': 'neither bischoppis neither popis curs byndith any man not, but him that is first cursed of God' (*Selections from English Wycliffite Writings* 19).
**525–6** *Of ... witnesse* The author sounds as if he has had first-hand experience with papal wrath and cursing. If so, this is a tantalizingly vague biographical detail.
**528** *viker in erth* The first specific reference to the pope in this tract. This expression is used throughout to refer to the pope.
**528–30** *For ... father* Matthew 23:9.
**530 Foxe side-note** 'the pope would be a father, but he beareth no loue.'
**531** *he* Ie, the pope.
**531** *fadur of fadurs* Cf Tyndale *The Practice of Prelates*: 'As soon as Nemroth, that mighty hunter had caught this prey, that he had compelled all bishops to be under him, and to swear obedience unto him, then he began to be great in the earth; and called himself Papa, with this interpretation, Father of fathers' (*Exposition and Notes* 259).
**532** *maketh ... fadur* Cf Tyndale *The Practice of Prelates*: 'The apostles chose priests to preach Christ only, all other things laid apart, and chose none but learned and virtuous. The pope shaveth whosoever cometh, lever out of the stews than from study' (*Expositions and Notes* 275). See also *Obedience of a Christian Man*: 'The spirituality increaseth daily. More prelates, more priests, more monks, friars, canons, nuns, and more heretics, (I would say heremites,) with like draff' (*Doctrinal Treatises* 302).
**535–6** *nor ... order* The jealousy and hatred of the orders of friars for each other is the subject of *Pierce the Ploughmans Crede*. See also the antimendicant tract *Jack Upland* (*Six Ecclesiastical Satires* 119–32), a late-fourteenth, early-fifteenth-century tract, published in the sixteenth century in about 1536. Barlowe and Roye in *Rede Me and be Nott Wrothe* (2141–2) refer to the 'murmuracion' and the 'backbytynge' of the friars.
**536** *and it is agenward* Ie, the fact that friars do not like monks, that secular priests like neither friars nor monks, and that friars do not like friars is backwards (not the way it should be). Three times in this work the author states that the world has been turned upside down by the spiritual orders (678, 862, 1341). The same thing is implied in this phrase.
**538–42** *For ... beestes* Ie, what charity, O Lord, do such men of religion possess, who know how sin might be resisted and yet avoid less intelligent men

than they are and suffer the unknowing to make their way through the world as beasts without their guidance? Cf Frith 'A Mirror to Know Thyself': 'I affirm that all our holy hypocrites and idle-bellied monks, canons, and priests, whether they be regular or secular, if they labour not to preach God's word, are thieves and also murderers; for they maintain their strong members in idleness, which ought to labour for the profit of their neighbours, that their perfect members might minister unto the necessity of them that lack their members' (*The Work of John Frith* 272).
**545–7** *And ... selfe* Ie, and Lord you didn't make one man more knowledgeable than another that he might keep his knowledge to himself.
**546** *o* Ie, one.
**548 Foxe side-note** 'To forsake the world is not to liue in ease from company.'
**552–6** *But ... worlde* Ie, but Lord where did you teach men to forsake their brethren and their work in order to live in ease and at the expense of those who work in the world, and, through anger and outrage with the world, appear to forsake it? The criticism is here directed at members of the spiritual orders who withdraw from the world but unjustly profit from those who live, work, and struggle within the world.
**560–2** *Lorde ... traueyle* These lines are a clearer expression of the sentiment found in 545–56. Cf Tyndale on monks and friars in *Obedience of a Christian Man*: 'They give not, but receive only. They labour not, but live idly of the sweat of the poor' (*Doctrinal Treatises* 300).
**568** The sentence is clearer if the colon after *seruauntes* is ignored.
**569–79** *And ... the* Cf Tyndale *Obedience of a Christian Man*: 'Pattering of prayer increaseth daily. Their service, as they call it waxeth longer and longer, and the labour of their lips greater' (*Doctrinal Treatises* 302).
**571** *preyen ... shortlych* Matthew 6:5–7.
**572** The sense of the sentence is clearer if the full stop after *preynge* is read as a comma.
**575–6** *woo ... ypocriets* See Matthew 23:13–15, 23, 25, 27, 29.
**578–80** *pharyseis ... commaundementes* Matthew 15:7–9.
**584–5** *graunten vs that vs nedeth* Ie, grant us what we need.
**586 Foxe side-note** 'True seruice of God standeth not in long praiers, but in keeping Gods comandements.'
**599 Foxe side-note** 'Singing in churches falsly called Gods seruice.'
**599–601** *Ezechiel ... tales* Ezekiel 33:31–2.
**609–10** *Christ ... yconforted* Matthew 5:4.
**610 Foxe side-note** 'Weeping for sins better seruice then singing in church.'
**610–11** *woo ... world* Luke 6:25.
**612–13** *Christ ... ioie* John 16:20.

**614–17** *A ... masse* Cf *I plaine piers*: 'we must come to mattens masse and euensonge, and harken them babble I wot not how longe' (E8r); *Jack Upland*: 'Thei marren many matins and massis with-out devossioun' (p 120); 'Of Prelates': 'Also prelatis ben more bounden to this prechynge, for that is commaundement of crist bifore his deth and eke aftir, than to seie matynes, masse, euen song, or placebo, for that is mannus ordynaunce' (*The English Works of Wyclif* 57); 'The Order of Priesthood': 'Also thei disceyuen the peple to holde forth here olde cursed lif and synne; for thei seyn that thei wolen preie for hem, and thei schullen ben excused tofore gof for the almes that thei don in fyndynge to seie mass and matynes and euensong and placebo and dirige' (*The English Works of Wyclif* 177). The reference here may be to the Ordinal of Salisbury, a book, Sisam tells us, 'showing the order of church sevices and ceremonies ... developed at Salisbury Cathedral' after the Conquest (*Fourteenth Century Verse and Prose* 247). On this issue Wycliffe in 'Of Feigned Contemplative Life' states: 'Also the Ordynalle of Salisbury lettith moche prechynge of the Gospel; for folis chargen that more than the maundementis of God, and to studie and teche Cristis Gospel. For yif a man faile in his ordynale, men holden that grete synne, and reprouen hym therof faste; but yif a preste breke the hestis of God, men chargen that litel or nought. And so yif prestis seyn here matynes, masse, and euensong aftir Salisbury vsse, thei hemself and othere men demen it is ynowgh, though thei neither preche ne teche the hestis of God and the Gospel' (*Fourteenth Century Verse and Prose* 125). See also 'Sixteen Points on which the Bishops accuse Lollards': 'prestis weren not ordeyned to sey massis or mateynes, but onli to teche and preche the worde of God' (*Selections from English Wycliffite Writings* 19).
**621–5** *But ... telleth* Deuteronomy 18:1–4.
**625–33** *And ... Christ* Hebrews 7:11, 17.
**634–6** *For ... blode* Hebrews 9:12.
**637 Foxe side-note** 'The order of priestes, not made to offer Christs bodie.'
**637–77** *A ... Christ* Although it is not entirely clear that the speaker denies the doctrine of the real presence, it is certain that he does not believe in transubstantiation. And the fact that he argues that a good man who looks after his family is eating the body and blood of Christ (669–75) suggests that the sacrament of the Eucharist is a memorial event only. For a 'Piers' tract on the subject see *A godly dyalogue and disputacyon betwene Pyers plowman and apopysh* [sic] *preest ...* (*STC* 19903). Tyndale sums up the three prevalent views on the Eucharist, only the first of which – the Roman Catholic view – was condemned by all reformers, in *A Brief Declaration of the Sacraments*:

> Ye shall understand therefore that there is great dissension and three opinions, about the words of Christ, where he saith, in pronouncing the testament over the bread, 'This is my body;' and in pronouncing it over the wine, 'This is my blood.'
>
> One part say that these words ... compel us to believe under pain of damnation, that the breed and wine are changed into the very body and blood of Christ really: as the water at Cana Galilee was turned into very wine.
>
> The second part saith 'We be not bound to believe that bread and wine are changed; but only that his body and blood are there presently.'
>
> The third say, 'We be bound by these words only to believe that Christ's body was broken, and his blood shed for the remission of our sins; and that there is no other satisfaction for sin than the death and passion of Christ.' (*Doctrinal Treatises* 366–7)

The difficulty of determining a fixed Lollard position on the Eucharist is made clear by Rubin: 'The most dangerous and frequent stand taken by Lollards was that against transubstantiation. Wycliffite understanding of the transformation is captured, albeit not very clearly, in the term remanence or consubstantiation. This view admits that through consecration the bread and wine underwent a spiritual change, one which now incorporated Christ's sacramental, spiritual and yet *real* presence ... Even though Wyclif and the first generation of his followers were not thoroughly anti-sacramental but rather assigned subtle symbolic value to the eucharist, their fine distinctions were lost throughout the fifteenth century as strong anti-sacramental attitudes became increasingly pronounced' (326).

**643–4** *eteth ... hym* John 6:56.

**645** *who ... ende* John 6:54.

**645–6** *But ... worde* John 6:60.

**646–8** *thou ... lyfe* John 6:62–3.

**651–2** *and doth after hem* Ie, and follows those words. A redundant expression reiterating *that kepeth thy wordes*.

**657–61** *take ... me* Luke 22:19–20. See also Matthew 26:26–8 and Mark 14:22–4.

**662–4** The author is trying to show that the mass has no sacrificial value nor is it a means for the forgiveness of sin.

**662 Foxe side-note** 'The sacrament of the bodie of the Lord abused.'

**662–4** *A ... auter* Cf *I plaine piers*: 'I cannot vnderstande your mystery of transubstancyacion ... which was neuer thought to be necessary because nether any of the prophettes nor yet any of the Apostelles did teche the same' (B6r–B6v).

**664–7** *go ... you* Matthew 28:19–20.

**668 Foxe side-note** 'Priests principally sent to preach, not to say maise, or to make the Lords bodie.'
**669** *to make thy body in sacramente* Ie, to make a sacrament of thy body.
**669–72** *And ... dede* Cf *I plaine piers*: 'Aboute thre yeres paste when I Piers scripture myghte reade, and render and reporte to my wyffe and to my barnes, it semed then a goodly lyffe a houshold then to kepe and feade, both with broth and bacon, and bread of the Byble, to tel forth Christes trade ... then was I syr, then was I father, then was I shepherd and all, then nothinge fayled vnto my byddyng, nether in bourne nor hal, my wyfe for my wysdom dyd counte me her hed, my chylder theyr father, my seruauntes theyr syre, then al did obbaye me in the feare of the lorde' (A6r).
**669–77** *And ... Christ* A difficult passage. With a view to showing that eating Christ's body and blood is simply being true to Christ's words and injunctions the author claims that farmers who look after their wives and children and those under their authority are priests in their own right and live as true Christian men; and by caring for their families and teaching by good example they are in fact eating Christ's body and blood, just as much as the disciples, at an earlier time, took the sacrament of bread and wine in remembrance of Jesus Christ.
**678 Foxe side-note** 'He that speaketh Gods teaching, is holden an heretike.'
**678** *vpso doune* The first of three references to this expression; see Commentary 536. The world upside down seems to have been a popular concept in Lollard literature. I have found it in four tracts in Matthew's *The English Works of Wyclif*: 'Of Prelates' (98), 'Of Clerks Possessioners' (119), 'Satan and His Children' (210), and 'How Satan and His Priests' (268). The reference also appears in *The Lanterne of Light* (*STC* 15225): Lorde what proffyt were it to wyn thys worlde/ and brynge thy soull vnto dampnacyon/ and the body is a lothesume careyn when the soule is departed therfrom ... But howe thou [the church] tournest thys ordre vpsydowne' (A6r). Chaucer makes use of the concept as well in the 'Parson's Tale' X, 260ff (*The Complete Poetry and Prose of Geoffrey Chaucer* 356). The concept has biblical authority; see Psalm 146:6, Isaiah 24:1–2, Acts 17:1–6.
**681–2** *Lorde ... tyme* Ie, Lord, I'm not surprised that they react in this way because they said the same thing about you when you were on earth.
**691–701** In this paragraph the author is attacking clerical celibacy and the refusal of the clergy to undertake manual labour. In short, he is questioning the clergy's commitment to the active Christian life.
**693–4** *syth ... man* Genesis 2:18.
**694–5** *yn ... reson* Cf Ephesians 5:22–3.
**702 Foxe side-note** 'What inconuenience by the unmaried liues of priestes.'
**702–6** *Leue ... flesch* Ie, if men forsake the company of women (ie, are not

allowed to marry), and these men have governance over other men and take up with shrews (loose women), then marriage which you created as a sinless act is now transformed into concupiscence.
**706–14** *And ... not* Cf Tyndale *Exposition of Matthew v.vi.vii.*: 'If ye profess chastity, why desire ye above all other men the cumpany of women? What do ye with whores openly in many countries, and with secret dispensations to keep concubines? Why corrupt ye so much other men's wives?' (*Expositions and Notes* 123–4). See also 'The Order of Priesthood': 'Also many prestis vnwisly taken a vow of chastitie and defoulen wyues, widewis and maydens; For thei taken presthod for to lyuen esely and fare wel, and take no reward to here heighe hoot complexon, but norischen it in welfare of mete and drynk of the beste and riche clothis and softe beddis and traueilen not' (*The English Works of Wyclif* 170). Cf *A Lytle treatous or dialoge very necessary for all christen men to learne and to knowe*: 'yf thou refrayne thy silfe from wedlocke/ as though thus doynge/ thou shuldst suppose to deserve somwhat therfore/ as of duety/ truely thou arte farre out of the waye. ye thou temptest God/ as though he hade not taught us goode workes ynowe. For through oute the whole bibill we fynde no commaundment of virginite that ever God gave vs. Contrary wyse as sone as he hadd made the worlde/ he ordened matrimony sayinge/ It is nott goode that man schulde be alone' (B7v–B8r).
**711 Foxe side-note** 'He complaineth of the idlenes of priestes.'
**717ff** In an attempt to counter the priestly claim that physical labour is unworthy of one who touches Christ's body, the author argues that Mary and Joseph worked with their hands and touched Christ's body regularly, and Christ touched them in their souls.
**725 Foxe side-note** 'What is the true church of Christ.'
**725–32** *But ... deed* Cf *The Plowmans Tale*:

> Yet they mot have som stocke or stoon
> Gayly paynted, and proudly dight,
> To maken men [to] leven upon
> And say, that it is full of might;
> About such, men sette up greet light,
> Other such stockes shall stand therby
> As darke as it were midnight,
> For it may make no ma[i]srty. (893–900)

See also 'Of Poor Preaching Priests': 'That the pore comons be not chargid with taxis, the while clerkis, and namely religiouse, han superfluyte of riches of gold and siluer and riche vesselis and othere iewelis ... That the wast tresour hanged on stockis and stones be wisly spendid in defence of the rewme, and releuynge of the pore comouns; that the peple of oure lond be not brought to maumetrie' (*The English Writings of Wyclif* 279). See also Barlowe and Roye *Rede Me*:

O, the great whore of Babilon,
With her deadly cuppe of poyson,
  Hath brought theym to dronkenship.
That paynted bordes and ded stockes,
Carved ydols in stones and blockes,
  Above allmyghty god they worship. (3025–30)

Cf *A Lytle treatous or dialoge*: 'he that hhath [sic] power to avoyde soche falce ydols out of the waye/ and to clense churches/ ordened only for the administracion of goddis worde/ from all abominacions/ as are domme stonnes/ blynde stakes/ and deffe postes/ with all soche paynted mamettes on bordes/ or pilleres/ and negligently omitteth it vndone ... abuseth gretly his fredom. and maye with oute fayle wayte for the sharpe scourge/ and cruell iudgement of god' (c1v–c2r)

**730–1** *A ... mawmetes* See, for instance, Exodus 20:1–4.

**733–6** *Lorde ... trewthe* John 4:21, 23.

**738 Foxe side-note** 'He complaineth of images in churches.'

**740–2** *And ... thurst* Cf the appearance of the devout ploughman in *Piers the Ploughmans Crede*:

His cote was of a cloute that cary was y-called,
His hod was full of holes and his heer oute,
With his knopped schon clouted full thykke;
His tot toteden out as he the londe treddede,
His hosen ouerhongen his hokschynes on eueriche a side,
Al beslombred in fen as he the plow folwede. (422–7)

**740–4** *And ... seyen* The author wants to contrast the image of Christ as seen in the humble and devout Christian with the idolatrous images associated with the church: I see your image enduring cold and heat in torn clothes without shoes and hose, hungry and thirsty. What kind of worship is it to carry candles and torches before blind images that I cannot see or understand.

**749** *thyne quyck ymages* Ie, Christ as manifested in Christians truly obedient to God's word.

**753** *to fynden hem in lykynge of the world* Ie, *hem* are the worldly members of the spiritual hierarchy. The sense is as follows: why should dedicated and devout Christians (*thyne quyck ymages*) kneel before those who are imbued with worldly values?

**764–6** *Lorde ... heryenge* Ezekiel 8:16.

**770–2** *Amos ... woorde* Amos 8:11: 'Lo! the daies comen, seith the Lord, and Y schal sende out hungar in to erthe; not hungur of breed, nether thirst of water, but of herynge the word of God' (III 704).

**772 Foxe side-note** 'He complayneth of false pastors that liue by their flocke, but feede not them.'
**772–5** *And ... lyketh* The first reference in the work to the people of God as sheep requiring tending by caring shepherds. Naturally the spiritual hierarchy is seen throughout as uncaring shepherds who abuse the flock rather than look after it. The metaphor is a leitmotif in the work.
**776–85** *Ezechiel ... feelde* Ezekiel 34:2–5.
**785–7** *And ... lesew* Jeremiah 23:1.
**788ff** Cf Frith *Antithesis Wherein are Compared Together Christ's Acts and the Pope's*: 'The Pope and bishops say also, that they are good shepherds; howebeit they pill and shear the sheep so nigh, that they leave not one lock of wool on their backs. And in all points may be likened unto the shepherds that Zacharias prophesied of; which saith, I shall raise up a shepherd in the earth, which shall not visit the things that are forsaken, and shall not seek that which is gone astray, neither yet heal the diseased, nor nourish and maintain that which standeth; but such a shepherd that shall nourish himself and not the sheep: and cryeth out of him, saying, Oh! thou shepherd and idol, think you that this shepherd will give his life for the sheep?' (*The Work of John Frith* 316).
**788–9** *A ... schepe* John 10:11.
**789–92** *lorde ... distroye* John 10:1, 10.
**792–6** *Zacharie ... light* Zechariah 11:16–17.
**798 Foxe side-note** 'Against hirelings.'
**805–9** *I ... thoughtes* Jeremiah 23:21–2.
**810–11** *For ... stones* Jeremiah 23:29.
**811–15** *Lo ... puple* Jeremiah 23:32.
**815–17** *Ieremie ... gyle* Jeremiah 8:10.
**818** Foxe side-note 'Popish priestes neither teach themselues, nor will suffer others besides themselues to teach.'
**830–2** *from ... incertayne* Jeremiah 31:34.
**840–2** *Blessed ... tyme* Psalm 105.
**843–4** *for ... vs* Matthew 6:14; see Commentary 355–7.
**846** *eye ... toth* Exodus 21:23–4.
**846–50** *But ... officers* Ie, Christ ended this law (ie, an eye for an eye) so that one brother would not seek vengeance on another, but he did not mean by this that sin should go unpunished, and this is why he has ordained kings, dukes, and other lay officers.
**850–2** *sainte ... done* Romans 13:4.
**853–5** *one ... charite* Ie, one brother may not take vengeance against another without sinning because by taking vengeance he breaks the law of charity.
**857–9** *thou ... cote* Matthew 5:40. Cf Luke 6:29.

**862** *vpso downe* See 678 and 1341.
**863 Foxe side-note** 'He complaineth for punishing litle faults and to let great faulters escape.'
**865–6** *And ... leichours* See John 8:2–5 for the well-known story of the women taken in adultery, especially 4–5.
**867** *theues ... punishment* For example, Exodus 22:7.
**872 Foxe side-note** 'If he be an heritike that breaketh mans law, what is the Pope that breaketh Gods law?'
**881–2** *songes ... not* Cf Tyndale's *Answer to Sir Thomas More's Dialogue*: 'M.More may see that buzzing in Latin, on the holy days, helpeth not the hearts of the people' (126).
**892–7** *Lord ... lawes* Lord what kind of people are we that keep neither the commands of the Old Testament (a law based on fear) nor those of the New (based on love) but have our own laws and take from your laws what we like and combine these with heathen men's laws?
**895 Foxe side-note** 'Against the canon law.' This ambiguous note can lead to some difficulties of interpretation. In this note Foxe is stating that the text is against canon law because canon law is *'an other law and taken of both thy lawes that is lykynge to vs/ and the remenaunte of hethen mennes lawes.'* He is not pointing to a passage in the text that is in violation of canon law. It is canon law itself, he claims, that the text opposes.
**899–901** *O ... agenwarde* Matthew 7:1–2.
**901–2** *lorde ... hem* Matthew 7:16.
**904 Foxe side-note** 'The popes lawe against Gods lawe, in causing men to accuse themselues.'
**911–14** *olde ... hem* Deuteronomy 17:6.
**915–21** *And ... more* John 8:3–11.
**923–6** *O ... litel* Lord, if one of these merciless priests broke one of your commandments, he would ask you for mercy and not for the punishment that the sin demands; for even the pain of death is too little (for sins committed against you).
**926ff** In this whole section the author is demonstrating that God's law is more merciful and less severe than the laws of the Church. Compare the author's description of persecution with Frith's in *Antithesis Wherein are Compared Together Christ's Acts and the Pope's* (*The Work of John Frith* 313).
**927 Foxe side-note** 'The breaking of the popes lawe more punished, then the breaking of Gods lawe.'
**931–2** *penaunce ... burnt* This reference to the burning of supposed heretics by the church helps date this tract. The burning of heretics was promulgated first in 1401 in a government proclamation entitled *De Heretico Combu-*

*rendo*, which reads in part: 'And if any person within the said realm and dominions, upon the said wicked preachings, doctrines, opinions, schools, and heretical and erroneous informations, or any of them, be, before the diocesan of the same place, or his commissaries, convicted by sentence, and the same wicked sect, preachings, doctrines and opinions, schools and informations, do refuse duly to abjure, or be pronounced relapsed ... then the sheriff of the country of the same place ... shall be personally present in preferring of such sentences ... and ... shall receive the same persons, and every of them ... and ... cause [them] to be burnt, that such punishment may strike fear to the minds of others whereby no such wicked doctrine and heretical and erroneous opinions, nor their authors and favourers in the said realm and dominions, against the Catholic faith, Christian law, and determination of the Holy Church be sustained ... or in any wise suffered' (Gee and Harvey, eds *Documents Illustrative of English Church History* 137). The editors point out that letters patent against Lollards had been issued in 1382 and 1384 but that the above act 'was the earliest step taken by Parliament to suppress Lollardy' (133). The act was put into effect on 26 February 1401 (perhaps even before it was passed by Parliament) when a royal writ announcing the burning of one William Sawtre was issued. Sawtre, traditionally seen as the first Lollard martyr, has his story told by Foxe (III 221–9). Foxe concludes by saying 'As king, Henry IV., who was the deposer of king Richard, was the first of all English kings that began the unmerciful burning of Christ's saints for standing against the pope; so was this William Sautre, the true and faithful martyr of Christ, the first of all them in Wickliff's time, that I find to be burned in the reign of the aforesaid king which was in the year of our Lord, 1401.' Two famous and interesting Lollard trials, those of William Thorpe and Sir John Oldcastle, are also recorded in Foxe. Thorpe's (III 249–85) took place in 1407, and Oldcastle's (III 326–48) in 1413.

**932–4** *but ... synnes* Matthew 6:15.

**934–5** *henge ... enemyes* Luke 23:34.

**939–43** *phareses ... also* John 18:31, 19:12.

**948–51** *For ... thee* John 18:30.

**952–7** *But ... prefe* Luke 10:13–14. Cf 'Why Poor Priests Have No Benefice': 'it is gret wonder that god suffrith so longe this synne vnponyschid opynly, namely of prelatis courtis that ben dennys of theues and larderis of helle ... this is a thousand fold more vengaunce that yif god distroie bodely bothe partis and alle here goodis and erthe ther-with as he dide bi sodom and gomor; for the lengere that thei lyuen thus in synne, the grettere peynes schullen thei haue in helle but yif thei amenden hem' (*The English Works of Wyclif* 251).

**955 Foxe side-note** 'Pilate more commended then the pope.'

**960–1** *Saul ... me* Acts 9:4. See also Acts 22:7, 26:14.
**961–2** *ye ... me* Matthew 25:40. See also Matthew 25:40.
**966** *thridde commaundement* See text at 351–4. This sounds more like the author's fourth commandment than the third.
**967–8** *Lorde ... ageinstandinge* Cf Matthew 5:44.
**975–6** *men ... contrey* Cf 2 Kings 20:6. See also Isaiah 37:35.
**976** The *two swerdes* must refer to Matthew 26:47 and 51 where Christ, prior to his passion, is approached by a hostile crowd bearing swords. Peter, for his part, draws his sword and strikes off the ear of the servant of the high priest.
**979** *a temporall swerde* The author is attempting to show how the spiritual hierarchy (falsely) justifies its involvement in worldly affairs by alluding to the two swords (spiritual and temporal) that they claim Christ had prior to his death. This explains why the author refers to the argument of these clerks (ie, in general, 'learned' defenders of the Roman Church's hold on authority) as *a sligh speche* (980). See Commentary 1013–16.
**983** *straungers and pelgrimes* Hebrews 11:13.
**992–3** *lorde ... Sauter* Psalm 23:8.
**996–7** *bynomyn ... spere* John 19:23–24, 34.
**998 Foxe side-note** 'The pope breaketh patience.'
**1003–5** *But ... dede* Ie, men adhere to the old law as contained in the Old Testament but fail to pay attention to the true meaning of *the lighte* of your fighting that you taught in the New Testament both in word and deed. The 'fighting' that Christ taught looks like submission, defeat, and death, given the incidents of Christ's life, but this fighting is far more valuable than actual physical confrontations between foes, so prevalent in the Old Testament. Despite the allusions throughout *The praier* to the Old Testament, it is the New Testament and Christ's words and deeds that should serve as the true model for all Christians. Earlier the author summed up *the generall proces of the olde testamente* (298–9) and added: *And all this testamente and this doinge ne was but a schadewe and a fygure of a new testamente that was geuen in by Christ* (300–2), a sentiment reiterated on 1003.
**1012 Foxe side-note** 'Christes vicar and his priestes will suffer nothing.'
**1013–16** *And ... deth* Cf *The Plowmans Tale*:

> They take on hem royall powere,
> And say, they have swerdes two,
> Oon curse to hell, oon slee men here. (565–7)

Cf also Barlowe and Roye's *Rede Me*:

> Yt is not for nought they fayne,
> That the two sweardes to theym pertayne,
> Both spretuall and temporall.
> Wherwith they playe on both hondes,

Most tyrannously in their bondes,
  Holdynge the worlde vniversall. (3337–42)

**1020–1** *For ... smitinge* John 18:10–11.
**1022** The meaning of this sentence is clearer if the full stop is ignored.
**1022–3** *for ... grounde* John 18:6.
**1034 Foxe side-note** 'No temporall sword geuen to Peter.'
**1036–7** *But ... smiten* Cf 1 Peter 3:8–9.
**1037–8** *he ... hym* John 21:15.
**1040–2** *O ... smytinge* Cf Tyndale's *Obedience of a Christian Man* (*Doctrinal Treatises* 207–8).
**1042–9** *Lorde ... men* Matthew 16:21–3.
**1050–1** *yif ... erth* The author questions the very origins of the papacy.
**1052 Foxe side-note** 'Faith commeth not by outward force.'
**1055–62** *A ... goodes* Cf *The Plowmans Tale*:

Moyses lawe forbood it tho,
That preestes shuld no lordshippes welde,
Christes gospel biddeth also
That they shuld no lordship helde. (701–4)

Cf 'Sixteen Points on which the Bishops accuse Lollards': 'it is agens the lawe of God that bischopis and other prelatis of the chirche schulden haue temperal possessions, for by Goddis lawe they schulden go oon fote preching the worde of God' (*Selections from English Wycliffite Writings* 19). The classic statement against clerical temporalities is 'The Lollard Disendowment Bill' (1406–7), the conclusion of which supports the claims made in *The praier*: 'And therfore alle the trewe comeners desireth to the worship of God and profyte of the rewme that thes worldely clerkes, bisshopes, abbotes and priours that arun so worldly lordes, that they be putte to leven by here spiritualtes, for they lyven nat now ne done the office of trewe curates other [as] prelates shulden ne they helpe nat the pore comens with here lordeshippes as that trewe sekulers lordes shulden, ne they lyve nat in penaunce ne in bodely travaylle as trewe religious shulden by here p[ro]fession. But of euery estate they take luste and ese and putte fro hem the travaylle and takyth profytes that shulden kome to trewe men, the which lyf and evyll ensample of hem hath be so longe vicious that alle the comen peple, bothe lordes and symple comvnes, beth now so vicious and enfecte thurh boldeship of here synne that vnneth eny man dredith God ne the devyll' (*Selections from English Wycliffite Writings* 135–7). The most important early-sixteenth-century commentary on the evils of temporalities held by the clergy is *A proper dyaloge betwene a Gentillman and an Husbandman* published in 1530. This tract is made up of an original dialogue to which is appended a Lollard essay on temporalities.

**1063 Foxe side-note** 'Pope breaketh the rule of charitie, of mercy, and of patience.'
**1068** *our cheueteyn* Ie, the pope.
**1074–5** *swerde ... mouth* Revelation 2:16.
**1081** *ye ... thinge* Matthew 5:36–7.
**1082–3** *a maundemente of mekenes and a nother of porenes* See text at 347–50 and 358–9.
**1086 Foxe side-note** 'The Pope breaketh the law of swearing.'
**1094–1100** *Lorde ... hestes* 1 Kings 28:16–18.
**1104–5** *false ... Babylon* The formidable king of Babylon, Nebuchadnezzar, is frequently mentioned in Jeremiah.
**1112** *swynes flesch* Leviticus 11:7. See also Deuteronomy 14:8.
**1114–15** *Lorde ... synne* John 8:34.
**1118–19** *no ... ones* Luke 16:13.
**1124 Foxe side-note** 'Seruant of seruants, the popes stile abused.'
**1125** *seruaunte of thy seruantes* Ie, servus servorum, the traditional way of opening a papal letter. See the opening of one of the letters of Innocent III reprinted in part in Cheney. Cf Barlowe and Roye's *Rede Me and Be Nott Wrothe*, where the pope is vilified in the following terms:

> Fye on his dyvlisshe interdiccions
> With his keyes lockes chaynes and fetters
> Fye apon all his iurisdiccions
> And apon those whiche to hym are detters
> Fye apon his bulles breves and letters
> Wherin he is named seruus servorum (89–94)

See also Tyndale *The Practice of Prelates*: 'thou be not a wolf in a lamb skin, as our holy father the pope is, which cometh unto us in a name of hypocrisy, and in the title of cursed Cham or Ham, calling himself *Servus servorum*, the servant of all servants, and is yet found *Tyrannus tyrannorum*, of all tyrants the most cruel' (*Expositions and Notes* 248).
**1125–6** *Lorde ... master* Matthew 23:10–11.
**1126–7** *but ... seruaunte* Matthew 20:25–7.
**1141–2** *For ... childern* Cf Galatians 3:7.
**1144–5** *clepedest ... brother* Cf Mark 3:35.
**1146–7** *clepe ... fader* Matthew 23:9.
**1156 Foxe side-note** 'Pride of priests.'
**1156** *lordschupis* Through this section (1013–1160) the word lordship often signifies authority. The author is stating that Christians should not have undue authority over other Christians. But at two points (1057, 1158) the word also means property, land, estates. Cf Barlowe and Roye's *Rede Me*:

Oure grete lordshippes and dominacions,
With oure ryche iuelles and somptous plate.
Oure places and large habitacions,
Adorned with hangynges and beddes of state
From our hondes shall nowe be seperate. (216–20)

**1162–4** *ybede ... sitteth* Luke 14:8–10.
**1167–9** *thilke ... heyghed* Matthew 23:12.
**1170** *ben ... phareses* Luke 12:1.
**1171–7** *they ... heven* Matthew 23:6–10.
**1179 Foxe side-note** 'Meeknes commended in minesters. Vicar in earth not tollerable in the pope.'
**1186ff** Cf *The Lanterne of Light* (*STC* 15225): 'For there ben many prechours but theyr bene fewe trewe prechours/ and yf any preche the trouthe/ the multytude shal agayne say him/ and thus men abyden styl in theyr gostly hungre for they wete neuer who to folowe: theyr prechynge is so wonderful/ ioynynge in theyr curyous wordes the trouth to the falshede who that hauntyth to thys brede for to sleke hys hungre thoughe he were so holye as euer was saynt Iohn the baptyst he shulde not fayle to be sclaundrede for a cursed lollarde/ and pursued as an heretyke of these euell enmyes' (G5v).
**1193–8** *Lord ... gospell* Ie, where is it stated that only masters can bear true and good witness to thy teaching, or where is it stated that masters by virtue of their state of being a master – which you have forbidden – can draw men away from sin any better than a man who is not a master and who would not be one since it is forbidden in your gospel?
**1200–1** *yhid ... children* Luke 10:21.
**1203 Foxe side-note** 'Mastership and lordship in preachers.'
**1207–8** *Trulich ... lesinge* Jeremiah 14:14.
**1209–14** *tyme ... wisdome* 2 Timothy 4:3–4.
**1226 Foxe side-note** 'False glosers.'
**1230–1** *there ... tyme* Mark 4:22.
**1242** *Nabugodonosor ... Babylon* See 1105 and Jeremiah, *passim*.
**1255–62** *O ... on* Cf 'The Function of the Secular Ruler': 'Lord! sith Criste had no thinge propur, as a house to rest in, what schulde moue his hyghest vicar thus to gete hym lordeschipe?' (*Selections from English Wycliffite Writings* 131).
**1257 Foxe side-note** 'Pouertie of Christ not folowed.'
**1258–9** *Zacharie ... man* Zechariah 9:9.
**1260–2** *foxes ... on* Matthew 8:20. See Luke 9:58.
**1262–3** *yblessed ... hern* Matthew 5:3.
**1263–4** *And ... world* Luke 6:24.
**1265 Foxe side-note** 'Couetise.'

**1265–6** *ben ... lyflode* Luke 12:15.
**1268–9** *but ... disciple* Luke 14:33.
**1270–1** *worde ... fruite* Mark 4:18–19.
**1277 Foxe side-note** 'Pouertie counted folly.'
**1287–9** *But ... mede* Luke 6:35.
**1294–5** *what ... thee* Matthew 25:40.
**1295 Foxe side-note** 'God is serued of the worst.'
**1297–8** *For ... haue* Speaking of monks and their duty of hospitality Barlowe and Roye comment in *Rede Me*:

But yf pover men thyther resorte,
They shall have full lytell comforte,
  Nether meate, dryncke, ne lodgynge.
Savynge wother whyles perhapes,
They gett a feawe broken scrapes,
  Of these cormorantes levynge. (2704–9)

And Frith has the following to say on the same subject in 'A Mirror to Know Thyself': 'they are thieves and murderers, because they distribute not that which was appointed by our faithful forefathers to the intent it should have been ministered unto the poor ... but now they bestow it upon hawks, hounds, horses, etc. upon gorgeous apparel and delicate fare: and glad are the poor when they may get the scraps' (*The Work of John Frith* 273).
**1298–9** The two sentences separated by a full stop are clearer if the full stop is read as a comma.
**1303–5** *And ... god* Ie, be aware that these goods that rich men have and keep are in fact God's goods given to you to see how you might use them to worship God.
**1305–7** *And ... more* Luke 19:17.
**1309 Foxe side-note** 'A lesson for them that have goods well to spend them.'
**1313–17** *O ... warde* In Barlowe and Roye's *Rede Me* Watkyn disingenuously suggests that the clergy help the poor, the same suggestion ironically made here:

Husbande men and labourers,
With all commen artificers,
  They cause to have grett ernynge.
Their townes and villages,
With out exaccions or pillages,
  Vnder theym have moche wynnynge.
They kepe also many servauntes,
Rataynynge fermers and tennauntes,
  Which by theym have their lyvynge. (2689–97)

**1334 Foxe side-note** 'The poverty of Christ rightly considered.'

**1341** *the worlde ys turned vpsedoune* See 536, 678, 862.
**1344 Foxe side-note** 'A poore king, and a proud uicar, how ioyne these two together?'
**1352 Foxe side-note** 'Christ a seruaunt vpon earth the pope a lord.'
**1352–3** *But ... cursen* The negative does not apply to *forsaken*; hence, thou taught a man to forsake his goods and not to plead, fight, and curse for them.
**1356–8** *For ... nede* In *A proper dyaloge betwene a Gentillman and an Husbandman* the author of the Lollard tract appended to the work anticipates the excuse the clergy will use for possessing property. He states: 'But yet I wote well that clarkes and relygyous folcke that loue vnkyndly these lordlynes wyll glose here and saye/ that they occupye not soche lordshyppes in proper as secular lordes doo/ but in comone/ lyke as the apostles and perfyte people dyde in the beginnynge of Christes chirche/ as wryteth Saynct Luke in the fourthe chaptre of the Actes of the apostles/ the whyche had all thynges in comone/ lyke as soche clarkes and religyous saye they haue nowe' (733–40). White cites lines 1249–73 to show 'the very radical theory of the nature of property which this unknown author apparently held' (27). She adds that this 'is for any age a radical version of the stewardship theory of possession' (28).
**1358 Foxe side-note** 'The pope for his right and riches will plead fight and curse.'
**1360** The full stop should be read as a comma.
**1370** *to ... nede* Ie, to share these goods with him in accordance with his needs.
**1377 Foxe side-note** 'Proprietie of goodes here, is now taken away, but charitie is required to help the neede of our neighbour.'
**1385** *so* Ie, thus.
**1396, 1418–19** *tenth party, tenth parte* Two references to the practice of tithing a tenth of earnings of various sorts. Cf Simon Fish *A Supplicacyon for the Beggers*. Commenting on the greed of the clergy, Fish states: 'they haue the tenth part of all the corne, medowe, pasture, grasse, wolle, coltes, calues, lambes, pigges, gese, and chikens. Ouer and bisides the tenth part of euery seruauntes wages, the tenth part of the wolle, milke, hony, waxe, chese, and butter. Ye and they loke so narowly vppon theyre proufittes that the poore wyues must be countable to theym of euery tenth eg or elles she gettith not her ryghtes at ester, shalbe taken as an heretike' (More VII 412).
**1399–1400** *they ... rich* Ie, they will have their titles against their will (ie the will of those from whom they seek titles) and make themselves rich by mastery and cursing.
**1401 Foxe side-note** 'The Pope a mainteyner of theeues and robbers.'
**1401–4** *Lorde ... theves* Cf Barlowe and Roye's *Rede Me*:

... they temporall goodes reape,
  And sowe nothynge spretually.
Their parisshons they sheare and clippe,
But they never open their lippe,
  To geve theym eny fode gostly. (2834–8)

**1412–13** *Peter ... scheep* John 21:16.
**1413 Foxe side-note** 'Christ a good shepeheard in drede.'
**1414–15** *For ... dore* John 10:7.
**1417 Foxe side-note** 'Comparison between the popes sheepherds and Christ.'
**1417–20** *For ... scheepe* Cf *I plaine piers*: 'you do persecute the flocke of Christe dayly, and slaye the shepe almost so faste as euer dyd the heathen' (B5v). See also Gower *Confessio Amantis*:

Lo, thus tobroke is Cristes folde,
Wherof the flock withoute guide
Devoured is on every side,
In lacke of hem that ben unware
Schepherdes, whiche her wit beware
Upon the worlde in other halve. (XII 390–5)

**1431–3** *comen ... wolfes* Matthew 7:15.
**1450** The full stop should be read as a comma.
**1452–3** *walisch ... wallys* Cf Barlowe and Roye *Rede Me* (3669–71), where the authors comment on the mountains of Wales and the rudeness of its inhabitants. My guess is that the Welsh, largely because of their isolation and their doctrinal conservatism (see Williams *The Welsh Church*), may have been the butt of jokes not unlike the one made here:

I will gett me then into Wales,
To dwell amonge hilles and dales,
  With folke that be simple and rude.

**1455** The full stop should be read as a comma.
**1458** The full stop should be read as a comma.
**1463 Foxe side-note** 'Wolues in lambeskins described.'
**1474 Foxe side-note** 'He complaineth against the valiant begers and friers.'
**1474–92** *O ... shame* See 359.
**1484–7** *poule ... man* 1 Timothy 5:8.
**1497 Foxe side-note** 'Wilfull pouertie abhorred.'
**1508 Foxe side-note** 'The propertie of good shepheards.'
**1512–15** *when ... it* Matthew 21:13. See also Mark 11:17 and Luke 19:46.
**1517** *Salomons temple* See 1 Kings 5–6.
**1518–22** *But ... rych* Cf John Frith *Antithesis Wherein are Compared Together Christ's Acts and the Pope's*: 'The Pope and bishops suffer chapmen in the church, that minister the sacraments for money daily unto the com-

mon people. And they give great pardon unto it, that they may be partakers of the winning' (*The Work of John Frith* 301).
**1520 Foxe side-note** 'The pope is a chapman in Gods temple.'
**1523–5** *what ... heven* Matthew 16:18–19.
**1528** *withouten any peyne* A reference to purgatory. See below 1596–1609.
**1530–1** *Byschopriches ... rych* Cf Tyndale *The Practice of Prelates* (*Expositions and Notes* 288).
**1533 Foxe side-note** 'Note good reader if Christ be where 2 or 3 be gathered in his name, what neede is therof a lieutenant.'
**1534–5** *thou ... world* Matthew 28:20.
**1536–7** *tweyne ... hem* Matthew 18:20.
**1540–4** *thou ... heven* Matthew 16:15–17.
**1544–9** *And ... heuen* Matthew 16:18–19. See 1525–6.
**1545 Foxe side-note** 'The place of giuing to Peter the keyes, expounded.'
**1546–51** *And ... telleth* In an attempt to take away exclusive authority from Peter and his successors the author claims that Christ gave power to Peter *and* the other disciples. Cf 'The Power of the Pope': 'And the same sentence is open pleynly ... wher Crist seide comunely to the apostlis "Whateuere thingis ye shulen bynde in erthe shulen be bounden in heuenes." And in the twentith capitel of *Ion* Crist seide generally to the apostles "Take ye the Holy Goost; whois synnes ye forgeuene ben forgouen to hem," where it is open that the same either euene power of byndynge and assoilinge was gouene of Crist generally to the apostles' (*Selections from English Wycliffite Writings* 123). See also Tyndale *The Obedience of a Christian Man*: 'As Peter answered in the name of all, so Christ promised him the keys in the person of all' (*Doctrinal Treatises* 205).
**1551** *In this place* Ie, here and now.
**1552** See 1041–3.
**1554–5** *taketh ... lyketh* Cf Tyndale *The Practice of Prelates*: 'Then he [the pope] goeth forth unto that which followeth: "Unto thee I will give the keys of the kingdom of heaven, and whatsoever thou bindest in earth, it shall be bound in heaven," etc. "Lo, saith he, in that he saith, whatsoever thou bindest in earth, he excepteth nothing; therefore, I may make laws, and bind both king and emperor."' (*Expositions and Notes* 282).
**1563** *Antichrist* The epistles of St John are the sources for the word. See 1 John 2:18, 1 John 2:22, 1 John 4:3, 2 John 7. The word 'Antichrist' is used by the reformers to refer to the pope and the papacy. In this sense the word appears in English as early as Wycliffe, although King suggests that the identification of the papacy with Antichrist was first made by the twelfth-century writer Joachim de Fiore (198). The fullest and most inventive definition of the term I have been able to locate is in *The Plowmans Tale* (493–521).

**1567 Foxe side-note** 'The pope proued a false Antichrist in earth.'
**1571 Foxe side-note** 'The popes abbommination described.'
**1573–4** *Nabugodnosor ... Babylon* Jeremiah *passim*; see 1105, 1242.
**1580–2** *For ... deeth* Once again a reference to the persecution and burning of Lollards. See Commentary 931–2.
**1589–90** *thou ... more* John 8:11.
**1596 Foxe side-note** 'Purgatorie.'
**1596–1601** *And ... worlde* Cf Tyndale *Obedience of a Christian Man*: 'The pope with all his pardons, is grounded on purgatory. Priests, monks, canons, friars, with all other swarms of hypocrites, do but empty purgatory, and fill hell. Every mass, say they, delivereth one soul out of purgatory. If that were true, if ten masses were enough for one soul, yet were the parish priests and curates of every parish sufficient to scour purgatory' (*Doctrinal Treatises* 303); 'Of Prelates': 'Also it semeth that the pope and his ben out of charite yif there dwelle ony soule in purgatorie, for he may with ful herte with-outen ony other cost delyuere hem oout of purgatorie and thei ben able to resceyue suche helpe sith thei ben in grace; than yif he delyuere hem not out of purgatorie him lackith charite' (*The English Works of Wyclif* 82). The definitive contemporary work on purgatory is Le Goff, *The Birth of Purgatory* 1984. The most scholarly of the reformist refutations of the doctrine of purgatory is Frith's *A Disputation of Purgatory* (*STC* 11386.5), published in 1531 (*The Works of John Frith* 81–203). Frith's tract responds to three pro-purgatory documents: John Fisher's *Assertionis Lutheranae confutatio* published in 1523, Thomas More's response (in *Supplication of Souls*) to Simon Fish's attack on purgatory, and John Rastell's *A New Boke of Purgatory*. Fish's attack on purgatory, *A Supplicacyon for the Beggers*, defended by Frith, is perhaps one of the first sixteenth-century English reformist salvos against this profitable church doctrine: 'They sey also that if there were a purgatory, and also if that the pope with his pardons for money may deliuer one soule thens: he may deliuer him aswel without money: if he may deliuer one, he may deliuer a thousand:yf he may deliuer a thousand he may deliuer them all, and so destroy purgatory. And then is he a cruell tyrant without all charite if he kepe theim there in pryson and in paine till men will giue him money' (More VII 419).
**1610 Foxe side-note** 'Selling of bishopprickes and benefices.'
**1615–17** *thy ... erth* See lines 319–36 of the text.
**1618** *commaundemente of chastite* See 360–3.
**1620 Foxe side-note** 'Mariage.'
**1621–3** *frele ... hestes* See Ephesians 5:22 and Colossians 3:18.
**1625–6** *And ... lustes* A difficult phrase meaning, I believe, if his wife does not satisfy his lust ...

**1629** There is a discussion on marriage not unlike the one found here in *The Lantern of Light* (*STC* 15225; sig ɪr2ff).
**1632–3** *thilke ... departe* Matthew 19:6 and Mark 10:9.
**1633–5** *yif ... herte* Matthew 5:28.
**1638** Foxe side-note 'A lesson how to marrye.'
**1638–41** *Raguels ... power* From the apocryphal book of Tobit 7.
**1656ff** Following the general discussion on the nature and sanctity of marriage (1620), the author turns his attention to the controversial issue of clerical celibacy. For 1659–63 see Commentary 706–14.
**1662 Foxe side-note** 'Priests had wyues to the time of Anselmus.'
**1664–6** *Anselmus ... writes* In *The Chronicle of Henry of Huntingdon* we read that in A.D. 1093 'William, the younger fell sick at Gloucester during Lent, in the sixth year of his reign. He then gave the archbishopric of canterbury to Anselm the abbot [of bec], a holy man' (224). 'At the feast of St Michael, the same year [ie, 1102, the reign of Henry ɪ], Anselm, the archbishop, held a synod at London, in which he prohibited the English priests from living with concubines, a thing not before forbidden. Some thought it would greatly promote purity; while others saw danger in a strictness which, requiring a continence above their strength, might lead them to fall into horrible uncleanness, to the great disgrace of their Christian profession' (241). The editor, glossing the text's 'concubines,' states that 'Uxores' was 'a term commonly applied to either the wives or concubines of priests, the former being regarded as no better than the latter.'
**1678** *shorten these dayes* Matthew 24:22 and Mark 13:20.

# Press Variants in the Copy Text

**1** praierand *Huntington*; praier and *Pierpont Morgan*
**1116** forswering *(broken terminal 'e') Huntington*; forsweringe *Pierpont Morgan*

# Emendations

**Abbreviations**

A = Huntington (1531); B = Bodelian (1531); F = Foxe; H = Harleian; PM = Pierpont Morgan

**1** praier and PM: praierand A: prayer and B: Praier and H
**38** onely B: ouly A: only H
**40** they. B: they A: they; H
**46** elders B,H: eldrrs crosse A
**54** the crosse B,H: te A
**98** slepe. B,H: slepe A
**120** foloweth ED: floweth A
**156** now. F: now A,B,H
**184** eyes B,F: yes A,H
**197** vnconnynge B: vncominge A: vncunning F: unconinge H
**217** worlde B,H: wrold A: world F
**292** 'they' they B,F: the A,H
**292** goddes. B: gods A: gods. F,H
**295** they B,H,H: the A
**342** the clere B,F,H: te clere A
**375** deuyl B: duuell A: deuill F: Devell H
**378** her B: hre A: their F: here H
**384** folke. B,D,H: folke A
**400** thynges. B: thinges A: things. F: thinges. h
**413** god. B: god A: God. F,H
**422** clene. B,F: cleue A: clene; H
**456** god. B: god A: God. F,H
**510** mysbeleued. B: misbyleued A: misbeleued, F: misbyleved; H

**536** agenward. B: ageinward A: agaynward. F: agein ward. H
**561** to forsake B,F,H: forsake A
**627** presthode. B,H: presthode A: priesthood F
**630** ordre. ED: ordre a,b: order F: ordre; H
**641** other B,F,H: othrr A
**703** they moten B,H: the moten A,H
**719** clenesse B,F,H: cleunesse A
**724** lykenes. B,H: lykenes A: likenesse H
**751** and putten B,F,H: nd putten A
**758** clothynge B: clotinghe A: clothings F: clothinghe H
**771** shall b,f: sall A,H
**780** the fatte B: they fatte A,H: the fat F
**787** lesew. B,F,H: lesew A
**828** then B,F,H: them A
**854** brother maye B,H: brother or maye A: brother ne may B
**862** downe. B,H: downe A: vpsedowne. F
**867** theues B: theres A: theeues F: theves H
**868** to B,F,H: te A
**961** to the B,F,H,: do the A
**969** geuen B,F: genen A: geven H
**1036** But B,H: Bnt A: but F
**1058** begynnynge B: beginninninge A: beginning F: beginninge H
**1067** Thus F,H: This A,B
**1089** hem. B,H: hem A: them F
**1116** forsweringe H, PM; forswering A; forsweryng B; forswearing F;
**1142** in B,F,H: n A
**1148** chyldren B: schildern A: children F: childern H
**1151** dysease B: descase A: desease F: disease H
**1200** from B,F,H: frow A
**1240** thus F,H: this a,b
**1260** haue B,F: hane A: have H
**1298** the B,H: they A,H
**1351** techynge B: techinhe A: teaching F: techinge H
**1374** brothers B,F: brothees A: brother's H
**1386** forsakynge B,H: forsaknnge A: forsaking F
**1396** party b,f: patye A: partye H
**1439** lesewe B,F,H: lelewe A
**1450** haue B: hane A: han F: have H
**1453** the hyredmen B: thiridmen A: the hyrid men F: thyrid men H
**1462** from B,F,H: frow A
**1467** the B,F,H: they A

**1486** mysbeleued B: misebleued A: misbeleved F,H
**1520** on B,F,H: ou A
**1610** byschoprychеs H: byschoryches A: Bysshopryches B: bishopricks F
**1658** vyker B: vi er A: vicar F: viker H

# Variants

**Abbreviations**

A = Huntington (1531); B = Bodelian (1531); F = Foxe; H = Harleian; PM = Pierpont Morgon

**1–150** *lacking in* F
**53** rose] arose B
**65** retayne] receyue B
**87** the last yere] Anno.M.d.xxx. B
**104** prayer and] prayer or B
**115** perceauinge] parteynynge B
**119** Anno.1531.] An.M.ccccc,xxxi, B
**158** drinke to] drinke tyll F
**158** mynstresies] mynstrels B: mynstrelsyes F
**169** bonde] boude B
**172** erth] ertly H
**178** to myne] myne F
**183** here ye] haue ye F: heveye H
**184** sight] fixt H
**184** not] uat B
**187** be] by F
**189** that cyties] that the cities F
**191** Here] There H
**213** thre] .iij. B
**220** eate of] eate F
**221** kowenge good] knowledge of good F
**223** eate] to eate B
**238** and the] and as the F

**240** yf] yet B
**245** was] were B
**246** cryeden] cry even H
**254** comen] camen B
**255** ten] .x. B: Ten H
**285** nolde] would F
**291** in to] to B
**295** they slowen] they haue slowen F
**302** sainte] s. B: S. F: Sainte H
**307** in the day] in that day F
**307** honde] bonde B
**317** and I nele] and I will F
**325** fette] sette F
**330** he] she F
**358** syxth] .vj. B
**367** clene] clere B
**368–9** water so] water is so F
**378** kele] kepe B
**379** for he hath] for now he hath B
**396–7** and thow shalt] and shalt F
**429** and other many] and manie F
**430** schryuinge] shriuings F
**519–20** and of mercy] and mercie F
**525** that thinge] what thing F
**529** fader] fathers B
**537** perfeccion] perfectyons B
**539** ageynstande] against and F
**542** beestes] yestes B
**554** defoul] trouble F
**565** hem good] her good H
**572** preynge.] prayer B
**592** that thou] thou B
**597** preyer] praiers F
**600** they turned in to] they turned thy wordes into F
**608** and they] and that they F
**623** prestes] priest F
**628** sacrifices] sacrfyce B
**655** to fore] before F
**687** deeth] deed B
**742** thurst] thrust F
**753** lykynge] lyuynge B

**756** thy] thee F,H
**757** roten] to rot F
**758** perish] to perish F
**790–1** and a thefe] a thefe H
**805** blyue] blyne B
**836** to oure] our F
**846** a toth for a toth] and tooth for a tooth F
**850** sainte] s. B
**852** wrakers] warkers H
**857** we se] wele H
**860** thy] the B
**889** ys a] is b,f
**917** dome] dout B
**926** doren] daren B,F,H
**929** hem and helpe and mainteynen] them, and mantaine F
**933** forgeve other] forgeue not other F
**955** lighte] lyghter B
**967** byddist] dyddest B
**971** And all] All F
**990** ouercome] ouercame B,F
**1005** in dede] dede H
**1014** clerkes] seruantes B
**1014** and he] anon he F
**1018** thou axsedist] axsedest thou F
**1023** to grounde] to the ground F
**1033** thou geue] geue thou B
**1037** smiten] sauten B
**1043** Christ/ that thou] Christ, and that thou B
**1050** on] in B
**1053** to the] vnto B
**1055** thou bede] bede thou B
**1064** thy] that B
**1066** broken also] also broken F
**1081** byddinge vs] byddinge H
**1084** ybroken these] ybroken both these F
**1087** and of his] and his F
**1090** soule] soules F
**1097** Saul kynge] Saule the king F
**1098** heriennge] worshipping F
**1099** nole] nyll B
**1116** lesinge] lesynges B

**1121** and becometh] becommeth F
**1124** of] to B
**1126** but yet in] but in B
**1128** thou bede] bid thou F
**1137** do her] doe to their F
**1140** lettin] let F
**1141** in fredom] in all freedom F
**1151** defoule] befoule B
**1155** desyringe] deseruynge B
**1157** lesewes] pastures F
**1157** but houses and lesewes for her beestes] *lacking in* B
**1167** hyeth] bigbeth B
**1168** ylowed] plowed H
**1169** an heyghed] highed B
**1169–70** to ben ware of the ypocresye of phareses] to beware of the Pharisies F
**1172** at the sopeer] at supper F
**1187** seggeth] obiect F
**1193** the] that F
**1195** mowe] now F
**1198** no] to F
**1209** there] where F
**1229** her falsheed] falsheed H
**1231–2** that it schall] that shal F
**1233** wisdome] wisedomes F
**1235** mayster] the maister F
**1238–9** the worldes] worldes F
**1250** nele] nyll B
**1268** that but yif] but gif F
**1270** saist also] sayest B
**1285** nole leue] nyll lende B: nele lean F
**1297** ordeynen both] ordeynen H
**1305** by setten to the worshupe] be setten them to the worshipping F
**1318** man] men F
**1363** that dispendinge] the dispendinge H
**1369** worlde/ yif] worlde, and yif H
**1399** these] the F
**1410** in soule] soule F
**1419** case] ease F
**1423** disparpled] dispearsed F
**1427** han they] they han F
**1451** highe ther] high, that there F

**1458** thy] that F
**1487** mowe] now F
**1492** in begginge] begging F
**1494** other] and F
**1499** ones oder twyes] oder ones twyes F
**1505** that] the F
**1523** gret a power] gret power B
**1535** in to] vnto F
**1573** the] that H
**1579** techinge] preaching F
**1592** dare] done B
**1599** were in waye of saluacion] were in saluacyon B
**1615** and] but F
**1620** thy] the F
**1639** seven] .vij. B
**1641** to] in F
**1651** his] the B
**1657** to] so F
**1661** money] mon H
**1665** a leven hundert and twenty and nyne] a.xi.hundreth and twenty and nyne B

# Glossary

Unless otherwise indicated, all definitions are taken from the *Oxford English Dictionary*. The initial entry for each item in the glossary is based on the spelling and form of the word as it first appears in the text. Alternative spellings and forms are given in parentheses, and uninflected forms of the verbs that appear in the text are given in square brackets. In entering a phrase the most important word is given first and the rest of the phrase appears in parentheses. In the glossary I have not included Middle English pronouns (e.g., *hem* for 'them' and *her* for 'their'), assuming that most readers are aware of these forms and their modern English meanings.

*accumbred* [accumber] overwhelmed 1429
*acorded* [accord] reconciled 1076
*agenstondinges* (*ageynstande, ageinstandinge, ageinstondeth*) [againstand] resisting 354, 539, 968, 971
*agyenwarde* back again or backward 291, 536, 901, 1324
*alwise* in every way or in any way 1570
*amydde* in the middle of 221
*antiquate* antiquated 109
*Apayed* (*apayred*) [apay] contented, satisfied, pleased 121, 469
*aperty* (*apert*) openly, plainly 495, 729
*ar* ere, before 380, 1074
*assayed* [assay] tried, tested 231
*assoylen* (*assoyled, assoyle, assoyledest*) [assoil] absolve from sin, grant absolution 412, 424, 462, 474, 476, 1354, 1406, 1527, 1585, 1592, 1607
*awne* (*awn*) own 28, 90, 107, 218
*bayly* ie, bailiff: agent, steward 1368
*begilen* (*begylen, begyled*) [beguile] cheat, deceive, delude 382, 384, 387
*begooten* [beget] begotten 271

*Behizte (behight, byhight, byhighted)* [behight] vow, promise 123, 239, 244, 284, 585
*Beneman (bynemen, bynemeth, bynemyth, bynomen, bynomyn, bynome)* take away 127, 286, 388, 391, 408, 416, 423, 432, 496
*betokeneth* [betoken] signify, denote 442, 978
*bith (beth, ben)* be, is 158, 197, 208, 209, 213, 214, 215, 216, 217, 240, 385, 386, 388, 484, 784, 794 (2), 797, 838 (2), 1279, 1280, 1283, 1356
*Bliue (blyue)* ie, belive: quickly, eagerly 126, 805
*bonsshell* bushel 746
*bowes* boughs 31
*brunt* burnt 932
*but yif (but if)* unless 370, 425, 432, 930, 1141, 1268, 1286, 1355
*buxumnes (buxum)* obedience 237, 1649, 1651
*byelden* build 206
*Byhest (beheest, byheste)* land of promise 124, 240, 245, 253, 265, 277, 279
*byhoten (byhighted)* [behight] promised 302, 585
*catell* property, goods 1367
*cesede* [cease] ceased 626
*chaffre (chaffare, chaffares)* wares, merchandise, goods 1513, 1522, 1530
*chapmen* merchant, trader, dealer 597, 1520, 1521
*chargen* [charge] to attach weight or importance to 579
*chargeth* [charge] to impose a duty or task 617, 802
*chees* [choose] choose 261, 263
*Chepinge* market 130, 1173
*Cheueteyn* chieftain, captain 129, 1068
*Clepe (clepeth, clepen, clepedest, cleped)* [clepe] call 128, 396, 518, 529, 530, 531, 602, 619, 726, 766, 1028, 1063, 1083, 1123, 1144, 1146, 1147, 1175, 1176, 1180, 1279, 1344, 1394, 1514, 1518, 1556, 1617
*comen* [come] come 243, 254
*complaynte* grief, lamentation, complaint 2, 105
*conferred* [confer] compare 112
*connynge (conning)* knowledge 162, 194, 195, 823
*croftes* enclosed grounds used for tillage or pasture, often adjacent to a house 277
*defaute (for defaute of)* in the absence of 708, 1424, 1502
*defoul (defoule)* outrage 554
*deme (demen, demed, demyn)* [deem] judge 329, 393, 873, 899, 900, 903, 906, 923, 926, 936, 937, 947, 949, 956
*deyeden* [die] died 162
*discomfort* deprivation, absence 492
*disparpleth (disparpled)* [disparple] scattered, dispersed, divided 786, 1423

*dispite* (*in*) in contempt or in scorn 1149
*Dome* (*domes*) decree, judgment 133, 380, 840, 863, 868, 872, 875, 878, 883, 886, 893, 894, 917, 918, 922, 945, 953, 956 (2), 961
*don* do [do] 171
*doren* dare 926
*dredeles* ie, dreadless: without fear 1432
*dreynte* [drown] drowned 230
*eft sones* moreover, likewise 165
*eres* ears 183, 185
*erlich* early 157
*erthlyche* earthly 1597
*ertly* earthly 171
*erytage* (*eretage, eritage*) heritage 220, 240, 278, 292
*euerichone* everyone 499
*even* evening, night 158
*evensonge* the English name of the service celebrated before sunset, being the sixth of the seven canonical hours; also called vespers 616
*everich* each 532, 932, 1119
*eyres* heirs 488
*febelich* weakly, poorly 1315
*felaw* equal, peer 559
*fell* fierce, savage 1461
*ferforth* as far as, to an extent and no farther 107
*fette* [fetch] fetched 325
*foden* [feed] feed 1446
*foele* ie, fele: many 293
*fordone* [fordo] destroyed 963
*fore* (*to*) before 249, 655
*forfended* (*forfendest*) forbid 1662 (2)
*for that* but 854
*For to* until 189, 453–4
*Forwarde* bargain 136, 169
*foundement* (*foundemente*) foundation 205 (2)
*frele* frail 1621
*fullen* [full] baptize 664
*fuyre* fire 810
*fygure* type of 301, 1518
*fynden* (*fynde*) [find] supply, provide, furnish 619
*fyndes* fiends 227
*gerners* not in *OED*; Foxe spells it *ireners* and Harleian gives its meaning as journeymen 1498. 'Here foloweth the table' glosses it as chapmen 150

*glosers* those who gloss or comment on a text 1187, 1223
*good* pleasing 740
*goue* gave 1006, 1412
*gouernayle* authority, governance 703
*gravell* sand 238
*gyle* guile, deceit 817
*gylteth* [guilt] commit an offence 356
*harty* bold, courageous, daring 1026
*han* have 203, 581
*heestes* (*hestes*) bidding, command, behest 241, 582, 587, 588, 590, 593, 907, 1091, 1092, 1094, 1096, 1098, 1100, 1101, 1103 (2), 1152, 1225, 1227 (2), 1243, 1244, 1334, 1336, 1558, 1559, 1560, 1571, 1623
*heieth* (*highen, hyeth*) [high] to place above 435, 436, 1609
*hern* herein 1263
*herpe* harp 158
*hertilich* heartily 192
*heryers* hearers, worshippers 733, 735
*Heryinge* (*heringe, heryenge, heryeth, heryinges*) hearing, but also in the sense of obedience or worshipping (see glossary in text 137) 395, 398, 409, 730, 734, 736, 738, 743, 747, 754, 766, 772
*homelich* ie, homely: familiar, intimate, of the same household 1485
*horen* whores 708, 713, 1661
*hosen* hose, stockings 742
*husbande men* farmers 670
*hutchinge* itching 1211
*hyeth* place higher [high] 1609
*hylden* [hold] hold, believe, regard 1202
*hyre* [hire] to have care of 802
*iugled* [juggle] confused 33
*kepe* [keep] care 160
*kele* [keel] cool, refresh 378, 827
*knowlegen* (*knowlege*) [knowledge] acknowledge 425, 498
*kunnen* [can] can 596
*kunninge* [con] know 546, 693
*kynde* kin 1017
*kyndelich* naturally 755
*late* [let] let 231
*lefull* lawful 1281
*legge* [lay] lay 1261
*lene* (*leneth*) [lend] lend 1287, 1288
*leper* leaper 1452

*letteth* [let] prevents, denies 415
*lese* [leese] lose 796
*Lesewes* (*lesuvoys, lesew, lesewes, lesewe* ) ie, leasow: pasture, meadow land 140, 787, 1157, 1437, 1438, 1439, 1440, 1442 (2), 1445, 1446, 1450, 1455, 1456, 1457, 1458, 1463, 1497, 1504, 1506, 1669
*lesinge* (*lesinges, lesynges*) lies, lying 812, 1116, 1118, 1208, 1440, 1656
*leue* (*lęuen*) [leve] believe 693, 702, 766, 833, 938, 1183, 1215, 1667
*lewed* (*lewede*) one meaning is certainly 'lay person' as opposed to 'priest'; but the word also means 'simple' or 'unlettered' and both senses are implied in the text wherever the word is used 433, 547, 581, 591, 616, 617, 621, 692, 850, 875, 886, 1159, 1184, 1247, 1614, 1667
*lordshippe* (*lordeship, lordschupe, lordschupis*) dominion, authority, but possibly also, in certain cases, land, estate 309, 348, 1155, 1156, 1158, 1340, 1472
*lore* doctrine, teaching 689
*lyche* like 306
*lyeulood* (*lyuelode, lyfloode, lyfelode, lyflode*) livelihood, means of living 274, 738, 774, 870, 1266, 1392, 1395, 1478
*manquellers* murderers 761
*matens* one of the canonical hours; the midnight office but sometimes recited at daybreak; often used as a designation for the whole of the public service preceding the first mass on Sunday 616
*maundemente* [mandment] commandment 1082
*Mawmetis* (*mawmetys, mawmetes, mawmettes*) idols 141, 727, 731, 739, 744, 748, 763, 768 side-note 6
*medefull* (*mede*) meritorious, deserving of reward 1183, 1281
*mest* most 315, 816, 830, 1671
*meten* [mete] allot 900, 901, 1185
*meynye* ie meinie: family, household, dependents 671
*mo* more 1107
*mostest* [most] must 1044
*mote* (*moten*) [mote] might 379, 650, 683, 703, 1227, 1231, 1339
*mow* (*mowe, mown, mowen*) [mowe, may] might, must 366, 378, 426, 539, 699, 744, 748, 910, 1195, 1286
*mychel* much 191
*mynstresies* the practice of playing and singing 158
*myrilych* merrily 601
*myschefe* (*myscheues, mischefe, mischeuous*) evil 769, 1233, 1583, 1653, 1677
*nedes ben* necessity 688
*nele* (*nole*) [nill] to be unwilling 317, 1250

*nemeth* [nim] take 413
*nes* [nis] was not 155
*norscheth* [nourish] feed in the sense of foster, support 1484, 1495
*nother* neither 892, 1604
*noughtines* wickedness 716
*nygheth* [nigh] come near 174
*oder* or 1499
*ondone* (*ondoth*) [undo] undone 519, 1250
*open* unreserved 31
*or* before 250
*other* either, or 295, 896, 927, 1012, 1013, 1053, 1228, 1365, 1491, 1530, 1604, 1646, 1650
*other whiles* occasionally, from time to time 675
*parsones* persons 213, 214
*partie* part 207, 208, 275
*pleten* (*plete, pletedest*) [plead] plead 973, 1349, 1353, 1388
*poyntigh* points 1207
*prefe* (*preve*) proof 948, 957, 1652
*presoned* [imprison] imprisoned 81
*preysen* [pray] pray 596
*priuylich* (*priuilich*) privately 728
*processe* course, drift; *by processe of* in the course of 110
*prophe* prophet 302
*proued* [prove] tested 233
*publicane* one cut off from the church 509
*pyenen* [pine] to afflict with pain; cause to suffer 1420
*quaynte* odd, but also, cunning, crafty 586, 712, 1184
*quitte* [quit] set free, release 35
*quycke* (*quyck, quyke, quike*) alive 566, 749, 751, 756, 758
*ragmans rolle* a long discourse, rigmarole 59–60
*rather* earlier 648
*rauenours* robbers, plunderers 1403
*remnawnt* (*remenaunt, remenaunte*) that which remains, the rest 256, 263, 897, 1346
*reprouist* (*reproue, reproued*) [reprove] reject, reprehend 573, 633, 1240, 1243
*reren* raise [raise] 793
*retayne* [retain] keep 65
*retcheth* [reck] care 1427, 1434
*rooten* rotten 759
*reysseyuen* [receive] receive 455
*sauourest* [savour] relish, like 1048

*schadde* [shed] shed 636
*schone* [shun] shun 509
*schone* shoes 742
*schryuinge* (*schriuinge, schryuen, schrift*) confession, forgiveness of sins 430, 445, 450, 457
*scismatiques* those who break with the church not necessarily on doctrinal grounds 48
*sech* (*sechen*) [seek] seek 794, 1459
*secte* group of followers 712
*Seggen* (*seggeth, segge*) [say] say 146, 1187, 1189, 1204, 1313, 1325, 1327, 1350, 1358, 1375, 1401, 1404, 1435, 1466, 1487, 1551, 1657
*seker* sure, certain 1286, 1303
*selden* seldom 1447
*selue* same 1552
*semelych* seemly, appropriate 1333
*Sertes* assuredly, certainly 1324
*shortlych* briefly 571, 584
*shullen* (*shulden, shulen, schullen, schulden, schulde*) [should] should 171, 172, 198, 217, 254, 259, 260, 280, 313, 316, 500, 653, 830, 859, 973, 1024, 1132, 1133, 1137, 1138, 1140, 1146, 1147, 1165, 1315, 1436, 1598, 1650
*sith* so 377
*sleyghthes* sleights, tricks 374
*sligh* sly 980
*slowen* (*slow*) slay 295, 780
*sorylich* in a poor manner 1500
*soth* truth 511
*Souter* (*Sauter*) Psalter 839, 993
*stekede* stick 996
*Sternship* (*sternschip*) sternly, cruelly (not in *OED*) 143, 783
*steyed vp* (*steyn vp*) [sty] ascended 327, 647
*stockes* (*and of stones*) images, idols, statuary 728, 739, 763
*stondeth* [stand] consist 339
*stoon* stone 256
*suen* seek [seek] 854, 857, 859
*sugettes* subjects 1051, 1130
*Sweuens* (*swevenes, swevens, sweuens, swevennes*) dreams 145, 800, 812, 813, 1185, 1655
*sych* such 732
*tabernacle* in this context at least, the tent in which the Israelites dwelt and worshipped during their sojourn in the wilderness 262, 264, 268, 270, 273

*terith* [tear] rend, separate 787
*testified* [testify] bear witness, serve as evidence 20
*thiderwarde* towards that place 255
*thilke* (*thylke*) these, those 311, 387, 483, 484, 726, 781, 782, 789, 794, 822, 861, 1048, 1049, 1167, 1168, 1225, 1267, 1310, 1361, 1364, 1481, 1485, 1600
*tho* (*thoo*) then 224, 322
*Thralles* those in bondage, slaves 147, 1137
*thrydde* third 324, 351
*token* [take] take 922
*token* sign (*in token of*) as a sign of 1111, 1144
*trauel* (*travelen, trauele, traueyle, trauelen, traueleth, traveill, traueyll, traueyled*) [travail] work; struggle 226, 541, 548, 553, 555, 558, 562, 689, 699, 714, 722, 752, 1150, 1397, 1419, 1471, 1476, 1478, 1489 (2), 1491, 1500
*trauelouse* laborious, wearisome 1470
*trowe* (*trow, trowed, trouwe*) [trow] believe, think 387, 402, 447, 546, 585, 603, 605, 685, 801, 1035, 1102, 1330, 1343, 1344, 1415, 1540, 1608, 1611
*verelich* truly 209
*vnconnynge* (*unkunnynge, vnkunninge*) lacking in knowledge 197, 540, 692, 793, 886, 889–90
*walisch* Welsh 1452
*war* [aware] aware 1461
*warde* keeping 1009, 1508
*wardes* (*wardys*) controls 824, 826
*waxe* [wax] grow 172
*weer* [were] were 452
*weten* [weet] know 831
*wether* (*whether*) where 552, 1033, 1052, 1055, 1193, 1195
*wheder* how, in what way 533
*whilke* which 908
*wole* wool 1402, 1406, 1428
*woll* (*Wole, wolen*) [will] will 178, 193, 311, 692, 712, 793, 947, 1399
*wolte* [will] would 1539
*wonneth* dwell 171
*wonniers* (*wonnyers, wonnyer*) dwellers, inhabitants 149, 168, 190
*wood* crazy 172
*wote* [wot] know 466, 547, 857
*wrake* vengeance 848
*wrakers* workers 852
*wreken* revenge 855

*ych* (*Yche, Ich*) I 187, 267, 305, 309, 310, 311, 312, 313, 367, 396, 649, 667, 808, 1368, 1369, 1372, 1378, 1380, 1545, 1547, 1555
*yche* each 334
*ycleped* [clepe] called 482, 1131, 1174
*ydo* [do] done 1346
*ydrad* [dread] honour, venerate 176
*yeen* eyes 186
*yfigured* [figure] represented 510
*ygouen* [give] given 340
*yhightest* [hight] ordain, promise 829
*yholde* [hold] bound 820, 1380
*yit* yet 766
*ylich* (*ylych*) each 215, 216 (2)
*ynow* enough 1022, 1025
*ywit* know 461

# Sixteenth-Century Ploughman Texts

The ploughman texts published in the sixteenth century are listed here in chronological order. Tracts 16 and 17 are undated.

1 *God spede the plough* undated c.1500. Not in *STC*. *'Pierce the Ploughmans Crede' ... to which is appended 'God spede the Plough'* ed Walter W. Skeat (London: Trübner 1867; rpt New York: Greenwood Press 1969)

2 *Here begynneth a lytell geste how the plowman lerned his pater noster* 1510? (*STC* 20034)

3 *Of Gentylnes and Nobylyte: A dyaloge betwen the marchaunt the knyght and the plowman dysputyng who is a verey gentylman and who is a noblę man and how men shuld come to auctoryte/ compiled in a maner of an enterlude ...* 1525 (*STC* 20723)

4 *A proper dyaloge betwene a Gentillman and an Husbandman* 1530 (*STC* 1462.5)

5 *The praier and complaynte of the ploweman vnto Christe* 1531 (*STC* 20036); 1532 (*STC* 20036.5)

6 *The Plowman's Tale* 1536? Not in *STC*, although *STC* does list a 1606 edition (20035). *Supplement to the Works of Geoffey Chaucer* ed Walter W. Skeat *Being A Supplement to the Complete Works of Geoffrey Chaucer* VII 147–89

7 *John Bon and mast Parson* 1547–8. *Tudor Tracts 1532–1588* intro A.F. Pollard

8 Hugh Latimer 'Sermon on the Plowers' 1548, also known as 'Sermon of the Plough' (*STC* 15291). *Sermons by Hugh Latimer* ed George Elwes Corrie 59–78; *Selected Sermons of Hugh Latimer* ed Allan G. Chester 28–49

9 *The vision of Piers Plowman* printed three times in 1550 (*STC* 19906; 19907; 19907a) and again in 1561 (*STC* 19908)

10 *A godly dyalogue and dysputacion betwene Pyers plowman and apopysh [*sic*] preest concernyng the supper of the lorde* published twice in 1550 (*STC* 19903; 19903.5)

11 *I playne Piers which can not flatter* 1550 (*STC* 19903a); published again in 1589 as *O read me, for I am of great antiquite. I plaine Piers ... I am the gransier of Marten marprelatte* (*STC* 19903a.5)

12 *Pyers Plowmans exhortation, vnto the lordes, knightes and burgoysses of the Parlyamenthouse* 1550? (*STC* 19905)

13 *Pierce the Ploughmans Crede* 1553 (*STC* 19904); published again in 1561 as *The Crede of Pierce Plowman* (*STC* 19908)

14 *Newes from the North. Otherwise called the Conference between Simon Certain and Pierce Plowman* 1579 (*STC* 24062)

15 Edmund Spenser *The Shepheards Calender* 1579

## Undated Ploughman Texts

16 'Tale of the Ploughman' ('The Prologe of the Ploughman') anonymous, late fifteenth century? See *A New Ploughman's Tale: Thomas Hoccleve's legend 'Of the Virgin and her Sleeveless Garment,' With a Spurious Link* ed Arthur Beatty

17 *The Banckett of Iohan the reve vnto Peirs [*sic*] ploughman, Laurens laborer, Thomlyn tailyer and Hobb of the hille with other* mid-sixteenth century? (British Library MS Harley 207)

# Bibliography


Alford, John A. ed *A Companion to 'Piers Plowman'* (Berkeley and Los Angeles: University of California Press 1988)

Ames, Joseph *Typographical Antiquities or The History of Printing in England, Scotland, and Ireland* 4 vols ed Thomas F. Dibdin (facsimile of 3rd ed [1810–19] Hildesheim: George Olms Verlagsbuchhandlung 1969)

Aston, Margaret *Lollards and Reformers: Images and Literacy in Late Medieval Religion* (London: Hambleton Press 1984)

– 'Lollardy and the Reformation: Survival or Revival' *History* 49 (1964) 149–70

Auksi, Peter *Christian Plain Style: The Evolution of a Spiritual Ideal* (Montreal: McGill-Queen's University Press 1995)

Avis, Frederick C. 'Book Smuggling into England during the Sixteenth Century' *Gutenberg-Jahrbuch* 1972 180–7

– 'England's Use of Antwerp Printers 1500–1540' *Gutenberg-Jahrbuch* 1973 234–40

Bale, John *Illustrium Maioris Britanniae scriptorum summarium* 1548 (*STC* 1295)

*The Banckett of Iohan the reve vnto Peirs [*sic*] ploughman, Laurens laborer, Thomlyn tailyer and Hobb of the hille with other* (British Library MS Harley 207)

Barlowe, Jerome, and William Roye *Rede Me and Be Nott Wrothe* ed Douglas H. Parker (Toronto: University of Toronto Press 1992)

Barr, Helen *Signes and Sothe: Language in the 'Piers Plowman' Tradition* (Cambridge: D.S. Brewer 1994)

Beer, Barrett *Rebellion and Riot: Popular Disorder in England during the Reign of Edward VI* (Kent, Ohio: Kent State University Press 1982)

Brown, Andrew J. *William Tyndale on Priests and Preachers* (London: Inscriptor Imprints 1995)

Bush, M.L. *The Government Policy of Protector Somerset* (Montreal: McGill-Queen's University Press 1975)

Butterworth, Charles C. *The English Primers (1529–1545): Their Publication and Connection with the English Bible and the Reformation in England* (Philadelphia: University of Pennsylvania Press 1953)

Chaucer, Geoffrey *The Complete Poetry and Prose of Geoffrey Chaucer* ed John H. Fisher (New York: Holt, Rinehart and Winston 1977)

– *Supplement to the Works of Geoffrey Chaucer being a Supplement to the Complete Works of Geoffrey Chaucer* ed Walter W. Skeat vol VII (London: Oxford University Press 1897; rpt London 1935)

Cheke, John *The Hurt of Sedition* (*STC* 5109)

Cheney, C.R. *Medieval Texts and Studies* (Oxford: Clarendon Press 1973)

*Christian Humanism and the Reformation: Selected Writings* ed John C. Olin (New York: Harper and Row 1965)

*The Chronicle of Henry of Huntingdon Comprising The History of England, from the Invasion of Julius Caesar to the Accession of Henry II* trans and ed Thomas Forester (London: Bohn 1853; rpt New York: AMS Press 1968)

Clebsch, William A. *England's Earliest Protestants 1520–1535* (New Haven: Yale University Press 1964)

Collinson, Patrick 'William Tyndale and the Course of the English Reformation' *Reformation* 1 (1996) 72–97

Crowley, Robert *The Selected Works of Robert Crowley* ed. J.M. Cowper (London: Kegan Paul, Trench, Trübner 1872; rpt Millwood, New York: Kraus reprint 1973)

Cullen, Patrick *Spenser, Marvell, and Renaissance Pastoral* (Cambridge, Massachusetts: Harvard University Press 1970)

Daniell, David *William Tyndale: A Biography* (New Haven: Yale University Press 1994)

Deansley, Margaret *The Lollard Bible and Other Medieval Biblical Versions* (London: Cambridge University Press 1920; rpt 1966)

Devereux, E.J. *Renaissance English Translations of Erasmus: A Bibliography to 1700* (Toronto: University of Toronto Press 1983)

Dickens, A.G. *The English Reformation* 2nd ed (London: Batsford 1989)

Duff, E. Gordon *Hand-Lists of English Printers* (London: Blades, East and Blades 1895)

Duffy, Eamon *The Stripping of the Altars: Traditional Religion in England 1400–1580* (New Haven: Yale University Press 1992)

*English Reprints* ed Edward Arber vol XIV (London 1871; rpt Westminster: Constable 1895)

Erasmus, Desiderius *Collected Works of Erasmus* gen ed J.K. McConica (Toronto: University of Toronto Press 1974–)

*The examinacion of Master Thorpe* (*STC* 24045)
*Four Supplications* ed J. Meadows Cowper (London: Kegan Paul, Trench, Trübner 1871; rpt Millwood, New York: Kraus Reprint 1973)
*Fourteenth Century Verse and Prose* ed Kenneth Sisam (Oxford: Clarendon Press 1921; rpt 1955)
Foxe, John *The Acts and Monuments of John Foxe* ed George Townsend 8 vols (London 1843–9; rpt New York: AMS Press 1965)
Frith, John *A Book Made By John Frith* (*STC* 11381)
– *A Christian Sentence* (*STC* 5190)
– *A pistle to the christen reader: the revelation of antichrist* (*STC* 11394)
– *The Work of John Frith* ed N.T. Wright (Oxford: Sutton Courtenay Press 1978)
Gee, Henry, and William J. Harvey, eds *Documents Illustrative of English Church History* (London: Macmillan 1910; rpt New York: Kraus Reprint 1972)
*Gentleness and Noblility* ed A.C. Partridge and F.P. Wilson (Oxford: Oxford University Press 1948–9; Malone Society Reprints 1949–50; rpt 1963)
*A godly dyalogue and dysputacyon betwene Pyers plowman, and apopysh preest/ concernyng the supper of the lorde* (*STC* 19903)
Gower, John *Confessio Amantis* ed Russell A. Peck (New York, Chicago: Holt, Rinehart and Winston 1968)
Gray, Douglas, and E.G. Stanley eds *Middle English Studies* (Oxford: Clarendon Press 1983)
Hall, Edward *Hall's Chronicle; Containing the History of England, during the Reign of Henry the Fourth and the Succeeding Monarchs, to the End of the Reign of Henry VIII* (London: J. Johnson 1809)
*The Harleian Miscellany: A Collection of Scarce, Curious, and Entertaining Pamphlets and Tracts* ed William Oldys and Thomas Park 10 vols (London: White and Co. 1808–13; rpt New York: AMS Press 1965)
Heisermann, A.R. *Skelton and Satire* (Chicago: University of Chicago Press 1961)
*Here begynneth a lytell geste how the plowman lerned his pater noster* (*STC* 20034)
Hoccleve, Thomas *Hoccleve's Works: The Minor Poems* ed Frederick J. Furnivall and I. Gollancz; rev Jerome Mitchell and A.I. Doyle EETS (London: Oxford University Press 1892, 1925, 1970)
– *A New Ploughman's Tale: Thomas Hoccleve's Legend 'Of the Virgin and her Sleeveless Garment,' With a Spurious Link* ed Arthur Beatty (London: Kegan Paul, Trench, Trübner 1902)
Hudson, Anne 'Epilogue: The Legacy of *Piers Plowman*' in Alford, ed *A Companion to 'Piers Plowman'* 251–66

– '"No newe thyng": The Printing of Medieval Texts in the Early Reformation Period' in Gray and Stanley, eds *Middle English Studies* 153–74

Hume, Anthea 'English Protestant Books Printed Abroad 1525–1535: An Annotated Bibliography' in *The Complete Works of St. Thomas More* VIII Appendix B 1065–91

– *A Study of the Writings of the English Protestant Exiles 1525–1535* PHD diss University of London 1961)

– 'William Roye's "Brefe Dialoge" (1527): An English Version of a Strassburg Catechism' *Harvard Theological Review* 60 (1967) 307–21

*I playne Piers which can not flatter* (*STC* 19903a)

Justice, Steven 'The Genres of Piers Plowman,' *Viator* 19 (1988) 291–306

Kelly, Robert L. 'Hugh Latimer as Piers Plowman' *Studies in English Literature* 17 (Winter 1977) 12–26

Kerby-Fulton, Kathryn *Reformist Apocalypticism and Piers Plowman* (Cambridge: Cambridge University Press 1990)

King, John N. *English Reformation Literature: The Tudor Origins of the Protestant Tradition* (Princeton: Princeton University Press 1982)

Knappen, M.M. *Tudor Puritanism: A Chapter in the History of Idealism* (Chicago: University of Chicago Press 1939; rpt 1965)

Knowles, David *The Religious Orders in England* 3 vols (Cambridge: Cambridge University Press 1948–59)

Kronenberg, M.E. 'Notes on English Printing in the Low Countries (Early Sixteenth Century)' *The Library* 4th series 9 (1928–9) 139–63

Lampe, David 'The Satiric Strategy of *Peres the Ploughmans Crede*' in Levy and Szarmach, eds *The Alliterative Tradition in the Fourteenth Century* 69–80

Lane Robert *Shepheards Devises: Edmund Spenser's 'Shepheardes Calender' and the Institutions of Elizabethan Society* (Athens: University of Georgia Press 1993)

Langland, William *Piers the Ploughman* trans J.F. Goodridge (Harmondsworth: Penguin 1959)

– *The Vision of William Concerning Piers the Plowman* ed Walter W. Skeat (London: Oxford University Press 1869; rpt 1964 EETS)

– *The Vision of William Concerning Piers the Plowman in Three Parallel Texts* ed Walter W. Skeat 2 vols (London: Oxford University Press 1886; rpt 1954)

*The Lanterne of Light* (*STC* 15225)

Latimer, Hugh *Selected Sermons of Hugh Latimer* ed Allan G. Chester (Charlottesville: University of Virginia Press 1968)

– *Sermons by Hugh Latimer* ed George Elwes Corries (Cambridge: Cambridge University Press 1844; rpt Johnson Reprint 1968)

– *Sermons and Remains of Hugh Latimer* ed George Elwes Corrie (Cambridge: Cambridge University Press 1845; rpt Johnson Reprint 1968)

Le Goff, Jacques *The Birth of Purgatory* trans Arthur Goldhammer (Chicago: University of Chicago Press 1984)

Levy, Bernard S., and Paul E. Szarmach eds *The Alliterative Tradition in the Fourteenth Century* (Kent, Ohio: Kent State University Press 1981)

*A Lytle treatous or dialoge very necessary for all christen men to learne and to knowe* (*STC* 24223.3)

McConica, James K. *English Humanists and Reformation Politics Under Henry VIII and Edward VI* (Oxford: Clarendon Press 1965)

McCusker, Honor *John Bale: Dramatist and Antiquary* (Bryn Mawr, Pennsylvania: J.H. Furst 1942)

McFarlane, K.B. *John Wycliffe and the Beginnings of English Nonconformity* (London: The English Universities Press 1952; rpt 1966)

McLane, Paul E. *Spenser's 'Shepheardes Calender': A Study in Elizabethan Allegory* (Notre Dame, Indiana: University of Notre Dame Press 1961)

Maclure, Millar *The Paul's Cross Sermons 1534–1642* (Toronto: University of Toronto Press 1958)

Manning, Roger B. *Village Revolts: Social Protest and Popular Disturbances in England, 1509–1640* (Oxford: Clarendon Press 1988)

Marsilius of Padua *Defensor Pacis* trans Alan Gewirth (New York: Columbia University Press 1956; rpt Toronto: University of Toronto Press 1980)

More, Thomas *The Complete Works of St. Thomas More* ed Louis L. Martz, Richard S. Sylvester et al (New Haven: Yale University Press 1963– )

Mozley, J.F. *William Tyndale* (New York: Macmilliam 1937; rpt Westport, Connecticut: Greenwood Press 1971)

*New Catholic Encyclopedia* 15 vols (New York: McGraw-Hill 1967)

*Newes from the North. Otherwise called the Conference between Simon Certain and Pierce Plowman* 1579 (*STC* 24062)

Norbrook, David *Poetry and Politics in the English Renaissance* (London:: Routledge and Kegan Paul 1984)

*Of Gentylnes and Nobylyte: A dyaloge betwen the marchaunt the knyght and the plowman dysputyng who is a verey gentylman and who is a noble man and how men shuld come to auctoryte/ compiled in a maner of an enterlude* ... 1525 (*STC* 20723)

Owst, G.R. *Literature and Pulpit in Medieval England* (Cambridge: Cambridge University Press 1933; rpt Oxford: Basil Blackwell 1961)

– *Preaching in Medieval England: An Introduction to Sermon Manuscripts of the Period c.1350–1450* (Cambridge: Cambridge University Press 1926; rpt New York: Russell and Russell 1965)

Pearsall, Derek *Old English and Middle English Poetry* (London: Routledge and Kegan Paul 1977)

*The Penguin Dictionary of Saints* ed Donald Attwater (Harmondsworth: Penguin 1965)

Peter, John D. *Complaint and Satire in Early English Literature* (Oxford: Clarendon Press 1956)

*Pierce the Ploughmans Crede ... to which is appended God spede the Plough* ed Walter W. Skeat (London: Trübner 1867; rpt New York: Greenwood Press 1969)

*The praier and complaynte of the ploweman vnto Christe* 1531 (*STC* 20036)

*The prayer and complaynt of the ploweman vnto Christe* 1532 (*STC* 20036.5)

*A proper dyaloge betwene a Gentillman and an Husbandman* ed Douglas H. Parker (Toronto: University of Toronto Press 1996)

Puttenham, George *The Arte of English Poesie* ed Gladys Doidge Willcock and Alice Walker (Cambridge: Cambridge University Press 1936)

*Pyers Plowmans exhortation, vnto the lordes, knightes and burgoysses of the Parlyamenthouse* (*STC* 19905)

Rastell, John *Three Rastell Plays: Four Elements, Calisto and Melebea, Gentleness and Nobility* ed Richard Axton (London: D.S. Brewer, Rowman and Littlefield 1979)

Reed, Arthur W. 'The Regulation of the Book Trade Before the Proclamation of 1538' *Transactions of the Bibliographical Society* 15 (1920) 157–84

*Reliquiae Antiquae: Scraps from Ancient Manuscripts* ed Thomas Wright and James Halliwell 2 vols (London: William Pickering 1841; rpt New York: AMS Press 1966)

*Rerum Britannicorum Medii Aevi Scriptores or Chronicles and Memorials of Great Britain and Ireland: Political Poems and Songs Relating to English History* ed Thomas Wright (London: Longman, Green, Longman and Roberts 1859)

Rubin, Miri *Corpus Christi: The Eucharist in Late Medieval Culture* (Cambridge: Cambridge University Press 1991)

Rupp, E.G. *Studies in the Making of the English Protestant Tradition* (Cambridge: Cambridge University Press 1947; rpt 1966)

Scattergood, V.J. *Politics and Poetry in the Fifteenth Century* (London: Blandford 1971; rpt New York: Barnes and Noble 1972)

*Selections from English Wycliffite Writings* ed Anne Hudson (Cambridge: Cambridge University Press 1978)

*Six Ecclesiastical Satires* ed James Dean (Kalamazoo, Michagan: Medieval Institute Publications 1991)

Sloyan, Gerard ed *Shaping the Christian Message* (New York: Macmillan 1959)

Smeeton, Donald Dean *Lollard Themes in the Reformation Theology of William Tyndale* (Kirksville, Missouri: Sixteenth Century Journal Publishers 1986)

Spenser, Edmund *The Yale Edition of the Shorter Poems of Edmund Spenser* ed William A. Oram et al (New Haven: Yale University Press 1989)

Steele, Robert *A Bibliography of Royal Proclamations of the Tudor and Stuart Sovereigns* 4 vols in 3 (1910; rpt New York: Burt Franklin 1967

– 'Notes on English Books Printed Abroad, 1525–48' *Transactions of the Bibliographical Society* 11 (1911) 189–236

Sturge, Charles *Cuthbert Tunstal: Churchman, Scholar, Statesman, Administrator* (London: Longmans, Green 1938)

Szitta, Penn R. *The Antifraternal Tradition in Medieval Literature* (Princeton: New Jersey: Princeton University Press 1986)

Thomson, John A.F. *The Later Lollards 1414–1520* (Oxford: Oxford University Press 1965)

Trueman, Carl R. *Luther's Legacy: Salvation and English Reformers 1525–1556* (Oxford: Clarendon Press 1994)

*Tudor Economic Documents* ed R.H. Tawney and Eileen Power 3 vols (London: Longmans 1924)

*Tudor Tracts 1532–1588* intro A.F. Pollard (1903; rpt New York: Cooper Square Publishers 1964)

Turville-Petre, Thorlac *The Alliterative Revival* (Cambridge: D.S. Brewer 1977)

Tyndale, William *An Answer to Sir Thomas More's Dialogue 'The Supper of the Lord'* ed Henry Walter (Cambridge: Cambridge University Press for Parker Society 1850)

– *Doctrinal Treatises and Introductions to Different Portions of the Holy Scripture* ed Henry Walter (Cambridge: Cambridge University Press for Parker Society 1848)

– *Exposition and Notes on Sundry Portions of the Holy Scriptures, together with 'The Practice of Prelates'* ed Henry Walter (Cambridge: Cambridge University Press for Parker Society 1849)

– *Tyndale's New Testament* ed David Daniell (New Haven: Yale University Press 1989)

Wawn, Andrew N. 'Chaucer, "The Plowman's Tale" and Reformation Propaganda: the Testimonies of Thomas Godfray and "I Playne Piers"' *Bulletin of the John Rylands University Library of Manchester* 56/1 (Autumn 1973) 174–92

– 'The Genesis of "The Plowman's Tale"' *The Yearbook of English Studies* 2 (1972) 21–40

Wenzel, Siegfried 'Medieval Sermons' in Alford, ed *A Companion to Piers Plowman* 155–72

White, Helen C. *Social Criticism in Popular Religious Literature of the Sixteenth Century* (New York: Octagon Books 1965)

Williams, Glanmor *The Welsh Church from Conquest to Reformation* (Cardiff: University of Wales Press 1962)

Wycliffe, John *The English Works of Wyclif Hitherto Unpublished* ed F.D. Matthew (London: Trübner 1880)

– *John Wycliffe: The Holy Bible, Containing the Old and New Testaments* ed Rev Josiah Forshall and Sir Frederic Madden 4 vols (Oxford: Oxford University Press 1850; rpt New York: AMS Press 1982)

# Index

www.ingramcontent.com/pod-product-compliance
Lightning Source LLC
Chambersburg PA
CBHW021011120726
47905CB00009B/2960

*9781442655003*